SELECTED

Spain
& Portugal

Quality camping & caravanning sites

Rogers

007

Alan Rogers

Alan

Celebrating 40 Years

Compiled by: Alan Rogers Guides Ltd

Designed by: Paul Effenberg, Vine Design Ltd

Maps created by Customised Mapping (01769 540044)
contain background data provided by GisDATA Ltd
Maps are © Alan Rogers Guides and Gis DATA Ltd 2006

© Alan Rogers Guides Ltd 2007

Published by: Alan Rogers Guides Ltd,
Spelmonden Old Oast, Goudhurst, Kent TN17 1HE
www.alanrogers.com Tel: 01580 214000

British Library Cataloguing-in-Publication Data:
A catalogue record for this book is available from the
British Library.

ISBN-13 978-0-9550486-6-1
ISBN-10 0-9550486-6-4

Printed in Great Britain by J H Haynes & Co Ltd

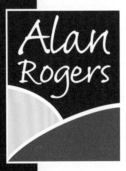

Contents

the Alan Rogers
approach

THIS YEAR WE CELEBRATE THE PUBLICATION OF THE FORTIETH EDITIONS OF THE ALAN ROGERS GUIDES. SINCE ALAN ROGERS PUBLISHED THE FIRST CAMPSITE GUIDE THAT BORE HIS NAME, THE RANGE HAS EXPANDED TO SIX TITLES COVERING 27 COUNTRIES. NO FEWER THAN 20 OF THE CAMPSITES SELECTED BY ALAN FOR THE FIRST GUIDE ARE STILL FEATURED IN OUR 2007 EDITIONS – LOOK OUT FOR THE 'CELEBRATING 40 YEARS' SYMBOL BESIDE OUR REPORTS.

THERE ARE MANY THOUSANDS OF CAMPSITES IN SPAIN AND PORTUGAL OF VARYING QUALITY: THIS GUIDE CONTAINS IMPARTIALLY WRITTEN REPORTS ON OVER 240 OF THE VERY FINEST, EACH BEING INDIVIDUALLY INSPECTED AND SELECTED. IT ALSO INCORPORATES A SECTION ON OUR POPULAR TRAVEL SERVICE, AS WELL AS ALL THE USUAL MAPS AND INDEXES, DESIGNED TO HELP YOU FIND THE CHOICE OF CAMPSITE THAT'S RIGHT FOR YOU. WE HOPE YOU ENJOY SOME HAPPY AND SAFE TRAVELS – AND SOME PLEASURABLE 'ARMCHAIR TOURING' IN THE MEANTIME!

A question of quality

The criteria we use when inspecting and selecting sites are numerous, but the most important by far is the question of good quality. People want different things from their choice of campsite so we try to include a range of campsite 'styles' to cater for a wide variety of preferences: from those seeking a small peaceful campsite in the heart of the countryside, to visitors looking for an 'all singing, all dancing' site in a popular seaside resort. Those with more specific interests, such as sporting facilities, cultural events or historical attractions, are also catered for.

The size of the site, whether it's part of a chain or privately owned, makes no difference in terms of it being required to meet our exacting standards in respect of its quality and it being 'fit for purpose'. In other words, irrespective of the size of the site, or the number of facilities it offers, we consider and evaluate the welcome, the pitches, the sanitary facilities, the cleanliness, the general maintenance and even the location.

".the campsites included in this book have been chosen entirely on merit, and no payment of any sort is made by them for their inclusion."

Alan Rogers, 1968

Independent and honest

Whilst the content and scope of the Alan Rogers guides have expanded considerably since the early editions, our selection of campsites still employs exactly the same philosophy and criteria as defined by Alan Rogers in 1968.

'telling it how it is'

Firstly, and most importantly, our selection is based entirely on our own rigorous and independent inspection and selection process. Campsites cannot buy their way into our guides – indeed the extensive Site Report which is written by us, not by the site owner, is provided free of charge so we are free to say what we think and to provide an honest, 'warts and all' description. This is written in plain English and without the use of confusing icons or symbols.

Expert opinions

We rely on our dedicated team of Site Assessors, all of whom are experienced campers, caravanners or motorcaravanners, to visit and recommend sites. Each year they travel some 100,000 miles around Europe inspecting new campsites for the guide and re-inspecting the existing ones. Our thanks are due to them for their enthusiastic efforts, their diligence and integrity.

We also appreciate the feedback we receive from many of our readers and we always make a point of following up complaints, suggestions or recommendations for possible new sites. Of course we get a few grumbles too – but it really is a few, and those we do receive usually relate to overcrowding or to poor maintenance during the peak school holiday period.

Please bear in mind that, although we are interested to hear about any complaints, we have no contractual relationship with the campsites featured in our guides and are therefore not in a position to intervene in any dispute between a reader and a campsite.

Highly respected by site owners and readers alike, there is no better guide when it comes to forming an independent view of a campsite's quality. When you need to be confident in your choice of campsite, you need the Alan Rogers Guide.

- ☑ **Parks only included on merit**
- ☑ **Parks cannot pay to be included**
- ☑ **Independently inspected, rigorously assessed**
- ☑ **Impartial reviews**
- ☑ **40** years of expertise

WRITTEN IN PLAIN ENGLISH, OUR GUIDES ARE EXCEPTIONALLY EASY TO USE, BUT A FEW WORDS OF EXPLANATION REGARDING THE LAYOUT AND CONTENT MAY BE HELPFUL. IN SPAIN WE HAVE USED THE 15 OFFICIAL ADMINISTRATIVE REGIONS, WHILST IN PORTUGAL WE USE THE FIVE REGIONS DEFINED BY THE PORTUGUESE TOURIST BOARD. A FULL PAGE INTRODUCTION TO EACH REGION HIGHLIGHTS ITS MAIN AREAS OF INTEREST, PLACES TO VISIT AND THE LOCAL CUISINE.

Region

The Site Reports – *Example of an entry*

Site Number **Site name**
Postal Address (including region)
Telephone number. Email address

A description of the site in which we try to give an idea of its general features – its size, its situation, its strengths and its weaknesses. This section should provide a picture of the site itself with reference to the facilities that are provided and if they impact on its appearance or character. We include details on pitch numbers, electricity (with amperage), hardstandings etc. in this section as pitch design, planning and terracing affects the site's overall appearance. Similarly we include reference to pitches used for caravan holiday homes, chalets, and the like. Importantly at the end of this column we indicate if there are any restrictions, e.g. no tents, no children, naturist sites.

Facilities

Lists more specific information on the site's facilities and amenities and, where available, the dates when these facilities are open (if not for the whole season). Off site: here we give distances to various local amenities, for example, local shops, the nearest beach, plus our featured activities (bicycle hire, fishing, horse riding, boat launching). Where we have space we list suggestions for activities and local tourist attractions.

Open: Site opening dates.

Directions

Separated from the main text in order that they may be read and assimilated more easily by a navigator en-route. Bear in mind that road improvement schemes can result in road numbers being altered.

GPS: references are provided as we obtain them for satellite navigation systems (in degrees and minutes).

Charges 2007

Indexes

Our three indexes allow you to find sites by their number and name, by region and site name or by the town or village where the site is situated. See also the handy Quick Reference sections at the back.

Campsite Maps

The maps will help you identify the approximate position of each campsite within its region. The colour of the campsite number indicates whether it is open all year or not. You will certainly need more detailed maps and we have found the Michelin atlas to be particularly useful.

Facilities

Toilet blocks

We assume that toilet blocks will be equipped with a reasonable number of British style WCs, washbasins with hot and cold water and hot showers with dividers or curtains, and will have all necessary shelves, hooks, plugs and mirrors. We also assume that there will be an identified chemical toilet disposal point, and that the campsite will provide water and waste water drainage points and bin areas. If not the case, we comment. We do mention certain features that some readers find important: washbasins in cubicles, facilities for babies, facilities for those with disabilities and motorcaravan service points. Readers with disabilities are advised to contact the site of their choice to ensure that facilities are appropriate to their needs.

Shop

Basic or fully supplied, and opening dates.

Bars, restaurants, takeaway facilities and entertainment

We try hard to supply opening and closing dates (if other than the campsite opening dates) and to identify if there are discos or other entertainment.

Children's play areas

Fenced and with safety surface (e.g. sand, bark or pea-gravel).

Swimming pools

If particularly special, we cover in detail in our main campsite description but reference is always included under our Facilities listings. Opening dates, charges and levels of supervision are provided where we have been notified.

Leisure facilities

For example, playing fields, bicycle hire, organised activities and entertainment.

Dogs

If dogs are not accepted or restrictions apply, we state it here. Check the quick reference list at the back of the guide.

Off site

This briefly covers leisure facilities, tourist attractions, restaurants etc. nearby.

Charges

These are the latest provided to us by the sites. In those few cases where 2006 or 2007 prices are not given, we try to give a general guide.

Reservations

Necessary for high season (roughly mid-July to mid-August) in popular holiday areas (ie beach areas). You can reserve via our own Alan Rogers Travel Service or through tour operators. Or be wholly independent and contact the campsite(s) of your choice direct, using the phone or e-mail numbers shown in the site reports, but please bear in mind that many sites are closed all winter.

Telephone numbers

All numbers assume that you are phoning from within Spain or Portugal. To phone Spain from outside that country, prefix the number shown with the International Code '00 34' and then the number indicated. To phone Portugal pefix the number shown with the International Code '00 351'.

Opening dates

These are advised to us during the early autumn of the previous year – sites can, and sometimes do, alter these dates before the start of the following season, often for good reasons. If you intend to visit shortly after a published opening date, or shortly before the closing date, it is wise to check that it will actually be open at the time required. Similarly some sites operate a restricted service during the low season, only opening some of their facilities (e.g. swimming pools) during the main season; where we know about this, and have the relevant dates, we indicate it – again if you are at all doubtful it is wise to check.

INSPECTED CAMPSITES & SELECTED

Some site owners are very laid back when it comes to opening and closing dates. They may not be fully ready by their stated opening dates – grass and hedges may not all be cut or perhaps only limited sanitary facilities open. At the end of the season they also tend to close down some facilities and generally wind down prior to the closing date. Bear this in mind if you are travelling early or late in the season – it is worth phoning ahead.

The Camping Cheque low season touring system goes some way to addressing this in that participating campsites are encouraged to have all key facilities open and running by the opening date and to remain fully operational until the closing date.

Whether you're an 'old hand' in terms of camping and caravanning or are contemplating your first trip, a regular reader of our Guides or a new 'convert', we wish you well in your travels and hope we have been able to help in some way. We are, of course, also out and about ourselves, visiting sites, talking to owners and readers, and generally checking on standards and new developments.

We wish all our readers thoroughly enjoyable Camping and Caravanning in 2007 – favoured by good weather of course!

THE ALAN ROGERS TEAM

have you visited
www.alanrogers.com
yet?

INSPECTED CAMPSITES & SELECTED

Alan Rogers

Our website has fast become the first-stop for countless caravanners, motorhome owners and campers all wanting reliable, impartial and detailed information for their next trip.

It features a fully searchable database of the best campsites in the UK & Ireland, and the rest of Europe: over 2,000 campsites in 26 countries. All are Alan Rogers inspected and selected, allowing you to find the site that's perfect for you, with the reassurance of knowing we've been there first.

Regions

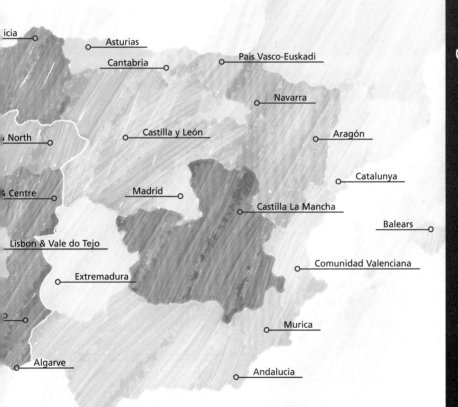

icia

Asturias

Cantabria

Pais Vasco-Euskadi

Navarra

North

Castilla y León

Aragón

Catalunya

Centre

Madrid

Castilla La Mancha

Balears

Lisbon & Vale do Tejo

Comunidad Valenciana

Extremadura

Murica

Algarve

Andalucia

In 2004 we introduced the first ever Alan Rogers Campsite Awards.

BEFORE MAKING OUR AWARDS, WE CAREFULLY CONSIDER MORE THAN 2000 CAMPSITES FEATURED IN OUR GUIDES, TAKING INTO ACCOUNT COMMENTS FROM OUR SITE ASSESSORS, OUR HEAD OFFICE TEAM AND, OF COURSE, OUR READERS.

OUR AWARD WINNERS COVER A MASSIVE GEOGRAPHICAL AREA FROM THE IBERIAN PENINSULA TO HUNGARY, AND THIS YEAR WE ARE MAKING AWARDS TO CAMPSITES IN 12 DIFFERENT COUNTRIES.

NEEDLESS TO SAY, IT'S AN EXTREMELY DIFFICULT TASK TO CHOOSE OUR EVENTUAL WINNERS, BUT WE BELIEVE THAT WE HAVE IDENTIFIED A NUMBER OF CAMPSITES WITH TRULY OUTSTANDING CHARACTERISTICS.

IN EACH CASE, WE HAVE SELECTED AN OUTRIGHT WINNER, ALONG WITH TWO HIGHLY COMMENDED RUNNERS-UP.

Listed below are full details of each of our award categories and our winners for 2006.

Alan Rogers Progress Award 2006

This award reflects the hard work and commitment undertaken by particular site owners to improve and upgrade their site.

WINNER
Camping International Marina, Spain

RUNNERS-UP
Camping La Grande Métairie, France
Newlands Caravan Park, England

Alan Rogers Welcome Award 2006

This award takes account of sites offering a particularly friendly welcome and maintaining a friendly ambience throughout reader's holidays.

WINNER
Mannix Point Caravan Park, Ireland

RUNNERS-UP
Castel Camping Sequoia Park, France
Balatontourist Napfeny, Hungary

Alan Rogers Active Holiday Award 2006

This award reflects sites in outstanding locations which are ideally suited for active holidays, notably walking or cycling, but which could extend to include such activities as winter sports or water sports

WINNER
Sportcamp Woferlgut, Austria

RUNNERS-UP
Klim Strand Camping, Denmark
Camping Bijela Uvala, Croatia

Alan Rogers Motorhome Award 2006

Motorhome sales are increasing and this award acknowledges sites which, in our opinion, have made outstanding efforts to welcome motorhome clients.

WINNER
Spessart-Camping Schönrain, Germany

RUNNERS-UP
Camping El Astral, Spain
Gaasper Camping, Netherlands

Alan Rogers 4 Seasons Award 2006

This award is made to outstanding sites with extended opening dates and which welcome clients to a uniformly high standard throughout the year.

WINNER
Komfort-Campingpark Burgstaller, Austria

RUNNERS-UP
Recreatiecentrum de Schatberg, Netherlands
Caravaning La Manga, Spain

Alan Rogers Seaside Award 2006

This award is made for sites which we feel are outstandingly suitable for a really excellent seaside holiday.

WINNER
Playa Montroig Camping Resort, Spain

RUNNERS-UP
Camping Baia Blu La Tortuga, Italy
Camping Bois Soleil, France

Alan Rogers Country Award 2006

This award contrasts with our former award and acknowledges sites which are attractively located in delightful, rural locations.

WINNER

Stowford Farm Meadows, England

RUNNERS-UP

Castel Camping La Paille Basse, France

Camping Romantische Strasse, Germany

Alan Rogers Rented Accommodation Award 2006

Given the increasing importance of rented accommodation on many campsites, and the inclusion in many Alan Rogers guides, of a rented accommodation section, we feel that it is important to acknowledge sites which have made a particular effort in creating a high quality 'rented accommodation' park.

WINNER

Camping Cambrils Park, Spain

RUNNERS-UP

Castel Camping Caravaning Esterel, France

Camping Kovacine, Croatia

Alan Rogers Unique Site Award 2006

This award acknowledges sites with unique, outstanding features – something which simply cannot be found elsewhere and which is an important attraction of the site.

WINNER

Camping Jésolo International, Italy

RUNNERS-UP

The Plassey Touring Park, Wales

Vakantiepark Duinrell, Netherlands

Alan Rogers Family Site Award 2006

Many sites claim to be child friendly but this award acknowledges the sites we feel to be the very best in this respect.

WINNER

Camping Capalonga, Italy

RUNNERS-UP

Beverley Park Holiday Centre, England

Domaine Le Pommier, France

Alan Rogers Readers' Award 2006

In 2005 we introduced a new award, which we believe to be the most important, our Readers' Award. We simply invited our readers (by means of an on-line poll at www.alanrogers.com) to nominate the site they enjoyed most. The outright winner for 2006 is:

WINNER

Camping Le Paradis, France

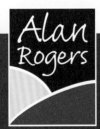

Alan Rogers.trave

The Alan Rogers Travel Service was set up to provide a low cost booking service for readers. We pride ourselves on being able to put together a bespoke holiday, taking advantage of our experience, knowledge and contacts. We can tailor-make a holiday to suit your requirements, giving you maximum choice and flexibility: exactly what we have been offering for some 7 years now.

2007 PRICE CRASH

For 2007 we offer more choice than ever before (around 500 campsites) and have thousands of holidays at significantly reduced prices - guaranteed.

unbeatable ferry deals

- ☑ CARAVANS GO FREE
- ☑ TRAILERS GO FREE
- ☑ MOTORHOMES PRICED AS CARS

ON CERTAIN ROUTES
- CONDITIONS APPLY

At the Alan Rogers Travel Service we're always keen to find the best deals and keenest prices. There are always great savings on offer, and we're constantly negotiating new ferry rates and money-saving offers, so just call us on

0870 405 4055

and ask about the latest deals.

or visit

Alan Rogers.travel

Whether you book on-line or book by phone, you will be allocated an experienced Personal Travel Consultant to provide you with personal advice and manage every stage of your booking. Our Personal Travel Consultants have first-hand experience of many of our campsites and access to a wealth of information. They can 'paint a picture' of individual campsites, check availability, provide a competitive price and tailor your holiday arrangements to your specific needs.

- Discuss your holiday plans with a friendly person with first-hand experience

- Let us reassure you that your holiday arrangements really are taken care of

- Tell us about your special requests and allow us to pass these on

- Benefit from advice which will save you money – the latest ferry deals and more

- Remember, our offices are in Kent not overseas and we do NOT operate a queuing system!

THE AIMS OF THE TRAVEL SERVICE ARE SIMPLE

- To provide convenience - a one-stop shop to make life easier.
- To provide peace of mind - when you need it most.
- To provide a friendly, knowledgeable, efficient service – when this can be hard to find.
- To provide a low cost means of organising your holiday – when prices can be so complicated.

HOW IT WORKS

1 Choose your campsite(s) – we can book around 500 across Europe. Look for the yellow coloured campsite entries in this book. You'll find more info and images at www.alanrogers.travel.

Please note: the list of campsites we can book for you varies from time to time.

2 Choose your dates – choose when you arrive, when you leave.

3 Choose your ferry crossing – we can book most routes with most operators at extremely competitive rates.

Then just call us for an instant quote

0870 405 4055
or visit

*Alan Rogers.*travel

LOOK FOR A CAMPSITE ENTRY LIKE THIS TO INDICATE WHICH CAMPSITES WE CAN BOOK FOR YOU.

THE LIST IS GROWING SO PLEASE CALL FOR UP TO THE MINUTE INFORMATION.

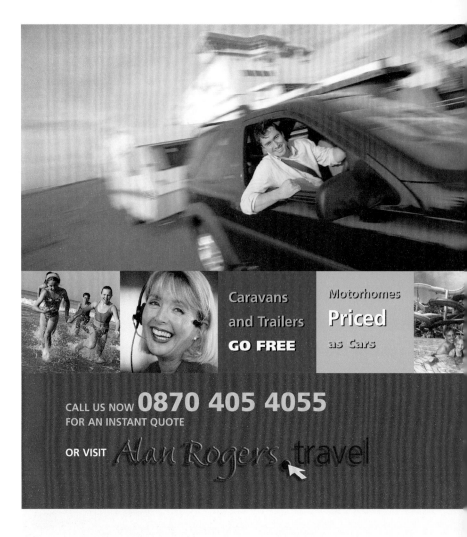

Leave The Hassle To Us

- All site fees paid in advance (nominal local tourist taxes may be payable on arrival).

- Your pitch is reserved for you – travel with peace of mind.

- No endless overseas phone calls or correspondence with foreign site owners.

- No need to pay foreign currency deposits and booking fees.

- Take advantage of our expert advice and experience of camping in Europe.

Already Booked Your Ferry?

We're confident that our ferry inclusive booking service offers unbeatable value. However, if you have already booked your ferry then we can still make a pitch-only reservation for you (minimum 5 nights). Since our prices are based on our ferry inclusive service, you need to be aware that a non-ferry booking may result in slightly higher prices than if you were to book direct with the site.

book
on-line
and save money

www.alanrogers.travel is a website designed to give you everything you need to know when it comes to booking your Alan Rogers inspected and selected campsite, and your low cost ferry.

Our friendly, expert team of travel consultants is always happy to help on **0870 405 4055** – but they do go home sometimes!

Visit www.alanrogers.travel and you'll find constantly updated information, latest ferry deals, special offers from campsites and much more. And you can visit it at any time of day or night!

www.alanrogers.travel

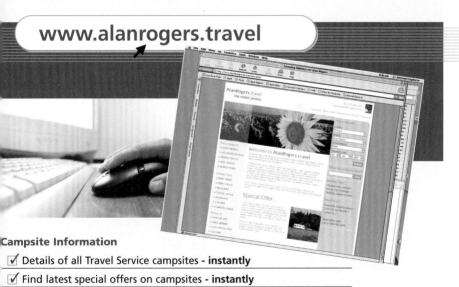

Campsite Information

☑ Details of all Travel Service campsites - **instantly**

☑ Find latest special offers on campsites - **instantly**

☑ Check campsite availability - **instantly**

Ferry Information

☑ Check ferry availability - **instantly**

☑ Find latest ferry deals - **instantly**

☑ Book your ferry online - **instantly**

☑ Save money - **instantly**

Crossing the Channel

One of the great advantages of booking your ferry-inclusive holiday with the Alan Rogers Travel Service is the tremendous value we offer. Our money-saving Ferry Deals have become legendary. As agents for all major cross-Channel operators we can book all your travel arrangements with the minimum of fuss and at the best possible rates.

Just call us for an instant quote

0870 405 4055

or visit
www.alanrogers.travel
Book on-line AND SAVE

Let us price your holiday for you

instantly!

The quickest and easiest way is to call us for advice and an instant quote. We can take details of your vehicle and party and, using our direct computer link to all the operators' reservations systems, can give you an instant price. We can even check availability for you and book a crossing while you're on the phone!

Please note we can only book ferry crossings in conjunction with a campsite holiday reservation.

One of the largest countries in Europe, with glorious beaches, a fantastic sunshine record, vibrant towns and laid back sleepy villages, plus a diversity of landscape, culture and artistic traditions, Spain has all the ingredients for a great holiday.

Spain has a huge choice of beach resorts to choose from. With charming villages and attractive towns, the Costa Brava boasts spectacular scenery with towering cliffs and sheltered coves. There are plenty of lively resorts, including Lloret, Tossa and Calella, plus several quieter ones. Further along the east coast, the Costa del Azahar stretches from Vinaros to Almanzora, with the great port of Valencia in the middle. Orange groves abound. The central section of the coastline, the Costa Blanca, has 170 miles or so of silvery-white beaches. Benidorm is the most popular resort. The Costa del Sol lies in the south, home to more beaches and brilliant sunshine, whilst in the north the Costa Verde is largely unspoiled, with clean water, sandy beaches and rocky coves against a backdrop of mountains.

Beaches and sunshine aside, Spain also has plenty of great cities and towns to explore, including Barcelona, Valencia, Seville, Madrid, Toledo and Bilbao, all offering an array of sights, galleries and museums.

Population: 39.5 million

Capital: Madrid

Climate: Spain has a very varied climate. The north is temperate with most of the rainfall; dry and very hot in the centre; subtropical along the Mediterranean

Language: Castilian Spanish is spoken by most people with Catalan (northeast), Basque (north) and Galician (northwest) used in their respective areas

Currency: The Euro (€).

Banks: Mon-Fri 09.00-14.00. Sat 09.00-13.00

Telephone The country code is 00 34

Shops: Mon-Sat 09.00-13.00/14.00 and 15.00/16.00-19.30/20.00. Many close later

Public Holidays: New Year; Epiphany; Saint's Day 19 Mar; Maundy Thurs; Good Fri; Easter Mon; Labour Day; Saint's Day 25 July; Assumption 15 Aug; National Day 12 Oct; All Saints Day 1 Nov; Constitution Day 6 Dec; Immaculate Conception 8 Dec; Christmas Day

Tourist office:
Spanish National Tourist Office
22/23 Manchester Square, London W1U 3PX

Tel: 020 7486 8077   E-mail: info.londres@tourspain.es
Fax: 020 7486 8034   Internet: http://www.tourspain.es

Flanked by the Pyrenees mountains and bathed b the Mediterranean Sea, Catalunya occupies the northeastern part of the Iberian peninsula. It has a strong identity, with a unique culture and language all of its own.

CATALUNYA IS COMPRISED OF FOUR PROVINCES: BARCELONA, TARRAGONA, LLEIDA AND GIRONA

THE REGIONAL CAPITAL IS BARCELONA

Barcelona is the historical capital of Catalunya and Spain's second leading city in both size and importance, after Madrid. The beautiful city has an impressive architectural heritage that includes the Gothic Quarter, with its cathedral, the old City Hall Building, the Episcopal Palace and the splendid Palace of the Generalitat. The city also boasts the work of the incomparable modernist architect Antonio Gaudí. In the centre of the fertile plain of the river Segre sits Lleida, capital of the province of the same name. Prominent atop a hill in the historic quarter of the city is the old cathedral or Seu Vella. The Costa Brava is the coastal zone that begins about 40 km. north of Barcelona and includes the entire shoreline of the province of Girona. It is an area of great natural beauty, formed by a succession of steep cliffs and small coves with finely grained sand. Some of its towns have been massively exploited for tourism but others, such as Tossa de Mar, still maintain their original size and fishing-village charm. The principal tourist centres on the coast include Roses, Sant Pere Pescador, L´Escala, L´Estartit, Palamos, Palafrugell, Platja d´Aro, S´Agaro, Sant Feliu de Guixols, Lloret de Mar and Blanes. There are daily boat services which operate along the coast for most of the year.

Places of interest

Empuries: Greco-Roman city.

Figueres: birthplace of Salvador Dali, museum displaying his finest work.

Girona: one of the oldest and most beautiful Catalan cities, 14th century cathedral.

La Costa Dorada: stretches south from the Costa Brava to Tarragona, with beautiful, open, well maintained beaches.

Parque Natural de Aigüamolls de L'Empordà: park made up of three reserves, with wildlife and over 320 bird species.

Sitges: attractive beach town, museum of Cau-Ferrat featuring paintings by El Greco.

Tarragona: Roman remains of Tarraco, the original Roman city.

Cuisine of the region

Mediterranean influence with lots of tomatoes, garlic, fresh herbs, olive oil, onions, fish. Wild mushrooms in the autumn. Locally produced wines from Penedés, Conca de Barberá, Pla de Bages and Alella.

Calçots: green onions grilled on a barbecue.

Cod esqueixada: cod soaked in cold water then mixed with tomatoes, olives and onion.

Escalivada: vegetable stew with roasted aubergine and peppers.

Fuet, llonganisa, butifarra: local sausages.

Suquet: seafood casserole.

Recao de binefar: rice cooked with white beans, potatoes and chorizo.

Cataluña-Catalunya North East

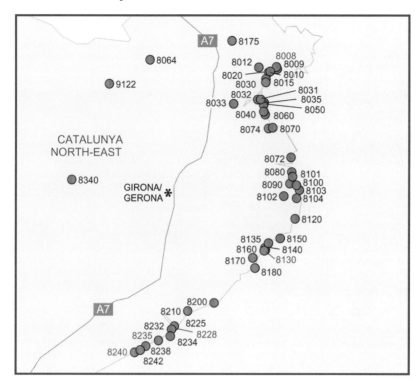

Cataluña-Catalunya South West

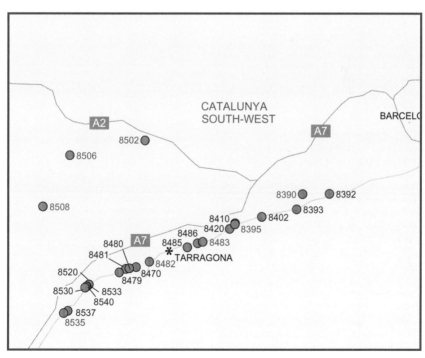

Check real time availability and at-the-gate prices...
www.alanrogers.com

ES8007 Camping Castell Montgri

Ctra Toroella - L'Estartit, km. 4.7, E-17258 L'Estartit (Girona)

Tel: **972 751 630**. Email: **cmontgri@campingparks.com**

This is a large bustling, expensive site with all the modern paraphernalia of holiday-making. Although over 50% of this site is dedicated to catering for tour operators, it does include three designated areas for independent campers. These provide 590 terraced and flat pitches, some shaded but all with electricity. On arrival you are processed by rather impersonal staff who retain your passport before inviting you to find your own place. The site could be of interest to families with teenagers, offering the possibility for parents to rest whilst the youngsters enjoy their own type of holiday within the confines of the site.

Facilities

Toilet facilities are adequate, if not that luxurious, each area having its own block. Cleaning is continual (06.00-22.00 hrs) but with the numbers on site, queuing and litter may be a problem. Bars and restaurants. Pizzeria. Takeaway. Swimming pools. Supermarket and souvenirs. Tennis. Minigolf. Playground. Large screen TV. Disco. Entertainment programme and excursions. Free bus to L'Estartit. Internet access. Torches required in some areas. Off site: Fishing 300 m. Riding 500 m. Bicycle hire 1 km. Golf 10 km.

Open: 13 May - 1 October.

Directions

Estartit is on the coast northeast of Girona. Leave the AP7/E15 and take the C66 towards Palamos. Then take the GI 642 towards Parlava and the GI 643 towards Torroella de Montgri. Site is well signed on the GI 641 Torroella de Montgri - L'Estartit road.

Charges 2006

Per person	€ 3,50
pitch incl. car and electricity	€ 9,00 - € 34,00

Prices include VAT. Minimum 7 day stay 6/7-18/8. Good discounts in low season. No credit cards.

ES8008 Camping Joncar Mar

Ctra Figueres s/n, E-17480 Roses (Girona)

Tel: **972 256 702**. Email: **info@campingjoncarmar.com**

Family owned since 1977, Jonca Mar is a mature, all year site with basic facilities. Its strength is its location with the beach promenade just outside the gate, and the many resort leisure facilities and local cultural attractions readily available to customers. The site is divided by a minor road and most leisure facilities are positioned on one side of the site. There are no views and the site has some apartment blocks around the periphery. Pitches are small (60 sq.m) with 6A electricity.

Facilities

Two dated, refurbished toilet blocks are well positioned on the main side of the site and the third very tired block on the other side is due for refurbishment. No formal facilities for disabled visitors but one toilet/shower has a wider door. Washing machine. Small shop. Small bar and buffet restaurant. Swimming pool. Basic play area. TV in bar. Limited animation programme. Internet. Torches useful. Off site: Nearest beach 50 m. Public transport 600 m. Bicycle hire 100 m. Riding 3 km. Golf 20 km.

Open: All year.

Directions

Roses is north of Girona and east of Figueres on the coast. From AP7/E15 take exit 3 south or exit 4 north (there is no exit 3 northbound) and then the N11 to the C260 and on to Roses. Site is well signed before you enter the town – follow camping signs initially.

Charges 2006

Per person	€ 5,15 - € 5,30
child (under 10 years)	€ 3,45 - € 3,55
pitch	€ 10,50 - € 11,65
electricity (10A)	€ 3,45 - € 3,55

ES8009 Camping Salatá

Port Reig s/n, Platja Salatá, E-17480 Roses (Girona)

Tel: **972 256 086**. Email: **info@campingsalata.com**

Situated in the heart of Roses, in one of the most attractive areas of the Costa Brava, Salatá is a short walk from the magnificent seafront promenade with its bars, restaurants and shops. Opposite the site entrance there is a landscaped sea inlet. There are 288 grass pitches with 16A electricity and some shade (80-110 sq.m). Buildings and amenities are well maintained. The campsite is part of a complex that includes apartments and the Hotel Terraza where a spa centre, indoor pool and other amenities can be enjoyed by campers in low season. The hotel bar/restaurant may be used at all times.

Facilities

Very clean toilet blocks have British style toilets and very good showers. Facilities for disabled visitors. Facilities for babies and children. Washing machines. Gas supplies. Bar with snacks. Swimming pool. Playground. Limited animation programme in high season. Internet. Barbecue area. Bicycle hire. Off site: Extra facilities at hotel. Tennis 300 m. Riding 5 km. Golf 15 km.

Open: February - December.

Directions

From the AP7/E15, take exit 3 south or exit 4 north (there is no exit 3 northbound) and then the N11 to the C260 and on to Roses. Site is well signed before you enter the town.

Charges 2006

Per person	€ 3,90 - € 5,35
pitch	€ 11,25 - € 22,50
incl. services	€ 16,10 - € 27,00

ES8010 Camping Castell Mar

Platja de la Rubina, E-17486 Castelló d'Empúries (Girona)

Tel: **972 450 822**. Email: **cmar@campingparks.com**

This friendly site is 350 metres from one of the very pleasant Gulf of Roses beaches, and within the large Aiguamolls de l'Empordá nature reserve. It is also convenient for (but quite separate from) the latest tourist development and facilities at Empuria Brava. With some 300 pitches, it is smaller than many sites in this part of Spain and is particularly suitable for families. The pitches, most with electricity, are of average size for the Costa Brava and are on level ground with some artificial shade mainly for tents, and natural shade from the trees and hedges.

Facilities

The large, well maintained, modern toilet block is of a high standard. Some washbasins in cabins. Facilities for disabled visitors. Laundry facilities. Bar, restaurant/pizzeria and takeaway (all season). Supermarket. Play area. Swimming pools (all season). Many activities and entertainment over a long season. Riding. ATM. Security boxes. Torches required in some areas. Off site: Boat launching 500 m. Riding and bicycle hire 1 km. Golf 10 km. Discounts at local attractions.

Open: 19 May - 23 September.

Directions

Castello d'Empuries is north of Girona and east of Figueres on the coast. From AP7/E15 take exit 3 south or exit 4 north (note there is no exit 3 north) and then N11 to the C260 towards Roses. Site signed on right at km. 40.5, just after second turn for Empuriabrava; follow road for approx. 1.5 km. GPS: N42:15.310 E03:08.196

Charges 2006

Per person	€ 3,50
child (3-10 yrs)	€ 2,50
pitch incl. electricity	€ 8,00 - € 32,00

VAT included. No credit cards.

ES8012 Camping Mas Nou

Ctra Figueres - Roses, km. 38, E-17486 Castelló d'Empúries (Girona)

Tel: **972 454 175**. Email: **info@campingmasnou.com**

Some two kilometres from the sea on the Costa Brava, this is a surprisingly tranquil site in two parts on either side of the access road. One part contains the pitches and toilet blocks, the other houses the impressive leisure complex. There are 450 neat, level and marked pitches on grass and sand, a minimum of 70 sq.m. but most 80-100 sq.m, and 300 with electricity (6/10A). The leisure complex is across the road from reception and features a huge L-shaped swimming pool with a paddling area. A formal restaurant has ajoining bar, pleasant terrace crêperie and rotisseria under palms.

Facilities

Three excellent, fully equipped sanitary blocks include baby baths, good facilities for disabled visitors. Washing machines. Supermarket and other shops. Bar/restaurant. Takeaway. Swimming pool with life guard (from 1/6). Tennis. Minigolf. Mini club (July/Aug). Play area. Electronic games. Off site: Riding 1.5 km. Fishing or bicycle hire 2 km. Beach 2.5 km. Aquatic Park. Romanica tour of famous local churches.

Open: 31 March - 30 September.

Directions

From A7 use exit 3. Mas Nou is 2 km. east of Castelló d'Empúries, on the Roses road, 10 km. from Figueres. Do not turn left across the main road but continue to the roundabout and return. GPS: N42:15.935 E03:06.150

Charges 2007

Per person	€ 2,30 - € 4,40
child (4-11 yrs)	€ 1,60 - € 3,10
pitch	€ 7,50 - € 11,90
electricity	€ 2,90 - € 4,10
dog	free - € 1,90

All plus 7% VAT.

Camping Cheques accepted.

ES8015 Camping Caravaning La Laguna

Apdo. de Correos no. 55, E-17486 Castelló d'Empúries (Girona)

Tel: **972 45 05 53**. Email: **info@campinglaguna.com**

La Laguna is a relaxed, spacious site on an isthmus within a Catalan national maritime park, on the migratory path of many different birds. It has direct access to a sandy beach and the estuary of the river Muga. The owners continue to spend much time and effort on improvements. The double lagoons are a most attractive feature. The 750 pitches (with just 10 mobile homes) are shaded and clearly marked on grass and sand, all with 6/10A electricity. There are also 24 fully serviced pitches. An attractive bar restaurant overlooks the lagoons and there are two swimming pools (one is heated in low season). A disco operates across the road from reception, keeping the noise away from the main site. A large riding school operates (May-Sept) and there are many other activites. The beach frontage is large and has a sailing school. It is said to be possible to cross over to Empuria Brava when the tide is out. There are many pleasant walks in this area and this a good site for family holidays.

Facilities

Five toilets blocks, placed to avoid long walks. All have been completely rebuilt and provide solar heated water. Laundry room and dishwashing facilities. Bar, restaurant and takeaway (all 15/3-20/10). New supermarket. Swimming pools (15/5-30/9). Basketball. Football. Tennis (free in low seasons). ATM. Minigolf. Windsurfing and sailing schools (July/Aug). Fishing. Mini club. Bicycle hire. Riding. Animation programme and competitions. Satellite TV. Internet access. Off site: Boat launching. Golf 15 km. Birdwatching.

Open: 15 March - 21 October.

Directions

Castello d'Empuries is north of Girona and east of Figueres on the coast. From AP7/E15 take exit 3 south or exit 4 north (note there is no exit 3 north) and then N11 to the C260 towards Roses. At Castello d'Empuries follow camping signs and a 4 km. unmarked road will take you to the site. GPS: N42:14.238 E03:07.284

Charges 2006

Per person	€ 4,25 - € 7,40
child (3-10 yrs)	€ 3,45 - € 5,50
pitch	€ 7,95 - € 14,40

Discounts for longer stays and pensioners in low season. No credit cards.

www.campinglaguna.com
info@campinglaguna.com

Tel. (+34) 972 45 20 33 / 45 05 53
Fax (+34) 972 45 07.99
Info. & booking:
Camping LAGUNA. Apartado de Correos 55
E-17486 Castelló d'Empúries · COSTA BRAVA

ES8020 Camping Internacional de Amberes

Playa de la Rubina, E-17487 Empúria-brava (Girona)

Tel: **972 450 507**. Email: **info@inter-amberes.com**

Situated in the 'Venice of Spain', Empuria Brava is interlaced with inland waterways and canals, where many residents and holidaymakers moor their boats directly outside their homes on the canal banks. Internacional Amberes is a large friendly site 50 m. from the wide, sandy beach, which is bordered on the east and west by the waterway canals. The site has 950 touring pitches, most enjoying some shade from strategically placed trees. All have electricity and water connections.

Facilities

Toilet facilities are in five fully equipped blocks. Washing machines. Motorcaravan services. New supermarket, bakery and shop. Restaurant/bar. Disco bar. Takeaway. Pizzeria. Watersports - windsurfing school. Organised sports activities, children's programmes and entertainment. Swimming pool. Playgrounds. Tennis. Internet and WiFi. Apartments. Off site: Beach 200 m. Fishing 300 m. Bicycle hire 500 m. Riding 1 km. Golf 12 km.

Open: 1 April - 15 October.

Directions

Empuria Brava is north of Girona and east of Figueres on the coast. From AP7/E15 take exit 3 south or exit 4 north (note there is no exit 3 north) and then N11 to the C260 towards Roses. At Empuria Brava follow camping signs to site. GPS: N42:15.160 E03:07.902

Charges 2006

Per person over 3 yrs	€ 3,10 - € 3,30
pitch incl. electricity	€ 9,50 - € 28,50

ES8032 Camping Riu

Ctra de la Platja, s/n, E-17470 Sant Pere Pescador (Girona)

Tel: **972 520 216**. Email: **info@campingriu.com**

Camping Riu is an established campsite which has been purchased by the Senia group and is being comprehensively upgraded. The pool and gym areas are brilliant for such a small site. There are 200 pitches of which 190 are for tourers with 5/10A electricity on flat ground and are shaded by mature trees. The bungalows are in a separate area away from the touring pitches. The bar restaurant and terrace are very pleasant overlooking the floodlit pool and children's area, where some animation is held in high season. Riu is on the Fluvia river, 1.5 km. from the sea.

Facilities

Two toilet blocks, one refurbished (2006), are clean and well positioned with good showers. Almost all WCs are British style. Facilities for disabled visitors. Baby room. Washing machines. Gas supplies. Supermarket. Pleasant bar and restaurant. Swimming pool. Adventure playground. Internet. New gymnasium. Bicycle hire. Animation programme including entertainment for children (high season). Kayaking. Fishing. Barbecue area. Excursions. Torches useful. Off site: Public transport 400 m. Golf 20 km. Road train to beach from site in high season.

Open: 1 April - 16 September.

Directions

Sant Pere Pescadore is on the coast between Roses and L'Escala. From AP7/E15 exit 4 take N11 north towards Figueres and then the C31 towards Torroella de Fluvia. Take Vilamacolum road east and continue to Sant Pere Pescadore. Site is well signed in the town. GPS: N42:11.247 E03:05.340

Charges 2006

Per person	€ 2,60 - € 3,50
child (1-9 yrs)	free - € 2,70
pitch	€ 4,60 - € 21,00
electricity (5A)	€ 3,50

ES8040 Camping Las Dunas

Ctra Santa Marti d'Empuries - Sant Pere, E-17470 Sant Pere Pescador (Girona)

Tel: **972 521 717**. Email: **info@campinglasdunas.com**

Las Dunas is an extremely large, impressive and well organised site with many on site activities and an ongoing programme of improvements. It has direct access to a superb sandy beach that stretches along the site for nearly a kilometre with a windsurfing school and beach bar. There is also a much used swimming pool with large double children's pools. Las Dunas is very large, with 1,700 individual hedged pitches (1,479 for tourers) of around 100 sq.m. laid out on flat ground in long, regular parallel rows. All have electrical connections and 180 also have water and drainage. Shade is available in some parts of the site. Member of Leading Campings Group.

Facilities

Five excellent large toilet blocks (with resident cleaners 07.00-21.00) have British style toilets, controllable hot showers and washbasins in cabins. Excellent facilities for youngsters, babies and disabled people. Laundry facilities. Motorcaravan services. Extensive supermarket and other shops. Large bar with terrace. Large restaurant. Takeaway. Ice-cream parlour. Beach bar in main season. Disco club. Swimming pools. Playgrounds. Tennis. Minigolf. Sailing/windsurfing school and other watersports. Programme of sports, games and entertainment, partly in English (15/6-31/8). Exchange facilities. ATM. Safety deposit. Internet café. WiFi. Dogs taken in one section. Torches required in some areas.

Open: 19 May - 2 September.

Directions

L'Escala is northeast of Girona on coast between Palamos and Roses. From A7/E15 autostrada take exit 5 towards L'Escala on GI 623. Turn north 2 km. before reaching L'Escala towards Sant Marti d'Ampurias. Site well signed. GPS: N42:09.659 E03:08.087

Charges 2006

Per person	€ 3,00 - € 4,00
child (2-10 yrs)	€ 2,50 - € 3,00
standard pitch incl. electricity	€ 13,00 - € 39,00
water and drainage	€ 1,00 - € 3,00
dog	€ 3,00 - € 4,00
All plus 7% VAT.	

ES8030 Camping Nautic Almata

Ctra Sant Pere Pescador, km 11.6, E-17486 Castelló d'Empúries (Girona)

Tel: **972 454 477**. Email: **info@almata.com**

In the Bay of Roses, south of Empuria Brava and beside the Parc Natural dels Aiguamolls de l'Empordá, this is a site of particular interest for nature lovers (especially bird watchers). Beautifully laid out, it is arranged around the river and waterways, so will suit those who like to be close to water or who enjoy watersports and boating. It is worth visiting because of its unusual aspects and the feeling of being on the canals, as well as being a high quality beachside site. A large site, there are 1,109 well kept, large, numbered pitches, all with electricity and on flat, sandy ground. There are some pitches right on the beach. As you drive through the natural park to the site watch for the warning signs for frogs on the road and enjoy the wild flamingos alongside the road.. The name no doubt derives from the fact that boats can be tied up at the small marina within the site and a slipway also gives access to a river and thence to the sea. Throughout the season there is a varied entertainment programme for children and adults. The facilities on this site are impressive. Some tour operators use the site.

Facilities

Toilet blocks of a high standard include some en-suite showers with basins. Good facilities for disabled visitors. Washing machines. Gas supplies. Excellent supermarket. Restaurant and bar. Two separate bars by beach where discos held in main season. Water-ski and windsurfing schools. 300 sq.m. swimming pool. Tennis, squash, volleyball and 'fronton' (all free). Minigolf. Games room. Extensive riding tuition with own stables and stud. Children's play park (near river). Fishing (licence required). Car, motorcycle and bicycle hire. Hairdresser. Torches are useful near beach. Off site: Canal trips 18 km. Aquatic Park 20 km.

Open: 14 May - 18 September, including all facilities.

Directions

Site is signed at 26 km. marker on C252 between Castello d'Empuries and Vildemat, then 7 km. to site. Alternatively, on San Pescador - Castello d'Empuries road head north and site is signed,

Charges 2006

Per pitch	€ 18,60 - € 37,25
person (over 3 yrs)	€ 1,75 - € 3,50
dog	€ 4,00 - € 5,10
boat or jetski	€ 7,40 - € 10,00

All plus 7% VAT. No credit cards.

ES8031 Camping La Gaviota

Ctra de la Platja s/n, E-17470 Sant Pere Pescador (Girona)

Tel: **972 520 569**. Email: **info@lagaviota.com**

La Gaviota is a delightful, small, family run site at the end of a beach access road. This ensures a peaceful situation with a choice of the pleasant L-shaped pool or direct beach access to the fine clean beach and slowly shelving access to the water. Everything here is clean and smart and the Gonzales family are very keen that you will enjoy your time here. There are 165 touring pitches on flat ground with shade and 6A electricity supply. A lush green feel is given to the site by many palms and other semi-tropical trees and shrubs.

Facilities

One smart and clean toilet block is near reception. All WCs are British style and the showers are excellent. Superb facilities for disabled visitors. Two excellent family rooms plus two baby rooms. Washing machine. Gas supplies. Supermarket. Pleasant bar and small delightful restaurant. Swimming pool. Playground. Bar. Games room. Limited animation. Beach sports and windsurfing. Internet. Torches useful. Off site: Boat launching 2 km. Riding 4 km. Golf 15 km.

Open: 20 March - 30 October.

Directions

From the AP7/E15 take exit 4 onto the N11 north towards Figueres and then the C31 towards Torroella de Fluvia. Take the Vilamacolum road east and continue to Sant Pere Pescadore. Site is well signed in the town. GPS: N42:18 E03:10

Charges 2006

Per person	€ 2,50 - € 3,10
child (under 10 yrs)	€ 1,00 - € 2,10
pitch	€ 10,50 - € 28,80
electricity (5A)	€ 2,85 - € 3,00

www.almata.com

1ª Cat

N 42° 21.248
E 3° 08.645

Camping Nautic Almata
Ctra. Giv-6216
17486 Castelló d'Empuries
Costa Brava-Girona-España
Tel:(34)972 454477
Fax:(34)972 454686
info@almata.com
www.almata.com

ES8033 Camping Las Palmeras

Ctra de la Platja, E-17470 Sant Pere Pescador (Girona)

Tel: **972 520 506**. Email: **info@campinglaspalmeras.com**

A very polished site, the pleasant experience begins as you enter the palm bedecked site and are greeted at the air conditioned reception building. The 230 pitches are flat, very clean and well maintained, with some shade and 5A electricity. A few pitches are complete with water and drainage. 26 smart mobile homes are placed unobtrusively around the site. A very pleasant pool complex has a lifeguard and the brightly coloured play areas are clean and safe. The very pleasant beach is a 200 m. walk through a gate at the rear of the site. A full animation programme allows parents a break during the day and there is organised fun in the evenings in high season. The owner Juan Carlos Alcantara and his wife have many years experience in the campsite business which is clearly demonstrated. You will enjoy a stay here as there is a very happy atmosphere.

Facilities

Two excellent, very clean toilet blocks include first class facilities for disabled campers. Baby rooms. Facilites may become a little busy at peak periods. Washing machines. Motorcaravan services. Supermarket. Restaurant/bar (children's menu). Swimming pools (heated). Play areas. Tennis. Gym. Barbecue. Bicycle hire. Mini-club. Animation. Satellite TV. Internet access. ATM. Torches useful. Off site: Beach and fishing 200 m. Sailing and boat launching 2 km. Riding 4 km. Golf 7 km.

Open: 1 April - 31 October.

Directions

Sant Pere Pescadore is south of Perpignan on coast between Roses and L'Escala. From the AP7/E15 take exit 4 onto N11 north towards Figueres and then C31 towards Torroella de Fluvia. Take the Vilamacolum road east and continue to Sant Pere Pescadore. Site well signed in town.

Charges 2006

Per person	€ 2,10 - € 3,40
child (2-10 yrs)	€ 1,50 - € 2,00
pitch	€ 11,90 - € 30,40
electricity (5A)	€ 2,90
animal	€ 2,10 - € 3,50

ES8035 Camping L'Amfora

2 Avenida Josep Tarradellas, E-17470 Sant Pere Pescador (Girona)

Tel: **972 520540**. Email: **info@campingamfora.com**

This is a superb spacious and friendly family site with a Greek theme, which is manifested mainly in the restaurant and pool areas. The site is spotlessly clean and well maintained and the owner operates in an environmentally friendly way. There are 830 pitches (730 for touring), all with 10A electrical connections and most with a water tap, on level grass with trees and shrubs. Of these, 64 pitches are large (180 sq.m.), made for two units per pitch and each with an individual sanitary facility (toilet, shower and washbasin). In addition to the individual units, three main sanitary blocks (one heated) offer free hot water, washbasins in cabins, hairdryers and baby rooms. There is extra provision near the pool area. Access is good for disabled visitors. An inviting terraced bar and self-service restaurant overlook four large swimming pools (one for children) with two water slides. Ambitious evening entertainment (pub, disco, shows) and children's animation are organised in season and a choice of watersports activities is available on the beach.

Facilities

Three main toilet blocks, one heated, provide washbasins in cabins and free showers. Baby rooms. Laundry facilities. Motorcaravan services. Supermarket. Terraced bar, self service and waiter service restaurants. Takeaway. Restaurant and bar on the beach with limited menu (high season). Disco-bar. Swimming pools (1/5-30/9). Gymnasium. Petanque. Tennis. Bicycle hire. Minigolf. Playground. Entertainment and activities. Windsurfing. Boat launching and sailing. Fishing. Exchange facilities. Games and TV rooms. Internet room and WiFi. Car wash. Torches required in beach areas. Off site: Riding 2 km. Golf 8 km.

Open: 31 March - 30 September.

Directions

Sant Pere Pescadore is on the coast between Roses and L'Escala. From the AP7/E15 take exit 4 onto the N11 north towards Figueres and then C31 towards Torroella de Fluvia. Take Vilamacolum road east and continue to Sant Pere. Site well signed in town.

Charges 2006

Per person	€ 3,20 - € 4,20
pitch (100 sq.m.)	€ 13,00 - € 32,00
with individual sanitary unit	€ 19,00 - € 50,00

Children free low season. Senior citizens specials. Electricity (10A) included. Plus 7% No credit cards. Camping Cheques accepted.

ES8050 Camping Aquarius

Playa s/n, E-17470 Sant Pere Pescador (Girona)
Tel: **972 520 003**. Email: **camping@aquarius.es**

A smart and efficient family site, Aquarius has direct access to a quiet sandy beach that slopes gently and provides good bathing (the sea is shallow for quite a long way out). One third of the site has good shade with a park-like atmosphere. There are 447 pitches with electricity (6/16A). Markus Rupp and his wife are keen to make their visitors experience a happy one and even issue flags to denote the number of years they have stayed at the site. The site is ideal for those who really like sun and sea, with a quiet situation. Mr Rupp has a background in architecture and a wealth of knowledge on the whole Catalan area and culture. He has written a booklet of suggested tours (available from reception). The family is justifiably proud of their most attractive site which they continually upgrade and improve. The fountain at the entrance, the fishponds and the water features in the restaurant are soothing and pleasing. A small stage close to the restaurant is used for live entertainment in season. The spotless beach bar complex with shaded terraces, satellite TV and evening entertainment, has marvellous views over the Bay of Roses. The 'Surf Center' with rentals, school and shop is ideal for enthusiasts and beginners alike.

Facilities

Attractively tiled, fully equipped, large toilet blocks provide some cabins for each sex. Excellent facilities for disabled people, plus baths for children. Superb new block has under-floor heating and features family cabins with showers and basins. Laundry facilities. Gas supplies. Motorcaravan services. Full size refrigerators. Supermarket. Pleasant restaurant and bar with terrace. Takeaway. Children's play centre (with qualified attendant), playground near the beach and games hall. TV room. 'Surf Center'. Minigolf. Bicycle hire. Barbecue and dance once weekly when numbers justify. ATM. Internet access. WiFi. Dogs are accepted in one section. (Note: no pool). Off site: Fishing and boat launching 3 km. Riding 6 km. Golf 15 km.

Open: 15 March - 31 October.

Directions

Sant Pere Pescadore is south of Perpignan on coast between Roses and L'Escala. From the AP7/E15 take exit 4 onto N11 north towards Figueres and then the C31 towards Torroella de Fluvia. Take the Vilamacolum road east and continue to Sant Pere Pescadore. Site well signed in town.
GPS: N42:10.614 E03:06.478

Charges 2006

Per person	€ 2,75 - € 3,30
child (2-12 yrs)	free - € 2,40
pitch acc. to season and facilities	€ 7,15 - € 35,00
electricity	€ 2,80

All plus 7% VAT. Discounts for pensioners on longer stays. No credit cards.

ES8060 Camping La Ballena Alegre 2

Ctra San Marti d'Empuries s/n, E-17470 San Pere Pescador (Girona)

Tel: **902 510 520**. Email: **infb2@ballena-alegre.com**

La Ballena Alegre 2 is partly in a lightly wooded setting, partly open, and has some 1,800 m. of frontage directly onto an excellent beach of soft golden sand (cleaned daily). They claim that none of the 1,531 touring pitches is more than 100 m. from the beach. The site has won Spanish tourist board awards and is keen on ecological fitness. The grass pitches are individually numbered and there is a choice of size (up to 100 sq.m.). Electrical connections (5/10A) are available in all parts and there are 91 fully serviced pitches. It is a great site for families.

Facilities

Seven well maintined toilet blocks are of a very high standard. Facilities for children, babies and disabled campers. Launderette. Motorcaravan services. Gas supplies. Supermarket. New 'Linen' restaurant. Self-service restaurant and bar. Takeaway. Pizzeria and beach bar in high season. Swimming pool complex. Jacuzzi. Tennis. Watersports centre. Fitness centre. Bicycle hire. Playgrounds. Sound proofed disco. Dancing twice weekly and organised activities, sports, entertainment, etc. all season. ATM. Dogs allowed in one zone (dog showers). Wi-Fi. Torches useful in beach areas. Off site: Go-karting nearby with bus service. Fishing 300 m. Riding 2 km.

Open: 12 May - 24 September.

Directions

From A7 Figueres - Girona autopista take exit 5 to L'Escala GI 623 for 18.5 km. At roundabout take sign to Sant Marti d'Empúries and follow camp signs. Access has now been entirely asphalted.
GPS: N42:09.194 E03:06.749

Charges 2006

Per person	€ 3,30 - € 3,50
child (3-9 yrs)	€ 2,50 - € 2,75
pitch incl. electricity	€ 14,90 - € 39,50
drainage plus	€ 1,25 - € 2,10
serviced pitch plus	€ 6,00 - € 11,00

All plus 7% VAT. Discount of 10% on pitch charge for pensioners all season. No credit cards.

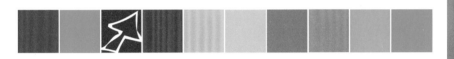

ES8064 Camping Bassegoda Park

Cami Camp de l'illa, E-17733 Albanya (Girona)

Tel: **972 542 020**. Email: **info@bassegodapark.com**

Surrounded by mountains alongside the river Muga, Bassegoda Park is a place to experience Spain in a natural environment but with a touch of luxury. This totally rebuilt site is in Albanya on the edge of the Alta Garrotxa National Park in an area of great beauty. In their own area, the 96 touring pitches are level and well shaded, all with electricity, water and drainage. Tents are dotted informally in the terraced forest areas. Particular care has been taken in the landscaping, layout and design of the whole site, but especially the most attractive pool, bar and restaurant, the hub of the site. These, with al fresco dining and night entertainment complement the natural setting. Regional wines and dishes are available in the reasonably priced restaurant. The enthusiastic young director, Estere Guerra (Steve) who speaks excellent English, and Laura have been working hard to make a stay at Bassegoda Park a unique experience. The site is designed with tourers in a separate area, 40 mobile homes in a pretty village setting and specially designed walkers' accommodation in the upper areas for those engaged in the famous G11 treks. The excellent sporting facilities, children's club and additional activities make this an ideal site for a family holiday whilst being in tune with nature.

Facilities

Three refurbished, clean toilet blocks are well positioned but could be busy at peak periods. Facilities for disabled visitors. Motorcaravan services. Washing machine. Gas supplies. Supermarket. Pleasant bar and restaurant. Swimming pool. Playground. Animation programme including children's entertainment. Walking, trekking and bicycle hire. Barbecue areas. Torches useful. Off site: Golf 20 km. Riding 15 km. Sailing 5 km. Beach 35 km. Limited public transport. The village outside the gate is unspoiled.

Open: March - December.

Directions

Site is north of Girona, west of Figures. From Barcelona on AP7/E15, take exit 4 and the N11 towards France. Then the GI 510 to Llers and GI 511 to St Llorenc de la Muga and Albanya. Site is well signed where the road ends. From France take exit 3 then the GI 510 to Llers. There is NO exit 3 northbound on the AP7/E15.

Charges 2006

Per person	€ 4,20 - € 4,75
child (0-4 yrs)	€ 3,80 - € 4,25
pitch incl. 3A electricity	€ 7,60 - € 8,60
10A electricity	€ 4,00

Camping Cheques accepted.

ES8070 Camping L'Escala

Cami Ample, E-17130 L'Escala (Girona)
Tel: **972 770 084**. Email: **info@campinglescala.com**

Under the same ownership as Las Dunas (no. ES8040), but a complete contrast in terms of size, this is a small, traditional site with limited facilities. The site has a canopy of fir trees giving excellent shade. There are 140 pitches of which 90 are for touring units, so reservation is essential. All pitches have electricity, water and drainage. In season there is a bar and restaurant offering very good food with a pleasant enclosed terrace with a retractable candy-striped canopy. There is some road noise despite the very high wall between the site and the busy road alongside.

Facilities

The central toilet block is basic but clean, with British style toilets, washbasins (two in cabins for ladies), free hot water and 25 free showers. Dishwashing and laundry sinks with hot water. Shop, bar and restaurant (all high season). Basic play area. Satellite TV. Off site: Public transport 500 m. Beach 100 m. Bicycle hire 500 m. Riding 3 km. Golf 15 km.

Open: Easter - 25 September.

Directions

L'Escala is northeast of Girona on the coast between Palamos and Roses. From A7/E15 autostrada take exit 5 towards L'Escala on GI 623. Turn north 2 km. before reaching L'Escala towards Sant Marti d'Ampurias. Site well signed on north side of town and beach. Watch for site name high on wall. GPS: N42:07.260 E03:08.087

Charges 2006

Per person	€ 2,50
child (2-10 yrs)	€ 1,80
pitch incl. electricity	€ 14,00 - € 18,00

All plus 7% VAT.

ES8072 Camping Les Medes

Paratge Camp de L'Arbre, E-17258 L'Estartit (Girona)
Tel: **972 751 805**. Email: **campinglesmedes@cambrescat.es**

Les Medes is different from some of the 'all singing, all dancing' sites so popular along this coast and the friendly family of Pla-Coll are rightly proud of their award wining site and provide a very warm welcome. With just 172 pitches, the site is small enough for the owners to know their visitors and, being campers themselves, they have been careful in planning their top class facilities and are aware of environmental issues. The level, grassy pitches range in size from 60-80 sq.m. depending on your unit. All have electricity (5,6 or 10A) and the larger ones (around half) also have water and drainage.

Facilities

Two modern spacious sanitary blocks can be heated and are extremely well maintained. Washbasins in cabins, top class facilities for disabled people and baby baths. Washing machines and dryer. Motorcaravan services. Bar with snacks (all year). Good value restaurant (1/4-31/10). Shop. Outdoor swimming and paddling pools (15/6-15/9). Indoor pool with sauna, solarium (15/9-15/6). Masseur. Play area. TV room. Internet access and Wifi. Excursions (July/Aug). Diving activities. Bicycle hire. Dogs only accepted at certain times. Torches are useful. Off site: Riding 400 m. Fishing 800 m. Beach 800 m. Medes Natural Reserve 1.5 km. Estartit 2 km. Golf 8 km.

Open: All year excl. November.

Directions

Site is signed from the main Torroella de Montgri - L'Estartit road GE641. Turn right after Camping Castel Montgri, at Joc's hamburger/pizzeria and follow signs. GPS: N42:02.900 E03:11.273

Charges 2007

Per person	€ 6,70
child (0-10 yrs)	€ 4,75
pitch	€ 15,00
electricity	€ 3,90

All plus 7% VAT. Discounts outside high season and special offers for low season longer stays. No credit cards.

ES8074 Camping Paradis

Avenida de Montgó 260, E-17130 L'Escala (Girona)
Tel: **972 770 200**. Email: **info@campingparadis.com**

If you prefer a quieter site out of the very busy resort of L'Escala then this site is an excellent option. This large, family run site has a dynamic owner Marti, who speaks excellent English. The site is divided by the beach access road and has its own private access to the very safe and unspoilt beach. There are 646 pitches, all with electricity (10A), some on sloping ground although the pitches themselves tend to be flat. Established pine trees provide shade for most places with more coverage on the western side of the site.

Facilities

Modern, fully equipped sanitary blocks are kept very clean. Washing machines and dryers. Shop, extensive modern complex of restaurants, bars and takeaways (all open all season). Swimming pools (1/5-20/9). Pool bar. Play areas. Fishing. Kayak hire. Organised activities for children in high season. ATM machine. Private access to beach. Off site: Cala Montgo beach 100 m. with a charming bay of soft sand offering all manner of watersports, pretty restaurants and a disco in season. Road train service to town centre from outside site. Riding 2 km. Golf 10 km.

Open: 17 March - 14 October.

Directions

Leave autopista A7 at exit 5 heading for Viladimat, then L'Escala. Site is well signed from town centre. Follow signs for Montgo and site is south of town beside the coast.

Charges 2007

Per person	€ 2,80 - € 5,00
child (3-10yrs)	€ 2,00 - € 3,50
pitch	€ 10,70 - € 23,60
electricity	€ 3,40

Plus 7% VAT. No credit cards.

ES8080 Camping El Delfin Verde

Ctra de Torroella de Montgri, E-17257 Torroella de Montgri (Girona)
Tel: **972 758 454**. Email: **info@eldelfinverde.com**

A large, popular and high quality site in a quiet location, El Delfin Verde has its own long beach stretching along its frontage. A prime feature of the site is an attractive large pool in the shape of a dolphin with a total area of 1,800 sq.m. This is a large site with 1420 touring pitches and approximately 6,000 visitors at peak times. It is well managed by friendly staff. Level grass pitches nearer the beach are marked and many are separated by small fences and hedging. All have electrical connections (5/6A) and access to water points. A stream runs through the centre of the site.

Facilities

Six excellent large and refurbished toilet blocks plus a seventh smaller block, all with resident cleaners, have showers using desalinated water and some washbasins in cabins. Laundry facilities. Motorcaravan services. Supermarket and shops. Swimming pools (with lifeguard). Two restaurants, grills and pizzerias. Three bars. 'La Vela' barbecue and party area. Large sports area. 2 km. exercise track. Dancing and floor shows weekly in season. Excursions. Bicycle hire. Minigolf. Playground. Trampolines. Fishing. Hairdresser. Car servicing. Gas supplies. Internet access. Dogs are not accepted in high season (11/7-14/8). Off site: Golf 4 km (20% discount). Riding 4 km.

Open: 8 April - 15 October

Directions

Torroella de Montgri is close to the coast east of Girona. From A7/E15 take exit 6 and C66 (Palafrugell). Then the GI 642 east to Parlava and turn north on C31 (L'Escala). Cross river Ter and turn east on C31 (Ulla and Torroella de Montgri). Site signed off the C31 and is at end of long approach road. Watch out for white dolphin marker and flags by road side on left. GPS: N42:00.718 E03:11.284

Charges 2006

Per person	€ 3,50 - € 4,00
child (2-9 yrs)	€ 3,00 - € 3,50
pitch incl. electricity	€ 13,00 - € 38,00
dog (excl 11/7-14/8)	€ 3,50

All plus 7% VAT. Special offers on long stays in low season.

ES8090 Camping Cypsela

Ctra de Pals - Platja de Pals, E-17256 Platja de Pals (Girona)

Tel: **972 667 696**. Email: **info@cypsela.com**

This impressive, de-luxe site with lush vegetation and trees is very efficiently run. The main part of the camping area is pinewood, with 661 clearly marked touring pitches of varying categories on sandy gravel, all with electricity and some with full facilities. The 228 'Elite' pitches of 120 sq.m. are impressive. The site has many striking features, one of which is the sumptuous complex of sport facilities and amenities near the entrance. This provides a fine large swimming pool, a good children's pool and playgrounds, two excellent squash courts, a tennis court, fitness room, and other entertainment rooms.

Facilities

Four sanitary blocks are of excellent quality with comprehensive cleaning schedules and solar heating. Three have washbasins in cabins and three have amazing children's rooms. Superb facilites for disabled people. Serviced launderette. Supermarket and other shops. Restaurant, cafeteria and takeaway. Bar. Hairdresser. Swimming pools. Tennis. Squash. Football. Minigolf. Skating rink. Fitness room. Solarium. Air conditioned social/TV room. Barbecue and party area. Children's club. Comprehensive animation programme in season. Organised sports and games activities. Games room. Business and internet centre. Medical centre. Gas supplies. ATM. Dogs are not accepted. Off site: Bicycle hire 150 m. Golf 1 km. Fishing 2 km.

Open: 12 May - 23 September.

Directions

Platja de Pals is southeast of Girona on the coast. From the AP7/E15 at Girona take exit 6 towards Palamos on the C66. This road changes number to the C31 near La Bisbal. 7.5 km past La Bisbal, exit to Pals on the GI 652. Follow signs for Platja de Pals. At El Masos take the 6502 for 1 km. Main entrance for Cypsela is on the left between the white metal fencing. GPS: N41:59.317 E03:11.083

Charges 2006

Per person	€ 5,40
child (2-10 yrs)	€ 4,25
pitch acc. to season and services	€ 17,30 - € 52,50

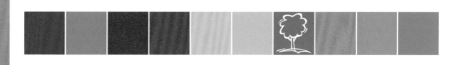

ES8170 Camping Valldaro

Apdo 57, Avenida Castell d'Aro 63, E-17250 Platja d'Aro (Girona)

Tel: **972 817 515**. Email: **info@valldaro.com**

Valldaro is 600 m. back from the sea at Platja d'Aro, a small, bright resort with a long, wide beach and plenty of amusements. It is particularly pleasant during out of peak weeks and is popular with British and Dutch visitors. Like a number of other large Spanish sites, Valldaro has been extended and many pitches have been made larger, bringing them up to 80 or 100 sq.m. There are now 1,200 pitches with 660 available for tourers. The site is flat, with pitches in rows divided up by access roads. You will probably find space here even at the height of the season.

Facilities

Four sanitary blocks are of a good standard and are well maintained. Child-size toilets. Washbasins (no cabins) and adjustable showers (temperature perhaps a bit variable). Two supermarkets and general shops. Two restaurants. Large bar. Swimming pools. Tennis. Minigolf with snack bar. Playgrounds. Sports ground. Children's club. Organised entertainment in season. Hairdresser. Internet. WiFi. Satellite TV. Gas supplies. Off site: Fishing, bicycle hire and golf 1 km. Riding 4 km.

Open: 23 March - 30 September.

Directions

Platja d'Aro is on the coast southeast of Girona. From Girona on the AP7/E15 take exit 7 to Sant Feliu on C65. On C65 at km. 313 take exit to Platja d'Aro (road number changes here to C31). In 200 m. at roundabout take GI 662 towards Platja d'Aro. Site is at km 4. If approaching from Palomas, access is via Platja d'Aro centre, exit on the GI 662 as the GI 662 cannot be accessed from the C31 southbound. GPS: N41:48.856 E03:02.622

Charges 2006

Per person	€ 3,35 - € 5,50
child (2-10 yrs)	€ 2,25 - € 3,15
pitch incl. electricity	€ 16,50 - € 37,20
dog	€ 2,35

All plus 7% VAT. Discounts in low seasons.
Camping Cheques accepted.

ES8100 Camping Inter-Pals

Avenida Mediterrania, E-17256 Platja de Pals (Girona)

Tel: **972 636 179**. Email: interpals@interpals.com

Set on sloping ground with tall pine trees providing shade and about 500 metres from the beach, Inter-Pals has 625 terraced pitches (including 280 for touring units and 250 for tents). It is sister site to no. ES8170 Valldaro. Arranged on level terraces, mostly with shade, some of the terraced pitches have views of the sea through the trees. The main entrance and its drive resembles a pretty village street as the bungalows are set on both sides of the street which is lined with traditional lamp-posts. Continuing the village theme is a row of shops where you will find most camper's needs. The formal restaurant with good value menu and choice of takeaway overlooks the pools. The site is close to Platja de Pals which is a long sandy unspoilt stretch of beach, a discreet area, part of which is now an official naturist beach. The pretty town of Pals is close by along with a good golf course. The site will assist with touring plans of the area.

Facilities

Three well maintained toilet blocks include facilities for disabled campers. Laundry facilities. Gas supplies. Fridge/TV rental. Shops. Restaurant/bar. Pizzeria with dancing and entertainment area. Café/bar by entrance. Swimming pool. Tennis. Playground. Organised activities and entertainment in high season. Excursions. Watersports arranged. ATM. Internet access. Some breeds of dog are excluded (check with site). New mini adventure park. Medical centre. Torch useful. Off site: Fishing 200 m. Bicycle hire 500 m. Golf 1 km. Riding 10 km.

Open: 19 March - 2 October

Directions

Site is on the road leading off the Torroella de Montgri-Bagur road north of Pals and going to Playa de Pals (Pals beach). GPS: N41:58.868 E03:11.985

Charges 2007

Per person	€ 3,60 - € 5,50
child (3-10 yrs)	€ 2,60 - € 3,25
pitch	€ 16,60 - € 29,30
small tent and car	€ 14,00 - € 19,00
dog	€ 2,80 - € 2,90

Plus 7% VAT. Discounts for long stays in low season. No credit cards. Camping Cheques accepted.

Check real time availability and at-the-gate prices...

www.**alanrogers**.com

ES8101 Camping Playa Brava

Avenida del Grau, 1, E-17256 Platja de Pals (Girona)

Tel: **972 636 894**. Email: **info@playabrava.com**

This is a pleasant site with an open feel which has access to a large sandy beach (200 m.) and a freshwater lagoon. On both you can enjoy watersports and you may launch your own boat. The ground is level and very grassy with shade provided for the 500 pitches by a mixture of conifer and broad-leaf trees. Electricity is provided (5A) and about a third of the pitches (75-85 sq m) have water and drainage. The air of spaciousness continues around the large swimming pool. There are no fences but huge grass sunbathing areas, the whole being overlooked by the restaurant terrace.

Facilities

Five modern, fully equipped toilet blocks include facilities for disabled visitors. Washing machines and dryers. Motorcaravan service point. Bar/restaurant. Takeaway. Supermarket. Swimming pool. Tennis. Volleyball. 5-a-side soccer. Minigolf. Play area on grass. Fishing. Watersports on river and beach, including sheltered lagoon for windsurfing learners. Internet access. Satellite TV. ATM. Gas supplies. Torches required in some areas. Dogs are not accepted. Off site: Two 18 hole golf courses 1 km. Bicycle hire 3 km. Riding 5 km.

Open: 14 May - 18 September.

Directions

Platja de Pals is southeast of Girona on the coast. From the AP7/E15 at Girona take exit 6 towards Palamos on the C66. This road changes number to the C31 near La Bisbal. 7.5 km past La Bisbal, exit to Pals on the GI 652. Follow signs for Platja de Pals. At El Masos take the 6502 east to the coast. Travel through Sa Piera (site signed). Site on left just before road ends at beach car park.
GPS: N42:00.106 E03:11.621

Charges 2007

Per person	€ 2,00 - € 3,00
child (2-9 yrs)	free - € 2,00
senior (over 60 yrs)	free - € 3,00
pitch incl. electricity	€ 23,00 - € 38,00

All plus 7% VAT. Discount for longer stays in low season. No credit cards.

ES8104 Camping Begur

Ctra d'Esclanya, km. 2, E-17255 Begur (Girona)

Tel: **972 623 201**. Email: **info@campingbegur.com**

The owners here have made a massive investment in making the site a pleasant place to spend some time. There are some good supporting facilities including a pleasant swimming pool at its centre. The bar and snack bar are part of this new pool complex and it has been well designed with terraces and sunbathing area. The touring areas are protected from the sun by mature trees and the 317 pitches are informally arranged on sloping sandy ground (chocks useful). Most pitches have electricity (10A), water and drainage. A few mobile homes and apartments are scattered around the slopes.

Facilities

Two modern toilet blocks are fully equipped and include really large showers. Excellent facilites for disabled campers. Baby bath. Washing machines and dryers. Motorcaravan services. Bar and snacks. Swimming pools (all season). Table tennis. Boules. Weight training room. Play area. Some animation in high season. Children's entertainment in high season. Little farm with ponies, goat and chickens. Internet access. Off site: Restaurant and supermarket just outside gate. Village and beaches 1.5 km. Fishing 3 km. Golf 10 km. Riding 15 km.

Open: 1 April - 30 September.

Directions

From Girona take road east to La Bisbal and Palafrugell then Begur. Turn south towards Fornells, the site is well signed 3 km. south of Begur.

Charges 2007

Per person	€ 3,00 - € 5,70
child (3-10 yrs)	€ 1,40 - € 3,10
pitch with electricity	€ 8,80 - € 18,90
animal	€ 2,60 - € 5,30

No credit cards.

ES8102 Camping Resort Mas Patoxas Bungalow Park

Ctra C31 Palafrugell-Pals, km. 339, E-17256 Pals (Girona)
Tel: **972 636 928**. Email: **info@campingmaspatoxas.com**

This is a mature and well laid out site for those who prefer to be apart from, but within easy travelling distance of, the beaches (5 km.) and town (1 km). It has a very easy access and is set on a slight slope with wide avenues on level terraces providing over 400 grassy pitches of a minimum 72 sq.m. All have electricity (5A) and water; many have drainage as well. There are some very pleasant views and shade from a variety of mature trees. Both bar and restaurant terraces give views over the pools and distant hills. The air-conditioned restaurant/bar provides both waiter service meals and takeaway food to order (weekends only mid Sept - April) and entertainment takes place on a stage below the terraces during high season. The restaurant menu is varied and very reasonable. We were impressed with the children's mini-club activity when we visited. There is a large, supervised irregularly shaped swimming pool with triple flume, a separate children's pool and a generous sunbathing area at the poolside and on the surrounding grass.

Facilities

Three modern sanitary blocks provide controllable hot showers, some washbasins with hot water. Baby bath and three cabins for children. No specific facilities for disabled people. Laundry facilities. Well stocked shop (1/4-30/9). Restaurant/bar, pizzeria and takeaway (all 1/4-30/9). Swimming pool (15/6-30/9). Tennis. Entertainment in high season. Fridges for rent. Gas supplies. Torches useful in some areas. Off site: Bus service from site gate. Bicycle hire or riding 2 km. Fishing or golf 4 km.

Open: 12 January - 16 December.

Directions

Site is east of Girona and approx. 1.5 km. south of Pals at km. 339 on the C31 Figueres-Palamos road, just north of Palafugel. GPS: N41:57.311 E03:09.478

Charges 2007

Per unit incl. 2 persons
and electricity	€ 15,00 - € 41,00
extra person	€ 3,60 - € 5,25
child (1-10 yrs)	€ 3,00 - € 3,75
dog	€ 2,10 - € 3,15

Plus 7% VAT. Special low season offers.

ES8103 Camping El Maset

Playa de Sa Riera, E-17255 Begur (Girona)

Tel: **972 623 023**. Email: **info@campingelmaset.com**

A delightful little gem of a site in lovely surroundings, El Maset has 116 pitches, of which just 20 are slightly larger for caravans or motorcaravans, the remainder suitable only for tents. The owner of some 40 years, Sr Juan Perez is delightful and his staff are very helpful. The site entrance is steep and access to the caravan pitches can be quite tricky. However, the owner's son will tow your caravan to your pitch. All these pitches have electricity, water and drainage with some shade. Tent pitches are more shaded on attractive rock-walled terraces on the hillside.

Facilities

Good sanitary facilities in three small blocks are kept very clean. Baby facilities. Washing machines and dryers. Unit for disabled campers but the ground is steep. Bar/restaurant, takeaway (all season). Shop (from May). Swimming pool (all season). Solarium. Play area. Area for football and basketball. Excellent games room. Internet access. Dogs are not accepted. Off site: Fishing 300 m. Golf and bicycle hire 1 km. Riding 8 km.

Open: Easter - 24 September.

Directions

From the C31 Figueres - Palamos road south of Pals, north of Palafrugell, take GI653 to Begur. Site is 2 km. north of the town; follow signs for Playa de Sa Riera and site (steep entrance). GPS: N41:58.116 E03:12.601

Charges 2007

Per person	€ 4,70 - € 6,70
pitch	€ 6,30 - € 14,00
electricity	€ 3,50 - € 4,70
Plus 7% VAT.	

ES8120 Kim's Camping

Font d'en Xeco, E-17211 Llafranc (Girona)

Tel: **972 301 156**. Email: **info@campingkims.com**

This attractive, terraced site (to which the owner has been welcoming guests for 50 years) is arranged on the wooded slopes of a narrow valley leading to the sea and there are many trees including huge eucalyptus. There are 350 grassy and partly shaded pitches, all with electricity (5A). Many of the larger pitches are on a plateau from which great views can be enjoyed. The terraced pitches are connected by winding drives, narrow in places. This is a pleasant place for holidays where you can enjoy the bustling atmosphere of the village and beach, while staying in a quieter environment. The site has an excellent swimming pool (with lifeguard) and children's pool, a bar, and a pleasant restaurant with 'al fresco' eating. An entertainment programme is provided. The site is under 1 km. from the resort of Llafranc. There is an outstanding view along the coastline and of the Pyrenees from Cap Sebastian close by. English and Dutch is spoken by the very friendly management and staff.

Facilities

All sanitary facilities are spotlessly clean and include a small new block and excellent toilet facilities for disabled visitors. Laundry facilities. Motorcaravan services. Gas supplies. Well stocked shop. Bar. Bakery and croissanterie. Cafe/restaurant (15/6-20/9). Swimming pools. Play areas and children's club. TV room. Excursions arranged - bus calls at site. Visits arranged to sub aqua schools for all levels of diving (high season). Torches required. WiFi. Off site: Beach, fishing, sailing and bicycle hire 500 m. Llafranc 1 km. Riding 4 km. Golf 9 km.

Open: Easter - 30 September.

Directions

Llafranc is southeast of Palafrugell. Turn off the Palafrugell - Tamariu road at turn (GIV 6542) signed 'Llafranc, Club de Tennis'. Site is on right 1 km. further on. GPS: N41:54.032 E03:11.361

Charges 2006

Per person	€ 2,50 - € 6,00
child (3-10 yrs)	free - € 3,00
pitch incl. electricity	€ 12,00 - € 25,00
Plus 7% VAT. Discounts for long stays and for senior citizens.	

Check real time availability and at-the-gate prices...

www.alanrogers.com

ES8130 Camping Internacional de Calonge

Ctra Sant Feliu/Guixols - Palamos, E-17251 Calonge (Girona)

Tel: **972 651 233**. Email: **info@intercalonge.com**

This spacious, well laid out site has access to the fine beach by a footbridge over the coast road, or you can take the little road train as the site is on very sloping ground. Calonge is a family site with two good sized pools on different levels, a paddling pool plus large sunbathing areas. The site's 800 pitches are on terraces and all have electricity (5A) with 167 available for winter use. A large proportion are suitable for touring units (the remainder for tents) being set on attractively landscaped terraces. Access to some pitches may be a little difficult. There is good shade from the tall pine trees and some views of the sea through the foliage, although the views from the upper levels are taken by the tour operator and mobile home pitches. The pools are overlooked by the restaurant terrace which has great views over the mountains. A nature area within the site is used for walks or picnics. A separate area within the site is set aside for visitors with dogs (including a dog shower!)

Facilities

Generous sanitary provision in new or renovated blocks include some washbasins in cabins. One block is heated in winter. Laundry facilities. Motorcaravan services. Gas supplies. Shop (31/3-31/10). Bar/restaurant (31/3-21/10). Patio bar (pizza and takeaway). Swimming pools (31/3-30/9). Playground. Electronic games. Rather noisy disco two nights a week (but not late). Bicycle hire. Tennis. Hairdresser. ATM. Internet. Torches necessary in some areas. Off site: Fishing 300 m. Golf 3 km. Riding 10 km. Supermarket 500 m.

Open: All year.

Directions

Site is on the inland side of the coast road between Palamos and Platja d'Aro. Take the C31 south to the 661 at Calonge. At Calonge follow signs to the C253 towards Platja d'Aro and on to site which is well signed.

Charges 2007

Per person	€ 3,40 - € 6,80
child (3-10 yrs)	€ 1,75 - € 3,85
pitch incl. electricity	€ 11,30 - € 25,00

All plus 7% VAT. Discounts for longer stays Oct - end May. No credit cards.

ES8135 Eurocamping

Ctra Palamós - Platja d'Aro, km. 49.2, E-17252 Sant Antoni di Calonge (Girona)

Tel: **972 650 879**. Email: **info@euro-camping.com**

This large campsite on the Costa Brava near Girona is attractively landscaped, with lawns, flowers and pretty features around the site, and 584 grass and gravel pitches (444 for touring). The size of the pitches varies, with some of good size and others that would struggle with larger units. Older areas of the campsite are shaded by tall trees creating a cooler zone, while the new areas have good size trees but are not yet under the same shade canopy. There are two pool complexes, one with an unusual feature where one large pool cascades into another at a slightly lower level.

Facilities

Four refurbished, clean toilet blocks vary in size and are well positioned. 11 private cabins for rent. Good facilities for disabled visitors. Rooms for babies and families. Washing machines. Gas supplies. Supermarket just outside gate. Pleasant bars and good restaurant. Swimming pools. Playgrounds. Full animation programme. Internet and WiFi. ATM. Excursions. Beach train (July/Aug). Torches useful. Off site: Beach 300 m. Fishing 300 m. Golf 6 km. Riding 15 km. Bicycle hire 100 m.

Open: 8 April - 24 September.

Directions

The town of Sant Antoni de Calonge is southeast of Girona on the coast. Leave the AP7/E15 at exit 6. Take the C66 towards Palomos which becomes the C31. Use the C31 (Girona - Palomos) road to avoid Palomas town. Take the C253 coast road. Site well signed at northern end of Sant Antoni de Calonge.

Charges 2006

Per person	€ 2,25 - € 5,55
pitch	€ 15,90 - € 26,05

37

ES8140 Camping Treumal

Ctra 253, km. 47.5, E-17250 Calonge (Girona)

Tel: **972 651 095**. Email: **info@campingtreumal.com**

This very attractive terraced site has been developed on a hillside around the attractive gardens of a large, spectacular estate house which is close to the sea. The house is the focus of the site's excellent facilities, including a superb restaurant with terraces overlooking two tranquil beaches, protected in pretty coves. The site has 550 pitches on well shaded terraces. Of these 447 are accessible to tourers and there are some 50 pitches on flat ground alongside the sea – the views are stunning and you wake to the sound of the waves. Electrical connections are available in all parts (5/16A).

Facilities

Four well maintained sanitary blocks have free hot water in the washbasins (with some private cabins) and controllable showers, and a tap to draw from for the sinks. New beach block. Washing machines. Motorcaravan services. Gas supplies. Supermarket, bar and takeaway (all season). Restaurant (15/6-15/9). Fishing. Play area. Sports area. Games room. Satellite TV. Internet access and WiFi. ATM. Off site: Bicycle hire 2 km. (delivered to site). Riding, golf 5 km.

Open: 1 April - 30 September.

Directions

Site is southeast of Girona on the coast 3 km. south of Palomos. It is best to avoid the town centre by using C31 (Girona - Palomós) road, leave at km 320, and take road south to Sant Anthoni de Calonge. Take C253 south towards Platja d'Aro. Site well signed. GPS: N41:50.185 E03:05.235

Charges 2007

Per person	€ 3,70 - € 6,70
child (4-10 yrs)	€ 2,20 - € 3,80
caravan, car and electricity	€ 13,80 - € 25,50
motorcaravan and electricity	€ 13,30 - € 24,50

Plus 7% VAT. Discounts in low seasons. No credit cards.

ES8150 Camping Internacional de Palamós

Apto. Correus 100, E-17230 Palamós (Girona)

Tel: **972 314 736**. Email: **info@internacionalpalamos.com**

This is a comfortable site which is clean, welcoming and useful for exploring the local area from a peaceful base. traditional in style, it is open for a long season and has a range of facilities. It might have space when others are full and has over 450 moderate sized pitches. The majority are level and terraced with some less defined under pine trees on a gentle slope. All pitches have a sink and variable shade, with electrical connections (6A) available in most parts. Some access roads are gravel and may suffer in the case of heavy rain.

Facilities

Two refurbished toilet blocks and one smart new one are fully equipped. Some washbasins in cabins. Facilities for disabled people. Laundry room. Small shop. Bar (1/4-29/9). Snack bar serving simple food and takeaway (from 1/6). Swimming pool (36 x 16 m.) with paddling pool. Torches necessary. Off site: Nearest beach 400 m. Fishing 500 m. Town 1 km. with hourly bus service. Bicycle hire or riding 1.5 km.

Open: 15 April - 30 September.

Directions

Central Palamós streets are too narrow for caravans which should turn off C255 road just outside Palamós. Continue north by large garage signed Kings Camping and La Fosca. Turn right just before Kings and follow Camping Internacional Palamos signs (not those for another site close by called Camping Palamos).

Charges 2006

Per person	€ 2,85 - € 3,15
child (under 10 yrs)	€ 2,10 - € 2,30
pitch with electricity	€ 20,80 - € 30,85
tent pitch	€ 5,90 - € 14,85

All plus 7% VAT. No credit cards.
Camping Cheques accepted.

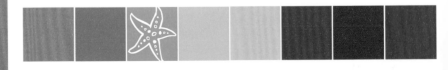

Check real time availability and at-the-gate prices...

www.alanrogers.com

ES8160 Camping Cala Gogo

Ctra Sant Feliu - Palamos, km 46.5, Platja d'Aro, E-17251 Calonge (Girona)

Tel: **972 651 564**. Email: **calagogo@calagogo.es**

Cala Gogo is a large traditional campsite with a pleasant situation on a wooded hillside with mature trees giving shade to most pitches. The 917 shaded touring pitches varying in size are in terraced rows, some with artificial shade, all have 10A electricity and 250 have water and drainage. There may be road noise in eastern parts of the site. Some pitches are now right by the beach, the remainder are up to 800 m. uphill, but the 'Gua gua' tractor train, operating all season, takes people between the centre of site and beach and adds to the general sense of fun.

Facilities

Seven toilet blocks are of a high standard. Some washbasins in private cabins. 2 private cabins for hire. New laundry room. Motorcaravan services. Supermarket. Restaurants and bars. Swimming and paddling pools (lifeguards). New playground. Crèche (extra charge). Sports centre. Programme of sports and entertainment. Bicycle hire. Kayaks (free). Fishing. Bureau de change. Internet access and WiFi. Dogs are not accepted mid June - end August. Off site: Bicycle hire and golf 4 km.

Open: 29 April - 24 September.

Directions

Leave AP7/E15 at exit 6. Take C66 towards Palomos which becomes the C31. Use the C31 (Girona - Palomos) road to avoid Palomas town. Take the C253 coast road. Site is 4 km. south of Palomas. GPS: N41:49.850 E03:04.948

Charges 2006

Per person	€ 3,25 - € 6,00
pitch	€ 10,10 - € 26,00

Electricity (5A) incl. Low season discounts.
All plus 7% VAT. No credit cards.

ES8175 Camping Mas Sant Josep

Ctra Santa Cristina - Platja d'Aro, km. 2, E-17246 Santa Cristina d'Aro (Girona)

Tel: **972 835 108**. Email: **info@msantjosep.com**

This is a very large well appointed site in two parts. The main side is centred around charming historic buildings, including a beautiful, but mysterious, locked and long unused chapel. Nearby are excellent lagoon style pools with a palm decorated island and a large complex including a bar, restaurant, takeaway foods and entertainment areas. The sporting facilities and fitness areas across the minor road are superb. Here there is another swimming pool and all manner of sport and training is possible. There are 868 pitches with 200 for tourers in a separate area which have shade from trees.

Facilities

Three older style toilet blocks and the facilities for tourers are better than the long stay areas. Facilities for disabled visitors and baby rooms. Washing machines. Motorcaravan service point. Supermarket. Bars, restaurant, snack bar and takeaway. Swimming pools. Playgrounds. Tennis. Spa room and gym. Internet. ATM. Bicycle hire. Torches useful. Off site: Nearest beach 3 km.

Open: 18 February - 12 December.

Directions

Site is at Santa Christiana d'Aro, 3 km. from the sea at San Feliu. From AP7 E15 (Girona - Barcelona) take exit 7 and C65 San Filiu road. Site is well signed at the Sant Christina d'Aro roundabout 3 km. from San Filiu. GPS: N41:80 E03:01

Charges 2006

Per person	€ 7,00 - € 9,00
pitch incl. electricity	€ 13,40 - € 17,95

ES8180 Camping Sant Pol

C Doctor Fleming No.1, E-17220 Sant Feliu de Guixols (Girona)

Tel: **972 327 269**. Email: **info@campingsantpol.com**

Sant Pol is a small, family owned site and Anna Genover speaks excellent English, with a firm understanding of campers needs. On the Costa Brava, this hillside site is on the edge of Sant Feliu, only 350 m. from the beach (there may be some road noise on one side of the site). An attractive pool, bar and restaurant are the central focus of the site with shaded terraces and pitches of differing sizes curving down the slope. Higher terraces have the chalets and bungalows. There are 17 pitches for tourers and the pleasant small terraces take 37 tents.

Facilities

The clean and modern sanitary block has British style WCs and hot water. WC for disabled campers, but no shower (terrain would be difficult for wheelchairs). Washing machines and dryer. Motorcaravan services. Small supermarket. Restaurant/bar. Solar heated swimming pools. Play area. Animation for children in high season. Minigolf. Internet point and WiFi. Excursions. Torches needed in some areas. Off site: Large supermarket 300 m. Beach 350 m. Regular bus service into town.

Open: 12 March - 30 November.

Directions

San Feliu is southeast of Girona and is reached via the C65 (Girona - Palomos) road. Leave this at km 312 signed to S'Agaró. Proceed towards Sant Feliu to outskirts of village. Site signed from first roundabout and is directly off second roundabout. Entrance is very steep. GPS: N41:47.196 E03:02.492

Charges 2006

Per person	€ 3,50 - € 7,00
child (5-10 yrs)	€ 2,00 - € 4,60
pitch incl. electricity	€ 11,00 - € 24,30

ES8210 Camping Tucan

Ctra de Blanes - Lloret, E-17310 Lloret de Mar (Girona)

Tel: **972 369 965**. Email: **info@campingtucan.com**

Situated on the busy Costa Brava near Lloret de Mar, Camping Tucan is well placed to access all the attractions of the area. Views over the mountains are mixed with views of the nearby town. The 250 good size pitches all have electricity, and are laid out in a herring-bone pattern with areas dedicated to singles, families with young children and couples who enjoy the quiet. Pitches are on terraces, flat surfaced with gravel and many are shaded. Tucan is a lively site with a variety of activities including an animation programme for children and modest entertainment at night.

Facilities

Two modern toilet blocks include washbasins with hot water and facilities for disabled visitors, although access is difficult. All very clean when seen. Washing machine. Gas supplies. Shop. Busy bar and good restaurant. Takeaway. Swimming pools and indoor solarium. Playground and fenced play area for toddlers. TV in bar. Bicycle hire. Animation in high season. Mini-club. Off site: Town 500 m. Nearest beach 600 m. Riding 1 km. Golf 4 km.

Open: 1 April - 30 September.

Directions

From A7/E4, A19 or N11 Girona - Barcelona roads take an exit for Lloret de Mar. Site is 1 km. west of the town, well signed and is at the base of the hill off the roundabout. The entrance can get congested in busy periods. GPS: N41:41.832 E02:49.310

Charges 2006

Per person	€ 4,20 - € 6,50
child (1-9 yrs)	€ 3,15 - € 4,40
pitch	€ 4,20 - € 10,30
electricity	€ 3,30 - € 4,30
animal	€ 1,80

ES8200 Camping Cala Llevadó

Ctra GI-682 de Tossa - Lloret, pk. 18,9, E-17320 Tossa de Mar (Girona)

Tel: **972 340 314**. Email: **info@calallevado.com**

For splendour of position Cala Llevadó can compare with almost any in this book. A beautifully situated cliff-side site, it has fine views of the sea and coast below. It is shaped something like half a bowl with steep slopes. High up in the site with a superb aspect, is the attractive restaurant/bar with a large terrace overlooking the pleasant swimming pool. There are terraced, flat areas for caravans and tents (with electricity) on the upper levels of the two slopes, with a great many individual pitches for tents scattered around the site. Some pitches have fantastic settings and views.

Facilities

Four very well equipped toilet blocks are immaculately maintained and well spaced around the site. Baby baths. Laundry facilities. Motorcaravan services. Gas supplies. Fridge hire. Large supermarket. Restaurant/bar (5/5-28/9). Swimming and paddling pools. Three play areas. Botanic garden. Entertainment for children (4-12 yrs). Sailing, water ski and windsurfing school. Fishing. Excursions. Internet access anf WiFi. Torches definitely needed in some areas. Off site: Bicycle hire 3 km. Large complex adjacent for sports, activities and swimming.

Open: 1 May - 30 September, including all amenities.

Directions

Cala Llevadó is southeast of Girona on the coast. Leave the AP7/E15 at exit 7 to the C65 Sant Feliu road and then take C35 southeast to the GI 681 to Tossa de Mare. Site is signed off the GI 682 Lloret - Tossa road at km 18.9, about 3 km. from Tossa. Route avoids difficult coastal road.
GPS: N41:42.769 E02:54.374

Charges 2006

Per person	€ 4,90 - € 7,90
child (4-12 yrs)	€ 3,00 - € 4,30
pitch incl. car	€ 8,25 - € 16,10
electricity	€ 3,95 - € 4,30
Plus 7% VAT.	

ES8225 Camping La Masia

C/Colon, 44, E-17300 Blanes (Girona)

Tel: **972 331013**. Email: **info@campinglamasia.com**

A large resort site, La Masia has 757 pitches with 300 for touring units. These pitches are flat, shaded by trees and in rows with some mobile homes inserted here and there. There is something for everyone in La Masia and the resort town is just outside the gate, as is the fine beach. A large, central building houses the main bar and restaurant. The jewel in the crown of the site is below this complex where you can enjoy an indoor heated pool, spas, massage, plunge pools and exercise pools, and pamper yourself in luxury in a Roman Bath type setting (extra charge).

Facilities

Six well maintained toilet blocks provide basic facilities with facilities for disabled campers and a well equipped baby room (key at reception). Motorcaravan services. Laundry facilities. Supermarket. Bakery. Restaurants. Snack bars. Swimming pools. Spa centre. Play areas. Boules. Bicycle hire. Barbecue area. Entertainment programme. Internet. WiFi. ATM. Exchange service. Security boxes. Torches useful. Off site: Resort town and beach outside the gate. Fishing. Boat launching 200 m. Bicycle hire 1 km. Riding 3 km. Golf 5 km.

Open: 1 April - 30 September.

Directions

Camping La Masia is on the southwest side of Blanes. From exit 9 on the AP7 Girona/Barcelona road follow the N11 to the B600 towards Blanes. Before entering Blanes turn southwest following site signs at the roundabouts which will direct you to La Masia avoiding Blanes town which has narrow roads and is best avoided by large units.

Charges 2006

Per persoon	€ 4,50 - € 6,10
pitch	€ 7,15 - € 23,75

Camping Cheques accepted.

ES8228 Camping Blanes

Avenida Villa de Madrid, 33, Apdo. Correus 72, E-17300 Blanes (Girona)

Tel: **972 331 591**. Email: **info@campingblanes.com**

Camping Blanes is the first of the sites which edge the pedestrian promenade here and probably the smallest. Open all year, it is family owned and run and indeed has been in the hands of the Boix family for 40 years. Antonio the son runs the site now with pride and care, speaking good English. With only 206 pitches, no bungalows or mobile homes and only 5 seasonal vans, there is a comfortable atmosphere. Shade is provided by tall pines and because of this, some of the pitches are a bit irregular in shape and average between 60-80 sq m.

Facilities

Traditional but well equipped sanitary block with provision for disabled visitors (by key). Baby changing unit. Washing machine and dryer. Shop (15/6-15/9). Bar (1/4-12/10). Restaurant (7/7-25/8). Takeaway (7/7-25/8). Swimming pool. Play area. No organized entertainment. Beach alongside site. Off site: All amenities of the town are within walking distance (500 m). Blanes is fishing port with a range watersports possible. Golf and riding 5 km.

Open: All year.

Directions

Site is south of the town beside the beach before Camping Bella Terra and El Pinar. Follow signs for 'campings' until individual site signs appear. GPS: N41:39.5 E02:46.8

Charges 2007

Per person	€ 4,40 - € 6,10
pitch incl. electricity	€ 12,95 - € 17,60

All plus 7% VAT. Less 10% in low season.

ES8232 Camping Bella Terra

Avenida Vila de Madrid 35-40, E-17300 Blanes (Girona)

Tel: **972 348017**. Email: **info@campingbellaterra.com**

Camping Bella Terra is set in a shady pine grove facing a white sandy beach on the Mediterranean coast. There are 906 pitches with 830 for touring units, the rest taken by bungalows to rent (75) and by Spanish 'residents' (200). All pitches have 5/6A electricity and 24 are fully serviced. The site is in two sections, each with its own reception, on either side of a road which leads to another campsite. The main reception is on the right of the road as you approach, as are the restaurant with its own bar and the two new swimming pools.

Facilities

The older sanitary blocks are just acceptable with provision for disabled visitors and laundry. The block on the newer side is much more modern and spacious. It includes very good facilities for children. Shop, restaurant, bar and takeaway and outdoor swimming pool (all May - Sept). Playground. Fishing. Bicycle hire. Internet. WiFi. Mini-club. Off site: Blanes town within walking distance.

Open: 1 April - 30 September.

Directions

Site is on the southwest side of Blanes. From exit 9 on the AP7 Girona/Barcelona road follow N11 to the B600 towards Blanes. Before entering Blanes turn southwest following site signs at the roundabouts. GPS: N41:39.696 E02:46.567

Charges 2006

Per person	€ 4,00 - € 5,00
pitch	€ 13,90 - € 32,60

ES9122 Camping Montagut

Ctra Montagut-Sadernes, km. 2, E-17855 Montagut (Girona)

Tel: **972 287 202**. Email: **info@campingmontagut.com**

This is a delightful, small family site where everything is kept in pristine condition. Jordi and Nuria, a brother and sister team, work hard to make you welcome and maintain the superb appearance of the site. Flowers and shrubs abound, with 90 pitches on attractively landscaped and carefully constructed terraces or on flat areas overlooking the pool. A tranquil atmosphere pervades the site and drinks on the pleasant restaurant terrace are recommended, along with sampling the authentic menu as you enjoy the views over the Alta Garrotxa.

Facilities

The modern sanitary block has free hot showers, washing and laundry facilities plus a modern section for babies and disabled campers; everything was spotless when seen. Motorcaravan services. Restaurant and bar (31/3-21/10; weekends only in low season). Supermarket. Medium sized swimming pool with large sunbathing area and children's pool (1/5-30/9). Playground. Petanque. Barbecue area. Torches are useful in some areas.

Open: 31 March - 21 October.

Directions

Going west from Figueres on N260 Olot road, approx. 10 km. past Besalu at km. 75, turn right towards Montagut. At end of village turn left towards Sadernes and site entrance is 3 km. GPS: N42:14.814 E02:35.826

Charges 2007

Per person	€ 4,65 - € 6,15
pitch incl. electricity	€ 13,15 - € 16,25

Plus 7% VAT. No credit cards.

ES9143 Camping Pirineus

Ctra Guils de Cerdanya, km. 2, E-17528 Guils de Cerdanya (Girona)

Tel: **972 881 062**. Email: **guils@stel.es**

This is a sister site to nos. ES8420 and ES9144, with a well organized entrance and an immediate impression of space, green trees and grass – there is always someone watering and clearing up to maintain the high standards here. The pitches are neat, marked, of average size and organized in rows. Generally flat with some on a gentle incline, many trees offer shade but watch overhanging branches if you have a high unit. From the restaurant terrace you have fine views of the mountains in the background and the pool in the foreground.

Facilities

Two fully equipped, sanitary blocks of top quality and decorated with boxes of bright flowers, are kept spotlessly clean and can be heated. Smart washing machines and dryers. Motorcaravan service point. Shop, bar and restaurant (all season). Heated swimming pool and circular paddling pool. Boules. Tennis. Outdoor sports. Play area. Excursions. Entertainment (high season). Dogs are not accepted. Off site: River fishing. Bicycle hire 2 km. Riding 4 km. Golf 6 km.

Open: 16 June - 11 September.

Directions

From Perpignan take N116 to Prades and Andorra. Exit at Piugcerda taking N-250 signed Le Seu d'Urgell and almost immediately take second right for Guils de Cerdanya. Follow for 2 km. to site on right. GPS: N42:26.587 E01:54.350

Charges 2006

Per person	€ 5,62
pitch incl. electricity	€ 24,18

All plus 7% VAT. No credit cards.

ES9144 Camping Stel

Ctra N-152 Ramal-Llivia s/n, E-17520 Puigcerdá (Girona)

Tel: **972 882 361**. Email: **puigcerda@stel.es**

Sister site to ES8420 and ES9143, this is an extremely efficient, if pricey site. Part of a large, attractive building, the spacious entrance houses a modern reception (English is spoken). From here you will quickly be on your way to one of the flat, terraced pitches. Many of the pitches have shade and all are marked, clean and organized in rows with a water tap for each row. There is some road noise so, in order to avoid this and have views of the Cerdanya valley and the eastern Pyrenées, take one of the pitches on the upper terraces. It is worth the trouble.

Facilities

Sanitary facilities in the main building are of very high standard and are kept very clean. A small, smart block serves the upper terraces. Both can be heated. Separate modern unit with facilities for disabled campers. Laundry facilities. Shop. Bar/restaurant (all season). Swimming pool (July-Sept). Boules. Novel adventure style play frame (supervision needed). Adventure club (watersports and outdoor activities). Animation (high season). Off site: Riding 5 km. Fishing and golf 7 km.

Open: 2 June - 24 September.

Directions

From Perpignan take N116 to Prades and Andorra. At roundabout at the border crossing at Puigcerdá take first right for Llivia (almost a turn back on yourself). Site is on left after 1 km. GPS: N42:26.492 E01:56.477

Charges 2006

Per person	€ 5,00
pitch incl. electricity	€ 21,40

All plus 7% VAT. No credit cards.
Camping Cheques accepted.

ES9121 Camping de la Vall d'Ager

Ctra Afores, s/n, E-256 Ager 91 (Lleida)

Tel: **973 455 200**. Email: **iniciatives@valldager.com**

Ager is not on a through-route to anywhere – hence the very peaceful situation. So, if you are coming here it is likely to be for a specific reason. One of the main reasons could be that it is a hang-glider's paradise. The Montsec mountain range (1,677 m.) towers over the site in the Catalan pre-Pyrenees. There are 132 pitches (85 for touring) on slightly sloping ground, marked out by trees and with some shade. Electricity (10A) is available to all. Site activities revolve around flying – one of the landing sites is just outside the perimeter and even the beer pump is in the form of a hang-glider!

Facilities

A central sanitary building provides large showers (with divider and lots of room to change). Separate facilities for disabled visitors. Washing machine and dryer downstairs. Bar, snack bar and restaurant (all year). Shop (July/Aug). Bicycle hire. Delta-wing store. Swimming pools (high season). Boules. Barbecue. Play area. Torches are required. Off site: Interesting village of Ager 300-400 m. Summer parties in the village. Riding 500 m. Fishing 7 km.

Open: All year.

Directions

Site is on northern edge of Ager village, at km. 201 on the C12 from Balaguer (which is 28 km. NNE of Lleida) to Tremp. Alternatively, use the excellent C13 Lleida - Tremp road and turn west near km. 67 onto the C12 (formerly L904) which has not yet been modernised and has old, narrow sections requiring attention. GPS: N42:00.250 E00:46.008

Charges 2006

Per person	€ 4,80
child (under 10 yrs)	€ 4,40
pitch incl. electricity	€ 14,80

ES9123 Camping El Solsones

Ctra Sant Llorenc, km. 2, E-25280 Solsona (Lleida)

Tel: **973 482 861**. Email: **info@campingsolsones.com**

Situated on a hillside, two kilometres from Solsona, this all year site has pleasant views of the hills on three sides and lots of mature trees giving a pleasant green shady appearance. With a lovely Spanish feel, it would be a pleasant spot for a short stay during any season. There are many weekend units here, and although only 72 of the 269 pitches are for touring (22 for caravans or motorcaravans and 50 for tents), we were told that finding a pitch was unlikely to be a problem. They are in separate sections of the site and are slightly sloping, with shade and 4/6A electricity.

Facilities

Modern sanitary facilities are in two buildings, with free hot water. Motorcaravan services. Large supermarket. Restaurant and bar (24/6-15/9 and winter weekends). Simple meals and snacks served indoors and outside on the terrace overlooking the pool. Swimming pool with lifeguard (24/6-16/9). Excellent sports complex. Minigolf. Tennis. Bicycle hire. Play area. Petanque. Aviary. Picnic area. Off site: Golf, riding and skiing nearby. Solsona is interesting with good bars, restaurants and cafés.

Open: All year.

Directions

Solsona is 45 km. northwest of Manresa, along the C55 and is on the C26 Lleida/Andorra - Barga road. Site is 2 km. out of town on the LV4241 signed to Sant Llorenc de Morunys and Ski Port del Comte. GPS: N42:00.799 E01:31.035

Charges 2006

Per person	€ 5,00
child (2-10 yrs)	€ 4,65
pitch incl. electricity	€ 12,50 - € 16,50
Plus 7% VAT.	

ES9142 Camping Solana del Segre

Ctra N260, km. 198, E-25720 Bellver de Cerdanya (Lleida)

Tel: **973 510 310**. Email: **sds@solanadelsegre.com**

The Sierra del Cadi offers some spectacular scenery and the Reserva Cerdanya is very popular with Spanish skiers. This site is situated in an open, sunny lower valley beside the River Segré where the far bank is a National Park (unfenced so children will need supervision). The immediate area is ideal for walkers and offers many opportunities for outdoor sports enthusiasts. The site is in two sections, the lower one nearer the river being for tourists, mainly flat and grassy with 200 pitches of 100 sq.m. or more, shaded by trees with 15A electricity. The upper area is taken by permanent units.

Facilities

Modern sanitary facilities are in a central building on the lower level, with extra 'portacabin' style units (unisex toilets/showers). Facilities for disabled campers are on the upper level (wheelchair users will experience problems). Laundry facilities. Motorcaravan services. Shop, bar and restaurant (1/6-15/9). Swimming and paddling pools (1/6-5/9). Indoor pool. Two play areas. Games room. River fishing. Dance area. Barbecue areas. Internet. Torches are required. Off site: Village has a range of shops bars and restaurants. Riding 2 km. Bicycle hire and golf 10 km. Skiing. Superb walking area.

Open: 1 June - 15 September.

Directions

Site is on left at the 198 km. marker on the N260 from Puigcerda to La Seu d'Urgell, well signed just beyond Bellver le Cerdanya.
GPS: N42:22.352 E01:45.629

Charges 2006

Per person	€ 4,68
child	€ 2,81
pitch incl. electricity	€ 17,29
dog	€ 2,81
Plus 7% VAT.	

ES8234 Camping del Mar

Avenida Pomareda s/n, E-08380 Malgrat de Mar (Barcelona)

Tel: **937 653 767**. Email: **delmar@campingsonline.com**

With such a wide choice of campsites along this part of the coast, standards have to be kept high and that is just what the Sisa family achieve at Camping del Mar. Beautifully manicured lawns and a well designed site help to create a relaxed atmosphere. All the facilities are kept immaculately clean. The 120 flat, grassy pitches all have electricity (6A) and easy access to a water point. The site is surrounded by a high hedge providing privacy and some shade to those pitches alongside. In time the many young trees and shrubs on the site will give plenty of shade.

Facilities

Modern, clean sanitary facilities are in the central building. Showers in large cubicles, open style washbasins and controllable hot water. Separate laundry room with washing machines. Small shop. Bar with TV and separate restaurant with varied menu. Games room. Swimming pool with separate children's pool. Multisports court. Tennis court. Large play area. Minigolf. Children's club and entertainment (July/Aug). Off site: Boat launching 4 km. Riding 5 km. Golf 20 km.

Open: 15 April - 30 October.

Directions

From Malgrat de Mar town centre follow signs to 'zona campings'. Cross railway line and head north along beach front. Site is the second campsite on the left.

Charges 2006

Per unit incl. 2 persons	
and electricity	€ 18,50 - € 26,70
extra person	€ 3,30 - € 5,10
child (4-10 yrs)	€ 2,50 - € 4,00

Widely regarded as the 'Bible' by site owners and readers alike, there is no better guide when it comes to forming an independent view of a campsite's quality. When you need to be confident in your choice of campsite, you need the Alan Rogers Guide.

- ✓ **Sites only included on merit**
- ✓ **Sites cannot pay to be included**
- ✓ **Independently inspected, rigorously assessed**
- ✓ **Impartial reviews**
- ✓ **40 years of expertise**

ES8235 Camping Bon Repos

Malgrat de Mar, E-08398 Santa Susana (Barcelona)

Tel: **937 678 475**. Email: **info@campingbonrepos.com**

If you enjoy the hustle and bustle of the Costa Brava in summer, then Bon Repos is ideal. It is a long, narrow coastal site with many pitches along the length of the attractive fine sandy beach with direct access and no fence. The 500 pitches are of reasonable size, flat with a sand surface and lots of shade, and with 10A electricity. The beach is a strong point of the site having rocky outcrops and close by is the bar/restaurant with huge terrace. The pool is overlooked from here through perspex screens and the terrace was buzzing when we visited.

Facilities

The two sanitary blocks are dated but clean. The number of showers is low and we suspect they are extremely busy at peak periods. Cold water at washbasins. Units for disabled campers. Baby room. Washing machines and dryers. Motorcaravan services. Supermarket. Restaurant. Chicken bar. Swimming pools (with lifeguard). Play area. Internet. Barbecue area. Tennis. Bicycle hire. Animation and happy hour. ATM. Torches useful. Off site: Resort town very close by. Boat launching 200 m. Bicycle hire 1 km. Riding 3 km. Golf 5 km.

Open: All year.

Directions

From A7 exit 9 (A19 exit 22) take road to Malgrat de Mar. Then turn south on coast road for Santa Susanna. Follow obvious campsite signs – they lead to site through a high tunnel under the railway line on a minor beach road.

Charges 2006

Per person	€ 4,50
child	€ 3,60
pitch incl. electricity	€ 29,00

ES8238 Camping Caballo de Mar

Passeig Maritim 52 - 54, E-08397 Pineda de Mar (Barcelona)

Tel: **937 671 706**. Email: **info@caballodemar.com**

This is definitely a site for lovers of the seaside with its direct access to a lovely, sandy beach. Actually divided into two parts by the railway and dual-carriageway, the main part of the site is neatly arranged off a central access road with plenty of colourful shrubs and trees providing shade. In total there are 400 pitches, 200 taken by seasonal visitors and a few bungalows. On the beach side of the site the pitches are generally smaller (60-70 sq.m.) with less shade (some artificial shade) but there is a bar and a toilet block on this side. All pitches have electricity (5/6A).

Facilities

Two toilet blocks, one in each area, are fully equipped and well maintained. En-suite units to rent (main side) with units for disabled visitors. Facilities for babies. Washing machines. Motorcaravan services. Shop (limited hours in low season). Main bar and restaurant (all season). Swimming pool. Play area. Entertainment organised. Off site: Beach activities. Town with bars and restaurants within walking distance. Bicycle hire 500 m. Riding 3 km.

Open: 1 April - 30 September.

Directions

Site is between Pineda and Calella with access off dual-carriageway linking the two places and runs parallel to the railway. GPS: N41:37.080 E02:40.603

Charges 2006

Per person	€ 3,90 - € 5,90
child (1-9 yrs)	€ 2,90 - € 4,40
pitch	€ 3,90 - € 9,60
electricity (3/6A)	€ 3,40 - € 4,40

45

ES8240 Camping Botánic Bona Vista

Ctra N-II, km 665,8, E-08370 Calella de la Costa (Barcelona)

Tel: **93 769 24 88**. Email: **info@botanic-bonavista.net**

While Calella itself may conjure up visions of mass tourism, this site is set on a steep hillside some 3 km. out of the town. Apart from perhaps some noise from the nearby coast road and railway, it is a quite delightful setting with an abundance of flowers, shrubs and roses (1,700, all planted by the knowledgeable owner Kim, who has won prizes for his roses). The site celebrated its 40th anniversary in 2006. Its design successfully marries the beautiful botanic surrounds with the attractive views of the bay. Of the 160 pitches, 130 are for tourers, all with electricity and on flat terraces on the slopes, with some shade.

Facilities

The standard of design in the three sanitary blocks is quite outstanding for a small site (indeed for any site). Some washbasins in cabins in the newest block. Baby room. Washing machines. Motorcaravan services. Bar/restaurant, takeaway and shop (1/4-1/10). Outdoor pool (1/5-30/9). Large play area. Recreation park. Satellite TV. Internet point. Games room. Barbecue and picnic area. No cycling on site. Off site: Fishing 100 m. Bicycle hire 1 km. Riding and golf 3 km. Watersports near.

Open: All year.

Directions

From N11 coast road, site is signed south of Calella (km. 665), and is on right hand side of road. The road is busy and sign is almost on top of turn (entrance shared with Camping Roca Grossa). Entrance is very steep. From Barcelona, pass through Sant Pol de Mar, go into outside lane shortly after 'Camping 800 m.' sign and keep signalling left. Site entrance is just before the two lanes merge. GPS: N41:36.411 E02:38.551

Charges 2007

Per person	€ 5,95
child (3-10 yrs)	€ 5,40
pitch incl. electricity	€ 17,90
All plus 7% VAT.	

ES8242 Camping Roca Grossa

Ctra N-II, km 665, E-08370 Calella de la Costa (Barcelona)

Tel: **937 691 297**. Email: **rocagrossa@rocagrossa.com**

Roca Grossa celebrated its 50th year in 2006. The owners, the Bachs family, are very friendly and there is a very happy atmosphere in the campsite. Very steep slopes predominate at this site and there is a 100 m. climb from reception to the swimming pool set at the top of the site. In high season a road train runs all day to ferry you to the amenities, but the site is unsuitable for disabled campers. The bonus is some great views over the sea from most of the terraced, but flat and reasonably sized pitches. Landrovers are used to site your unit.

Facilities

An amazing array of clean sanitary blocks means there is not far to walk from any area of the site. Large and small, all blocks are well kept with hot water throughout. Washing machines. Gas supplies. Shop. Pleasant bar (with internet) and restaurant. Swimming pools (May - Sept). Playground. Road train. Tennis. Animation programme including children's entertainment. Excursions. ATM. Torches useful. Off site: Beach, boat launching and fishing 50 m. Town 100 m. Riding 1 km. Golf 2 km. Watersports nearby.

Open: 1 April - 30 September.

Directions

From A7 (Girona - Barcelona) take exit 9 or 10 for Malgrat del Mar on the N11. Turn south towards Calella and site is at 665 km. marker sharing an entrance with another campsite. Caravans are placed on pitches with site Landrover.

Charges 2006

Per person		€ 5,85
child (under 10 yrs)		€ 5,15
pitch incl. electricity	€ 10,60 -	€ 16,45
dog		€ 3,50
No credit cards.		

ES8390 Camping Vilanova Park

Ctra de l'Arboc, km. 2.5, E-08800 Vilanova i la Geltru (Barcelona)

Tel: 93 893 34 02. Email: info@vilanovapark.es

Sitting on the terrace of the bustling but comfortable restaurant at Vilanova Park, it is difficult to believe that in 1908 this was a Catalan farm and then, quite lacking in trees, it was known as 'Rock Farm'. Since then imaginative planting has provided literally thousands of trees and gloriously colourful shrubs making a most attractive, large campsite, with an impressive range of high quality amenities and facilities open all year. There are 248 marked pitches for touring units in separate areas. All have 6A electricity, 133 also have water and some larger pitches (100 sq.m.) also have drainage. The terrain, hard surfaced and mostly on very gently sloping ground, has many trees and considerable shade. At present there are 865 pitches with a significant proportion occupied by bungalows and chalets carefully designed to fit into the environment. The really good amenities include a second pool higher up in the site with marvellous views across the town to the sea and a second, more intimate restaurant for that special romantic dinner overlooking the twinkling evening lights. The original pool has water jets and a coloured floodlit fountain playing at night time, which complement the dancing and entertainment taking place on the stage in the courtyard overlooking the pool. An unusual attraction is a Nature Park and mini-zoo with deer and birdlife, which has pleasant picnic areas and views. An indoor pool, sauna and gym are planned which will be appreciated by winter visitors as will the excursion programmes to Barcelona, Monserrat and Bodegas Torres for wine tasting. There is a transfer service from both Barcelona and Reus airports.

Facilities

All toilet blocks are of excellent quality, can be heated and have washbasins (over half in cabins) with free hot water, and others of standard type with cold water. Serviced laundry. Motorcaravan services. Supermarket. Souvenir shop. Restaurants. Bar with simple meals (all year). Swimming pools (outdoor 1/4 - 15/10, indoor all year). Play areas. Games room. Tennis. Bicycle hire. Tennis. ATM and exchange facilities. Off site: Fishing 4 km. Golf 5 km. Good train service from Vilanova to Barcelona, not so good the other way (to Tarragona). Vilanova town and beach are 4 km (local bus service).

Open: All year.

Directions

Site is 4 km. northwest of Vilanova i la Geltru towards L'Arboc (BV2115). From the A7 Tarragona - Barcelona take exit 29 onto C15 to Vilanova, then C31 El Vendrell road (km. 153) then onto BV2115.

Charges 2007

Per person	€ 4,40 - € 7,75
child (4-12 yrs)	€ 2,65 - € 4,86
pitch incl. electricity	€ 13,05 - € 20,35
with water	€ 15,80 - € 23,13

All plus 7% VAT. Excellent deals for retired people on longer stays.

Camping Cheques accepted.

ES8340 Camping Rupit

Ctra de Vic - Olot km. 31.5, E-08569 Rupit (Barcelona)

Tel: **93 852 21 53**. Email: **info@rupit.com**

The approach road to the site from the coast is not for the faint hearted, but if a rural setting is what you're looking for, then this is the site for you – we loved it! The Morell family who own the site (and others on the coast) will welcome you warmly and speak English very well. The mostly level, grass pitches are slightly terraced and some have shade from mature trees. Long leads will be necessary as the electricity points are well spread out. There are two beautiful stone buildings, one housing the reception, bar and restaurant, the other a toilet block.

Facilities

The central toilet block provides open washbasins and shower cubicles with curtains only. Baby bath. Facilities for disabled visitors in the men's side only. Laundry room with washing machines. No shop (essentials from the bar). Bar and restaurant. Outdoor swimming pool (all season) overlooked by restaurant terrace. Games room. Play area. Communal barbecue area. Bicycle hire. Off site: Rupit town 1 km. Riding 5 km. Fishing 15 km.

Open: March - December.

Directions

From the AP7 exit 6 (Gerona), take the C66 to Olot. From Olot follow C153 for 31.5 km. This road is steep and winding in places. Site is 1 km. before the town of Rupit. GPS: N42:01.51 E02:27.53

Charges 2006

Per person	€ 3,90 - € 5,20
pitch	€ 3,90 - € 5,20
electricity (6A)	€ 4,40

ES8392 Camping El Garrofer

Ctra 246 km 39, E-08870 Sitges (Barcelona)

Tel: **938 941 780**. Email: **info@garroferpark.com**

This large, pine covered site, alongside fields of vines, is 800 m. from the beach, close to the pleasant town of Sitges. It has over 500 pitches of which 380 with 6A electricity are for tourers, including 28 with water used for large motorcaravans. Everything is kept clean and the pitches are tidy and shaded, all with electricity (6A). The amenity buildings are along the site perimeter next to the road which absorbs most of the road noise.

Facilities

Two of the three sanitary blocks have been refurbished and provide roomy showers and special bright facilities for children. Separate baby room with bath. Good facilities for disabled campers. Laundry. Bar/restaurant. Shop (reception in low season). Swimming pool. Golf packages. Practice golf. Tennis. Play area for older children and fenced play area for toddlers. Bicycle hire. Boules. Off site: Bus from outside site to Barcelona. Golf, riding and fishing 0.5 km.

Open: All year excl. 18 December - 16 January.

Directions

From A16/C32 autopista take exit 26 towards Vilanova/St Pere Ribes. From Tarragona, go under autopista, around roundabout and back to the other side to pick up site sign (towards Sitges). Follow C-246 to km. 39; site entrance is not too easy to see beside old large tree. GPS: N41:14.033 E01:46.835

Charges 2006

Per person	€ 2,68 - € 4,71
child (1-9 yrs)	€ 1,82 - € 3,64
pitch incl. electricity	€ 14,35 - € 18,53
Plus 7% VAT.	

ES8393 Camping La Rueda

Ctra C31, km. 146.2, E-08880 Cubelles (Barcelona)

Tel: **938 950 207**. Email: **info@la-rueda.com**

On arrival at La Rueda, you are met with an impressive security barrier opposite the reception building. The staff here speak good English and are very welcoming. Just inside the gate is a small pine forest where a more casual camping area is to be found offering plenty of shade. The remainder of the 300 flat, grassy pitches are set amongst young trees where some artificial awnings provide shade. At the far end of the site is a railway underpass (some noise) which leads to a long sandy beach. At the centre of the site and up a few steps, are a bar and snack bar.

Facilities

Two identical sanitary blocks, one on each side of the site. Although kept clean, they offer adequate facilities and are kept very clean. Some washbasins in cabins. Baby cubicle. Separate laundry room. Shop (weekends only in low season). Bar and snack bar with takeaway pizzas. Formal restaurant. Swimming pool (July/Aug). Play area. Animation and entertainment (July/Aug). Off site: Fishing 200 m. Riding and bicycle hire 1 km. Golf 7 km.

Open: 15 April - 11 September.

Directions

La Rueda is very easy to find. It is on the C31 at 146.2 km. west of Cubelles.

Charges 2006

Per person	€ 3,28 - € 5,47
child	€ 2,30 - € 3,83
pitch	€ 9,84 - € 16,40
electricity	€ 3,28 - € 5,47

ES8395 Camping Arc de Bara

CN 340, km 1182, E-43883 Roda de Bará (Tarragona)

Tel: **977 800 902**. Email: **camping@campingarcdebara.com**

In comparison to the gigantic sites along this coastline, this smaller site has only 300 pitches of which most are taken up with static holiday caravans. The site is 200 m. from the impressive Roman monument, Arc de Bara, and 60 m. from the superb beach. The beach is accessed by a rear gate in the site perimeter and is soft sand shelving gently into the waves. The 30 pitches for tourers are generally shaded, are of average size (60-70 sq.m.) and are somewhat set apart from the very extensive permanent pitches but there is a distinct feeling of compression.

Facilities

Three very clean toilet blocks are of various designs (one a most unusual elevated circular building) and a fourth without showers. Units for disabled visitors. Limited facilities for babies. Washing machines and dryers. Swimming pools. Bars. Restaurant. Snack bars. Supermarket. Small play area. Some animation in season. Torches required in some areas.

Open: All year.

Directions

From the A7 take exit 31 towards Tarragona. Site is on CN340 Barcelona - Tarragona road at 1182 km. marker just 50 m. downhill from the Roman Arc which spans the road. Use the approach turn for Camping Stel. GPS: N41:10.210 E01:28.032

Charges 2006

Per person	€ 3,50 - € 5,50
pitchincl. electricity	€ 6,50 - € 8,80

Minimum charge € 23,40 per day for pitch and persons (1/7-31/8). All plus 7% VAT.

ES9140 Camping Repos del Pedraforca

Ctra B400, km. 13.5, E-08697 Saldés (Barcelona)

Tel: **938 258 044**. Email: **pedra@campingpedraforca.com**

Looking up through the trees in this steeply terraced campsite in the area of the Cadi-Moixero Natural Parc, you see the majestic Pedraforca mountain. A favourite for Catalan climbers and walkers, its amazing rugged peak in the shape of a massive stone fork gives it its name. Access to the site is via a steep, curving road which could challenge some units. Pitches vary in size and accessibility, although there are excellent pitches for larger units. The long scenic drive through the mountains to reach the site is breathtakingly beautiful. The campsite owner, Alicia Font, is a charming hostess.

Facilities

Two clean, modern sanitary blocks are fully equipped (but at peak periods there may be queues). Facilities for disabled campers. Separate family room. Washing machines and dryer. Small supermarket (w/ends all year, then 15/5-30/9). Restaurant/bar (1/6-30/9). Heated indoor pool, gym and spa. Outdoor pool (15/5-30/9). Play areas. Animation for all in high season. Games and social rooms. Rooftop relaxation area. Torches required. Off site: Motorcaravan service point close. Mountain biking.

Open: All year.

Directions

Site is approx. 90 minutes from Barcelona. Access to the site is gained from the C-16 Berga road. 2 km. south of Guardiola de Berguedá turn west to Saldes and site is well signed. It is 13.5 km. to site from the C-16. GPS: N42:13.847 E01:45.147

Charges 2007

Per person	€ 5,20
child (1-10 yrs)	€ 4,20
pitch incl. electricity	€ 18,90 - € 19,70

Camping Cheques accepted.

ES8402 Camping Vendrell Platja

Avenida del Sanatori, s/n, E-43880 Coma-ruga - El Vendrell (Tarragona)

Tel: **977 694 009**. Email: **vendrell@camping-vendrellplatja.com**

In the popular Calafell area, this site is set back from the beach across a minor road. Popular with tourists for many years, the area has apartment buildings, bars and restaurants, and is popular with families. The pitches (70 sq.m.) are partially shaded by trees which are growing well. Access to all the pitches is through one narrow central road which is busy with foot and vehicle traffic. An avenue of palms greets you on arrival here, and the pool has more tall palms and grassy areas.

Facilities

Two well located toilet blocks provide clean facilities with a new unit for disabled campers and well equipped baby rooms. Washing machines. Motorcaravan services. Supermarket. Restaurant. Snack bar. Swimming pools and pool bar. Play areas. Boules. Bicycle hire. Entertainment and activity programmes. ATM. Security boxes. Torches useful. Internet access. Off site: Resort town and beach outside the gate with usual attractions. Fishing. Bicycle hire 200 m. Riding 2 km. Golf 3 km.

Open: 7 April - 31 October.

Directions

From A7 or A16 take exits for El Vendrel. Then go east to Sant Salvador, and north on coast road towards Platja Calafell. Site is well signed on this road west of the town centre.

Charges 2006

Per person	€ 3,50 - € 7,00
child (3-11 yrs)	€ 1,50 - € 6,50
pitch incl. electricity	€ 11,00 - € 18,00

ES8479 Camping Playa Cambrils – Don Camilo

Ctra Cambrils - Salou km. 1.5, E-43850 Cambrils (Tarragona)

Tel: **977 361 490**. Email: **camping@playacambrils.com**

Almost completely canopied by trees which provide welcome shade on hot days, the site is 300 m. from the beach across a busy road. It is mature and has had some recent renovations. The small (60 sq.m.) pitches are on flat ground, divided by hedges. There are many permanent pitches and half the site is given up to chalet style accomodation. Large units are placed in a dedicated area where the trees are higher. The pool complex includes a functional glassed restaurant and bar with a distinct Spanish flavour reflected in the menu and tapas available all day. As this is a popular site with Spanish families it is a good place to practice your language. The pool is long and narrow with separate children's pool and a large paved area for soaking up the sun. Entertainment for children is organised by a good animation team. A big building at one end of the site consists of the supermarket, an attended electronic games room and a large play room.

Facilities

One modern sanitary building, and one large plus one small refurbished block offer reasonable facilities with British style WCs and free showers in separate buildings. Facilities for disabled campers. Laundry facilities. Supermarket (April-Sept). Bar/snacks and separate restaurant (April-Sept). Swimming pool. Playground. Animation in high season. Mini-club. Huge electronic games room. Torches useful. Off site: Resort town has a range of shops, bars and restaurants. Bicycle hire 500 m. Fishing and golf 1 km. Riding 1.5 km.

Open: 15 March - 12 October.

Directions

Leave A7 autopista at exit 37 and head for Cambrils and then to the beach. Turn left along beach road. Site is 1 km. east of Cambrils Playa and is well signed as you leave Cambrils marina.

Charges 2006

Per person	€ 2,15 - € 4,20
child (under 9 yrs)	free - € 3,15
pitch	€ 10,00 - € 24,00

ES8420 Camping Stel

Ctra N340, km. 1182, E-43883 Roda de Bará (Tarragona)

Tel: **977 802 002**. Email: **rodadebara@stel.es**

Camping Stel is situated between the pre-Littoral mountains and the sea. The rectangular site is between the N340 road and the excellent beach, with the railway running close to the bottom of the site. Beach access is gained through a gate and under the railway – there is rail noise on the lower pitches. The pitches are generally in rows with hedges around the rows but at the lower end of the site the layout is less formal. Many pitches have individual sinks. There is a separate area where no radio or TV is allowed ensuring peace and quiet.

Facilities

Four clean, fully equipped, sanitary blocks. One offers excellent facilities for children and disabled campers and four high standard private cabins. Baby baths. Large launderette. Motorcaravan service area. Supermarket and tourist shop. Bar/restaurant and snack bar. Swimming pools.(4/4-28/9) Outdoor sports area. Gym. Bicycle hire. Miniclub and some adult entertainment in high season. Internet room. Hairdresser. ATM. Dogs are not accepted. Off site: Fishing from beach. Golf and riding 4 km.

Open: 4 April - 30 September.

Directions

Site is at 1182 km. marker on the N340 near Arc de Bara, between Tarragona and Vilanova.
GPS: N41:10 E01:27.84

Charges 2006

Per person	€ 6,70
child (3-10 yrs)	€ 5,20
pitch incl. electricity	€ 20,80 - € 24,35
with water and drainage	€ 25,10 - € 29,35

All plus 7% VAT.
Camping Cheques accepted.

ES8410 Camping Playa Bara

Ctra N340, km. 1183, E-43883 Roda de Bará (Tarragona)

Tel: **977 802 701**. Email: **info@barapark.es**

This is a most impressive, family owned site near the beach, which has been carefully designed and developed. On entry you find yourself in a beautifully sculptured, tree-lined drive with an accompanying aroma of pine and woodlands and the sound of waterfalls close by. Considering its size, with over 850 pitches, it is still a very green and relaxing site with an immense range of activities. It is well situated with a 50 m. walk to a long sandy beach via a tunnel under the railway (some noise) to a new promenade with palms and a quality beach bar and restaurant. Much care with planning and in the use of natural stone; palms, shrubs and flowering plants gives a most pleasing tropical appearance to all aspects of the site. The owners have excelled themselves in the design of the impressive terraced Roman-style pool complex, which is the central feature of the site. This complex is really amazing. Sunbathe on the pretty terraces or sip a drink whilst seated at the bar stools submerged inside one of the pools or enjoy the panorama over the sea from the rooftop spa or the upper Roman galley bar surrounded by stylish friezes. A separate attractive amphitheatre seats 2,000 and is used to stage very professional entertainment in season. Pitches vary in size and are being progressively enlarged; the older ones terraced and well shaded with pine trees, the newer ones more open, with a variety of trees and bushes forming separators between them. All have electricity (5A) and a sink with water. Arrive early to find space in peak weeks.

Facilities

Excellent, fully equipped toilet blocks include private cabins and excellent facilities for children and disabled visitors. Private facilities to hire. Superb launderette. Triple motorcaravan service points. Supermarket and several other shops. Full restaurant. Large bar with simpler meals and takeaway. Three other bars. Pleasant bar/restaurant on beach. Swimming pools. Jacuzzi/hydro-massage. Fronton and tennis (floodlit). Junior club. Sports area. Windsurfing school. Gym. Massage. Petanque. Minigolf. Fishing. Entertainment centre. ATM. Hairdresser. Internet room. Medical centre. Flights and excursions booked. WiFi. Off site: Bicycle hire 2 km. Riding 3 km. Golf 4 km.

Open: 23 March - 25 September, with all amenities.

Directions

From the A7 take exit 31. Site entrance is at the 1183 km. marker on the main N340 just opposite the Arco de Bara Roman monument from which it takes its name.

Charges 2006

Per person	€ 3,00 - € 9,40
child (1-9 yrs)	€ 2,00 - € 6,60
pitch	€ 3,50 - € 9,40
electricity	€ 3,20

All plus 7% VAT. Low season reductions for pensioners and all sports charges reduced by 90%.

ES8480 Camping & Bungalows Sanguli

Prolongacion Calle, Apdo de Correos 123, E-43840 Salou (Tarragona)

Tel: **977 381 641**. Email: **mail@sanguli.es**

Sanguli is a superb site boasting excellent pools and ambitious entertainment. Owned, developed and managed by a local Spanish family, it provides for all the family with everything open when the site is open. There are 1,220 pitches of varying size (75-90 sq.m) and all have electricity. About 160 are used by tour operators and 140 for bungalows. A wonderful selection of trees, palms and shrubs provides natural shade. The good sandy beach is little more than 100 metres across the coast road and a small railway crossing (a little noise). Although large, Sanguli maintains a quality family atmosphere due to the efforts of the very keen and efficient staff. The owners are striving to achieve the 'Garden of Eden' that is their dream. There are three very attractive pool areas, one (heated) near the entrance with a grassy sunbathing area partly shaded and a second deep one with water slides that forms part of the excellent sports complex (with fitness centre, tennis courts, minigolf and football practice area). The third pool is the central part of the amphitheatre area at the top of the site which includes an impressive Roman style building with huge portals, containing a bar and restaurant with terraces. An amphitheatre seats 2,000 campers and treats them to very professional free nightly entertainment (1/5-30/9). All the pools have adjacent amenity areas and bars. A real effort is made to cater for the young including teenagers with a 'Hop Club' (entertainment for 13-17 year olds), along with an internet room. Located near the centre of Salou, the site can offer the attractions of a busy resort while still being private and it is only 3 km. from Port Aventura. This is a large, professional site providing something for all the family, but still capable of providing peace and quiet for those looking for it.

Facilities

The quality sanitary facilities are constantly improved and are always exceptional, including many individual cabins with en-suite facilities. A new block also has excellent facilities for babies. All are kept very clean. Launderette with service. Motorcaravan services. Bars and restaurant with takeaway. Swimming pools. Jacuzzi. Fitness centre. Sport complex. Fitness room (charged). Playgrounds including adventure play area. Mini-club, teenagers club. Internet room. Upmarket minigolf. First-aid room. Gas supplies. Off site: Fishing and bicycle hire 100 m. Riding 3 km. Golf 6 km. Resort entertainment.

Open: 24 March - 29 October.

Directions

On west side of Salou about 1 km. from the centre, site is well signed from the coast road to Cambrils and from the other town approaches.

Charges 2006

Per person	€ 6,00
child (4-12 yrs)	€ 4,00
pitch incl. electricity	€ 12,00 - € 37,00
incl. water	€ 14,00 - € 39,00

All plus 7% VAT. Less 25-45% outside high season for longer stays. Special long stay offers for senior citizens.

ES8470 Camping La Siesta

Calle Ctra Norte 37, E-43840 Salou (Tarragona)

Tel: **977 380 852**. Email: **info@camping-lasiesta.com**

The palm bedecked entrance of La Siesta is only 250 m. from the pleasant sandy beach and close to the life of the resort of Salou. The site is divided into 470 pitches which are large enough and have electricity (10A), with smaller ones for tents. Many pitches are provided with artificial shade and within some there is one box for the tent or caravan and a shared one for the car. There is considerable shade from the trees and shrubs that are part of the site's environment. In high season, the siting of units is carried out by the friendly management.

Facilities

Three bright and clean sanitary blocks provide very reasonable facilities. Motorcaravan services. Supermarket. Various vending machines. Self-service restaurant and bar with cooked dishes to take away. Dancing some evenings till 11 pm. Swimming pool (300 sq.m. open all season). Playground. Medical service daily in season. ATM point. Torches may be required. Off site: Many shops, restaurants and bars near. Port Aventura is close. Bicycle hire 200 m. Fishing 500 m. Riding amd golf 6 km.

Open: 14 March - 3 November.

Directions

Leave A7 at exit 35 for Salou. Site is signed off the Tarragona/Salou road and from the one way system in the town of Salou. The site is in the town so keep a sharp eye for the small signs.
GPS: N41:04.666 E01:08.352

Charges 2006

Per person	€ 3,90 - € 7,55
child (4-9 yrs)	€ 3,10 - € 4,00
pitch	€ 3,10 - € 15,10
electricity	€ 2,70 - € 3,20

All plus 7% VAT. No credit cards.

PARC DE VACANCES

Sangulí Salou
CAMPING & BUNGALOW PARK
★★★★ 1ª CAT.

✉ Apartat de Correus 123
43840 SALOU • Tarragona • España
☎ Camping   +34 977 38 16 41
☎ Bungalow +34 977 38 90 05
   Fax   +34 977 38 46 16
@ mail@sanguli.es
   www.sanguli.es

Online   Booking: www.sanguli.es

Luxurious holidays at the Costa Daurada

Salou • Costa Daurada • España

ES8478 Camping Joan

Ctra Pere iii, 14, E-43850 Cambrils (Tarragona)

Tel: **977 364 604**. Email: **info@campingjoan.com**

Recommended by our agent, we plan to conduct a full inspection of this site in 2007. Camping Joan is a family site to the south of the popular resort of Cambrils and with direct access to the sandy beach. Pitches are of a reasonable size (70m2) and are well shaded. Most have electrical connections. This is a lively site in peak season with a varied activity and entertainment programme for adults and children. Chalets and mobile homes available for rent.

Facilities	Directions
Six sanitary blocks. Bar, restaurant and takeaway meals. Supermarket. Swimming and paddling pools. Playground. Entertainment programme in high season, children's club. Direct access to beach. Off site: Cambrils 2 km. Golf 8 km. Universal Studios Port Aventura Theme Park 8 km,	Heading south on the AP7 motorway, leave at exit 37 (Costa Daurada) and join the southbound N340. Leave this road at the service station in La Dorada. GPS: N41:03.32 E01:01.40

Open: 1 April - 1 October.

Charges 2006

Per person	€ 3,10 - € 4,70
child (3-10 yrs)	€ 2,80 - € 3,95
minimum pitch fee	€ 3,10 - € 26,25
electricity	€ 3,50

BUNGALOW PARK - CAMPING CARAVANING
CAMPING JOAN

The quiet, small holiday site directly on the beach

Road A-7, exit nr. 37, than the N-340 direction Valencia and turn off at km 1.141 (Hotel La Daurada). Situated at 2 km south of Cambrils and 6 km of the theme park 'PORT AVENTURA'.
• Bungalows and caravans • very clean and quiet • swimming pool • organized leisure for grown ups and children • modern san. install. with free hot water • ideal for families w. children • nice, personal contact with the owner • large sites w. lots of shade • Considerable discounts off-season.

www.campingjoan.com • info@campingjoan.com
E-43850 CAMBRILS (Tarragona) COSTA DAURADA - Tel/Fax: (34) 977 36 15 57 / 977 36 46 04

ES8486 Camping Torre de la Mora

CN 340, km. 1171, E-43080 Tarragona (Tarragona)

Tel: **977 650277**. Email: **campmora@tinet.fut.es**

Located on a promontory in a pleasant corner of the Costa Daurada with a village like atmosphere, Torre de la Mora takes advantage of its wonderful location, offering some pitches with beautiful views over the white sandy beaches and rocky promontories of the coastline. The hinterland is pine forest and there are areas where you can pitch a tent, access electricity (6A) and feel close to nature. The 200 touring pitches vary in just about every way, some are on the lower flat area, including a few with beach frontage, others are on steep terraces around the promontory.

Facilities	Directions
Two large and three small sanitary blocks are mature but the facilities within are clean. There is a mixture of washing facilities some of which have hot water, others not and most are dated. Facilities for disabled campers (careful selection of pitch is required). Washing machine. Motorcaravan services. Supermarket. Restaurant. Chicken bar (high season). Swimming pool and sports area (in need of renovation when we visited). Play area. Entertainment. Torches useful. Off site: Pretty beach town outside the gate. Fishing. Bicycle hire 1 km. Golf 2 km. Riding 3 km. Boat launching 8 km.	From A7 (Barcelona - Tarragona) take exit 32, then N340 towards Tarragona. Turn off for Punta del la Mora and site is well signed approaching the village. The final approach is via some narrow streets so watch for one way signs and there is an unusual entry through a high wire fence alongside road.

Open: 18 March - 31 October.

Charges 2006

Per unit incl. 1 person and electricity	€ 17,10 - € 29,60
extra person	€ 4,00 - € 7,00
child (3-11 yrs)	€ 3,00 - € 4,00
dog	€ 1,00 - € 2,00

ES8482 Camping La Pineda de Salou

Ctra Costa Tarragona - Salou km 5, E-43481 La Pineda (Tarragona)

Tel: **977 37 30 80**. Email: **info@campinglapineda.com**

La Pineda is just outside Salou towards Tarragona and this site is just 300 m. from the Aquapark and 2.5 km. from Port Aventura, to which there is an hourly bus service from outside the site entrance. There is some noise from this road. The site has a fair-sized swimming pool adjoining a smaller, heated one, open from mid June, behind large hedges close to the entrance. A large terrace has sun loungers, and various entertainment aimed at young people is provided in season. The 366 flat pitches are mostly shaded and of about 70 sq.m. All have 5A electricity. The beach is about 400 m. The simple restaurant/bar is shaded and has a large cactus garden to the rear. This is a plain, friendly and convenient site, with reasonable rates, probably best used for visiting Tarragona and Port Aventura, or exploring the local area, rather than for extended stays. Note: the site is reasonably close to a large industrial centre.

Facilities

Sanitary facilities are mature but clean with baby bath, dishwashing and laundry sinks. Facilities for disabled visitors. Two washing machines in each block. The second building is opened in high season only. Gas supplies. Shop (1/7-31/8). Restaurant and snacks (1/7-31/8). Swimming pools (1/7-31/8). Bar (all season). Small TV room. Bicycle hire. Games room. Playground (3-12 yrs). Entertainment (1/7-30/8). Torches may be required. Off site: Beach and fishing 400 m. Golf 12 km.

Open: All year.

Directions

From A7 just southwest of Tarragona take exit 35 and follow signs to La Pineda and Port Aventura then campsite signs appear. GPS: N41:05.310 E01:10.947

Charges 2006

Per person	€ 4,30 - € 6,00
child (1-10 yrs)	€ 2,90 - € 4,50
pitch incl. car	€ 10,40 - € 20,20
electricity	€ 3,50

All plus 7% VAT.

ES8502 Camping Caravaning Montblanc Park

Ctra Prenafeta, km. 1,8, E-43400 Montblanc (Tarragona)

Tel: **977 862544**. Email: **info@montblancpark.com**

Taking current trends into account, Montblanc Park may be described as a campsite of the future. Purpose designed, there are 213 terraced pitches for touring units and about 60 for wooden chalets, with more being developed, on the upper terraces. The restaurant and terrace enjoy views of the exceptionally large, lagoon-style pool and further across the valley, over the autoroute towards the town of Montblanc and the Prades mountains of the Serra del Prades. The pitches are on terraces so take advantage of the mountain views and gentle cooling afternoon breezes. They vary in size, with hedging but little shade yet, and are sloping (chocks useful).

Facilities

Two purpose built toilet blocks feature en-suite facilities including superb facilities for disabled campers and a well equipped baby room. Washing machines and dryers. Supermarket. Restaurant. Snack bar. Swimming pool and large paddling pool. Play areas. Boules. Bicycle hire. Entertainment for children (weekends and main holiday season). Tents for hire. Barbecues may not be allowed in July and August. Off site: Riding 4 km. Beach or golf 35 km. Mountain activities: climbing, caving, canyoning.

Open: All year.

Directions

Site is 3 minutes off the autopista. From the A2 (Barcelona - Lleida) take exit 9 and follow N240 (Reus - Tarragona), then road to Prenafeta and site is on the left, 1.8 km. out of Montblanc and signed in the town. GPS: N41:22.612 E01:11.120

Charges 2006

Per person	€ 4,00 - € 6,00
child (0-10 yrs)	free
pitch incl. electricity	€ 12,00 - € 20,00
water	€ 2,00

ES8481 Camping Cambrils Park

Avenida Mas Clariana s/n., E-43850 Cambrils (Tarragona)

Tel: **977 351 031**. Email: **mail@cambrilspark.es**

This is a superb site for a camping holiday providing for all family members, whatever their age. A drive lined with palm trees and flowers leads from a large, very smart round reception building at this impressive modern site. Sister site to no. ES8480, it is set 500 metres back from the excellent beach in a generally quiet setting with outstanding facilities. The 684 slightly sloping, grassy pitches of around 90 sq.m. are numbered and separated by trees. All have 10A electricity, 55 have water and waste water connections, some having more shade than others. The marvellous central lagoon pool complex with three pools and water slides is the main focus of the site with a raised wooden 'poop deck' sunbathing area with palm surrounds that doubles as an entertainment stage at night. There is a huge bar/terrace area for watching the magnificent floodlit spectacles, along with an excellent restaurant in the old farmhouse with an adjacent takeaway. By day there is a small bar at a lower level in the pool where you can enjoy a cool drink from submerged stools, plus a dryer version on the far side of the bar or just relax on the spacious grass sunbathing areas. There are a number of tour operator pitches and attractive thatched chalets. A fabulous jungle theme children's pool is nearer the entrance – they love it, especially the elephants! An extra pool for adults has been added here, along with a snack bar.

Facilities

Four excellent sanitary buildings provide some washbasins in cabins, superb units for disabled visitors and immaculate, decorated baby sections. Dishwashing and laundry sinks. Huge serviced laundry. Motorcaravan services. Car wash. Restaurant. Takeaway. Huge supermarket, souvenir shop and 'panaderia' (fresh-baked bread and croissants). Swimming pools with lifeguards. Minigolf. Tennis Multi-games court. Petanque. Animation and entertainment all season. Mini-club. Internet café. Medical centre. ATM. Gas supplies. Dogs are not accepted. Off site: Beach 500 m. Fishing, bicycle hire 400 m. Riding 3 km. Port Aventura theme park 4 km. Golf 7 km.

Open: 7 April - 8 October.

Directions

Site is about 1.5 km west of Salou. From the A7 take exit 35 and at roundabout take signs for Cambrils. Follow new dual-carriageway around the back of Salou and site is signed at last roundabout towards Cambrils. GPS: N41:04.584 E01:06.527

Charges 2006

Per person	€ 6,00
child (4-12 yrs)	€ 4,00
pitch incl. electricity	€ 12,00 - € 37,00
pitch with water and waste water	€ 14,00 - € 39,00

All plus 7% VAT. Special offers, plus low season discounts for pensioners.
Camping Cheques accepted.

ES8506 Camping & Bungalow Park Serra de Prades

Sant Antoni, s/n, E-43439 Vilanova de Prades (Tarragona)

Tel: **977 869 050**. Email: **info@serradeprades.com**

On the edge of the village of Vilanova, nestling in granite foothills with superb views from its elevation of 950 m, this is a welcoming and peaceful site. The 215 pitches are on terraces formed with natural stone and with good access. Many are occupied by seasonal units and touring units may be placed on the smaller pitches at the higher levels. The upper tent pitches have wonderful views although you have a trek to the sanitary facility on the lower level. Hedges and trees separate pitches providing a pleasant green environment and some shade, and 90% of the pitches have electricity.

Facilities

The modern, heated, well equipped toilet block has washbasins in cabins and is well maintained. Facilities for disabled visitors and babies. Laundry facilities. Motorcaravan service point. Shop. Bar and good quality restaurant. Swimming pool (open and heated 1/4-15/10). Internet points. Archery. Quad bike and 4x4 hire. Paint ball. Tennis. Riding with guided treks. Activities organised. Sports area. Entertainment in season. Safety deposit. Exchange facilities. Gas supplies. Torches required in some areas.

Open: All year.

Directions

From Tarragona on A2 take exit 9 (Montblanc) and continue towards Lleida on N240. At km. 48 just west of Vimbodi, turn left towards Vallclara and Vilanova de Prades. Site is on the right after the roundabout at entrance to village. From Lleida leave A2 at exit 8 towards Tarragona on N240, then as above from km. 48 just before Vimbodi.

Charges 2006

Per person	€ 5,45
child (3-10 yrs)	€ 4,65
pitch	€ 5,45 - € 10,00
electricity (6A)	€ 4,65

Plus 7% VAT.
Camping Cheques accepted.

The only luxury **Camping** on the **Costa Daurada**

PARC DE VACANCES
Cambrils-Park
CAMPING - BUNGALOW
●●●●● LUXE

✉ Apartat de Correus 123
43840 SALOU • Tarragona • España
☎ Camping +34 977 35 10 31
☎ Bungalow +34 977 38 90 04
   Fax   +34 977 35 22 10
@ mail@cambrilspark.es
   www.cambrilspark.es

ES8485 Camping Las Palmeras

Ctra N340 km 1168, E-43080 Tarragona (Tarragona)

Tel: **977 20 80 81**. Email: **laspalmeras@laspalmeras.com**

Situated amongst pine, poplar and palm trees, running parallel to a fine, white sandy beach, Camping Las Palmeras has a wonderful location. Care must be taken on the final approach as you pass under the railway (some noise) and take a sharp turn into the parking area. Most of the 655 pitches are on grass with plenty of shade. All have access to 5A electricity, although long leads may be necessary in places. For its beach side location alone, Las Palmeras is worthy of a visit and, with so many facilities on offer, it is a great site for the whole family.

Facilities

Four large toilet blocks attractively tiled in a traditional style, are evenly located and kept to a high standard. Open style washbasins and good sized shower cubicles. Baby rooms. Laundry in each block. Shop. Bar and beach restaurant. Smaller bar and snack bar (high season only). Two swimming pools (June - Sept). Tennis court. Two large play areas. Children's club in high season.

Open: 1 April - 15 October.

Directions

Las Palmeras is easily accessed from the N340 (Barcelona – Tarragona) and is signed after the 1169 km. marker. Beware of the sharp bend at the entrance.

Charges 2006

Per pitch incl. electricity	€ 9,00 - € 26,00
person	€ 5,00 - € 8,00
child (under 10 yrs)	€ 4,50 - € 6,00

ES8508 Camping Poboleda

Placa de les Casetes s/n, E-43376 Poboleda (Tarragona)

Tel: **977 827197**. Email: **poboleda@campingsonline.com**

Time stands still at this unique site hidden away in a corner of the village, watched over by La Morera de Montsant, a peak of the Serra del Montsant. Situated among olive groves, yet almost in the heart of the lovely old village of Poboleda, it is an idyllic site for tents, small caravans and motorcaravans. Large units may have problems negotiating the narrow village streets. The 151 pitches of 80 sq.m. are set under olive and almond trees. Fairly level and 70 with 4A electricity, they provide a peaceful haven broken only by the peal of church bells or bird song. The young manager is enthusiastic and proud of the facilities offered which are quite unexpected and special. Behind the modern reception is a traditional, comfortablly furnished room with piano and TV, which doubles as a peaceful cool area for relaxing if it is too hot on the terrace. Here you can have breakfast or order a drink. The village is on the doorstep for other needs. The mellow terraced pool area is a lovely surprise and very welcome, as is the tennis court. There is plenty to do, walking or climbing, visiting the region's vineyards and enjoying the local cuisine. A must to visit is the monastery of Poblet nearby.

Facilities

One small block, open all year, is fully equipped, as is a larger block open for high season. Shower for children. Facilities for disabled people (key). Dishwashing and laundry sinks. Laundry service. Breakfast can be ordered. Bar. Swimming pool (24/6-11/9). Tennis. Boules. Reception has tourist information, postcards and basic bits and pieces. Off site: Beach and Port Aventura 30 km. Fishing 12 km. Bicycle hire 10 km.

Open: All year.

Directions

Bypass Reus (west of Tarragona) on N420. After Borges del Camp pick up C242, signed Alforja. Continue over Coll d'Alforja (the road is OK and the views magnificent). Watch for left turn (T702) for Pobodeda. Continue for 6 km. to village. Watch for tent signs and follow carefully through narrow village streets. Not recommended for large units.

Charges 2007

Per person	€ 4,50
pitch incl. electricity	€ 12,50 - € 13,00

ES8483 Camping Tamarit Park

N340 km 1172, Tamarit, E-43008 Tarragona (Tarragona)

Tel: **977 650 128**. Email: **tamaritpark@tamarit.com**

This is a marvellous, beach-side site, attractively situated at the foot of Tamarit castle at one end of a superb one kilometre long beach of fine sand. Parts are landscaped with lush Mediterranean palms and shrubs; other areas have natural pine shade, all home to mischievous red squirrels. The 734 pitches, 50 of which are virtually on the beach, are marked out on hard sand and grass and some are attractively separated by green vegetation which provides good shade. There are about 120 tour operator pitches, a number of seasonal pitches and about 120 bungalows. All pitches have electricity (6A). Long electricity leads and metal awning pegs may be required in places but wide internal roads give good access for even the largest of units (American motorhomes accepted). Catering includes a beach-side waiter service restaurant with superb views and a terrace with tables just a few metres from the sea. A vast, attractively designed, lagoon-type swimming pool with bar and sun terrace has recently been added. The site is approached by a long access road, rather narrow but with passing places, reached across a bridge (6 m.) over the railway line (there is train noise on the site). Security is provided but the very low wall which is the site beach boundary must be viewed with caution. Tamarit would be a good choice for windsurfing enthusiasts or a family holiday by the sea. The early morning sun shining on the blue sea and the golden stone of Tamarit castle high above is a memorable sight! It is only 9 km. from Tarragona and 16 km. from Port Aventura.

Facilities

Sanitary blocks (one heated) are modern and tiled, providing good facilities. An unfortunate economy feature in the showers is push-button controlled hot water with tap controlled cold, leading to a confusing mix of temperatures. Private bathrooms to rent. Laundry facilities. Motorcaravan services. Gas supplies. Shop, bar/restaurant and takeaway (all until 15/10). Swimming pool (15/5-15/10). Tennis. Petanque. Minigolf. Playground. Animation programme in season. Fishing. Internet access. Barbecues not permtted on pitches. Off site: Riding 1 km. Bicycle hire 2 km. Golf 8 km.

Open: All year.

Directions

From A7 take exit 32 towards Tarragona and continue for 4.5 km. At roundabout (km. 1172) turn back towards Atafulla/Tamarit and after just 200 m. turn right to Tamarit. Take care over railway bridge, then turn immediately sharp right. Site entrance is 1 km. GPS: N41:07.943 E01:21.652

Charges 2006

Per person	€ 4,50
child (1-12 yrs)	€ 3,50
pitch acc. to size and season	€ 16,00 - € 44,00

All plus 7% VAT. Discounts for students, pensioners, large families and longer stays in low season.

ES8520 Camping Marius

Ctra N340, km 1137, E-43892 Miami-Playa (Tarragona)

Tel: **977 810 684**. Email: **schmid@teleline.es**

Quiet, well tended and not too huge, this agreeable site has a family atmosphere and a personal touch. One perimeter is on a good sandy beach with direct access and no roads to cross – you can almost fall out of bed and onto the beach and a large beach bar will provide resuscitation when required! The site is divided into 345 individual pitches of adequate size so it does not become too overcrowded. They are quite shady and all have electrical connections, 8 pitches with water and drainage. Some train noise may be expected.

Facilities

Two of the sanitary blocks are quite elderly but clean and well maintained, with a third of excellent standards. Free hot water in the showers and half the washbasins, plus 21 private cabins. Facilities for babies and disabled campers. Laundry room. Motorcaravan services. Bar and restaurant (1/6-30/9). Supermarket (15/4-30/9). Souvenir shop. Gas supplies. Children's club and playground. Hairdresser. Fishing. Torches required at night.
Off site: Windsurfing, water ski and pedaloes nearby. Riding 4 km. Golf 10 km.

Open: 1 April - 15 October.

Directions

The site entrance is 28 km. from Tarragona on the Valencia road (N340). GPS: N41:02.426 E00:58.922

Charges 2006

Per person	€ 5,00 - € 7,00
child (1- 10 yrs)	€ 2,50 - € 3,50
pitch incl. electricity	€ 12,00 - € 18,00
dog	€ 2,50 - € 3,50

Plus 7% VAT.
Less 10-20% for longer stays.

ES8530 Playa Montroig Camping Resort

Apdo 3, N340 km. 1136, E-43300 Montroig (Tarragona)

Tel: **977 810 637**. Email: **info@playamontroig.com**

What a superb site! Playa Montroig is about 30 kilometres beyond Tarragona set in its own tropical gardens with direct access to a very long soft sand beach. The main part of the site lies between the sea, road and railway (as at other sites on this coast, there is some train noise) with a huge underpass. The site is divided into spacious, marked pitches with excellent shade provided by a variety of lush vegetation including very impressive palms set in wide avenues. There are 1,950 pitches, all with electricity and 330 with water and drainage. Some 48 pitches are directly alongside the beach. Member of Leading Campings Group.

Facilities

Fifteen sanitary buildings, some small, but of very good quality with toilets and washbasins, others really excellent, air conditioned larger buildings housing large showers, washbasins (many in private cabins) and separate WCs. Facilities for disabled campers and for babies. Several launderettes. Motorcaravan services. Good shopping centre. Restaurants and bars. The 'Eurocentre' with 250 person capacity and equipped for entertainment (air conditioned). Fitness suite. Eco-park. TV lounges (3). Beach bar. Playground. Free kindergarten with multi-lingual staff. Skate-boarding. Jogging track. Sports area. Tennis. Minigolf. Organised activities including pottery and gardening classes. Windsurfing and water skiing courses. Surfboard and pedalo hire. Boat mooring. Hairdressers. Bicycle hire. Internet café. Gas supplies. Dogs are not accepted. Off site: Riding and golf 3 km.

Open: 1 March - 31 October.

Directions

Site entrance is off main N340 nearly 30 km. southwest from Tarragona. From motorway take Cambrils exit and turn west on N340 at 1136 km marker.

Charges 2006

Per unit incl 2 persons and electricity	€ 13,00 - € 30,00
premium pitch	€ 26,00 - € 95,00
extra person	€ 5,00 - € 6,00
child (1-9 yrs)	free - € 5,00

All plus 7% VAT. Discounts for longer stays and for pensioners.

ES8535 Camping-Pension Cala d'Oques

Via Augusta s/n, E-43890 Hospitalet del Infante (Tarragona)

Tel: **977 823 254**. Email: **kroller@tinet.org**

This peaceful and delightful site has been developed with care and dedication by Elisa Roller over 30 years or so and she now runs it with the help of her daughter Kim. Part of its appeal lies in its situation beside the sea with a wide beach of sand and pebbles, its amazing mountain backdrop and the views across the bay to the town and part by the atmosphere created by Elisa, and staff – friendly, relaxed and comfortable. There are 255 pitches, mostly level and laid out beside the beach, with more behind on wide, informal terracing. Odd pine and olive trees are an attractive feature and provide some shade. Electricity is available although long leads may be needed in places. The restaurant with its homely touches has a super menu and a reputation extending well outside the site (the excellent cook has been there for many years) and the family type entertainment is in total contrast to that provided at the larger, brasher sites of the Costa Daurada. Gates provide access to the pleasant beach with useful cold showers to wash the sand away. Torches are needed at night. For those interested, there is a naturist beach of fine sand around the little headland just south of the site. This is a pretty place to stay and Elisa gives a pleasant personal service but do not expect 'Costa' type entertainment. Ask how the nearby village of Hospitalet del Infante got its name – it's a royal riddle! The village itself is well worth exploring and if you are here in June watch for the fabulous fireworks of the celebration of St John. It is interesting to note that Cala d'Oques (Goose Bay) was where the migrant geese landed on return from wintering in South Africa, hence the geese featured on the site logo and the guard goose that watches the entrance.

Facilities

Toilet facilities are in the front part of the main building. Clean and neat, there is hot water to showers (hot water by token but free to campers - a device to guard against unauthorized visitors from the beach). New heated unit with toilets and washbasins for winter use. Additional small block with toilets and washbasins at the far end of the site. Motorcaravan service point. Restaurant/bar and shop (1/4-30/9). Play area. Kim's kids club. Fishing. Internet point. Gas supplies. Off site: Village facilities, incl. shop and restaurant 1.5 km. Bicycle hire or riding 2 km.

Open: All year.

Directions

Hospitalet del Infante is south of Tarragona, accessed from the A7 (exit 38) or from the N340. From the north take first exit to Hospitalet del Infante at the 1128 km. marker. Follow signs in village, site is 2 km, by the sea. GPS: N40:58.666 E00:54.203

Charges 2006

Per person	€ 4,85 - € 8,25
child (0-10 yrs)	free
pitch incl. electricity	€ 8,35 - € 15,90

Discounts for seniors and for longer stays.
No credit cards.

ES8536 Camping Caravanning Ametlla Village Platja

Apdo. Correus 240, Paraje Santes Creus, E-43860 Ametlla de Mar (Tarragona)

Tel: **977 267 784**. Email: **info@campingametlla.com**

This site within a protected area has been well thought out and is startling in the quality of service provided, the finish and the materials used in construction. The 373 pitches are on a terraced hillside above colourful coves with shingle beaches and two small associated lagoons (with a protected fish species). The many bungalows here have been tastefully incorporated. There are great views, particularly from the friendly restaurant. There is some train noise. The site is used by tour operators (30 pitches). It is a very good site for families or for just relaxing. The site is environmentally correct and local planning regulations are extremely tight including the types of trees that may be planted. No transit traffic is allowed within the site in high season. Animation is organised for children in high season and there is a well equipped fitness room (free). There are good quality pools (with lifeguard) and a sub-aqua diving school operates on the site in high season and beginners may try a dive. This most attractive small site is in an idyllic situation near the picturesque fishing village of L'Ametlla de Mar, famous for its fish restaurants, and within the Ebro Delta nature reserve. It is about 20 minutes from Europe's second largest theme park, Port Aventura, but as there is no regular bus service your own transport is required (the owners arrange free buses to the local disco each Wednesday).

Facilities

Three really good toilet blocks. Some private cabins with WC and washbasin. Motorcaravan services. Gas supplies. Supermarket (1/4-30/9; small shop incl. bread at other times). Good restaurant with snack menu and bar with TV (1/4-30/9). Swimming pool. Sub-aqua diving. Kayaking. Fishing. Children's club and play area. Fitness room. Bicycle hire. Entertainment (July/Aug). Barbecue area. Fishing. Off site: Boat launching 3 km. Golf 15 km.

Open: All year.

Directions

From A7/E15 (Barcelona - Valencia) take exit 39 for L'Ametlla de Mar. Follow large white signs and site is 2.5 km. south of the village.

Charges 2006

Per person	€ 2,30 - € 5,30
child (under 10 yrs)	€ 1,85 - € 4,30
pitch incl. electricity	€ 7,70 - € 18,50

All plus 7% VAT. Less for longer stays, especially in low season.

www.campingametlla.com · info@campingametlla.com

Open throughout the year

WI-FI **20 min. from the theme park Port Aventura!**

At the sea, quiet situation in midst of nature. All facilities of a first class site, incl. swimming pools, diving centre, sports centre, medical service, etc. **New, fully furnished bungalows for hire, fitness centre.**

Tel.: +34 977 267 784 · Fax: +34 977 267 868 · Postadr.: Apartado 240
Paratge Santes Creus · E-43860 L'Ametlla de Mar (Tarragona) · A-7, exit 39

ES8533 Camping Els Prats

Ctra N340, km 1137, E-43892 Miami-Playa (Tarragona)

Tel: **977 810 027**. Email: **info@campingelsprats.com**

A medium size, beach resort site with 203 pitches, El Prats is situated in a very popular part of the Costa Daurada, not far from Tarragona and the Port Adventura theme park. The pitches are fairly close together, mostly flat and shaded. Bungalows are in one corner of the site, with an apartment block in another. A feature is the tropical style beach bar. Attractive tropical plants adorn the site including many banana trees. There is some road and rail noise on the western side of the site.

Facilities

Two blocks, one for each sex, provide clean facilities. Separate unit for disabled campers. Children's bathroom. Washing machines. Motorcaravan services. Supermarket. Restaurant, takeaway and three bars. Swimming pool (3/4-17/10). Play area. Bicycle hire (organised trips). Windsurfing, canoeing and diving. Animation programme in high season. Dogs not accepted 1/7-31/8. Torches useful. Off site: Riding 3 km. Golf 5 km. Cambrils 7 km.

Open: 6 March - 1 November.

Directions

Site is between Miami Playa and Cambrils on the N340. Take exit 37 from the A7 towards Cambrils, then 7 km. southwest of Cambrils take exit for Torre del Mar. Go under railway bridge and immediately right – site is 100 m. up this road.

Charges 2006

Per person	€ 3,50 - € 6,20
pitch incl. electricity (5A)	€ 11,00 - € 17,50

Camping Cheques accepted.

ES8540 Camping Caravaning La Torre del Sol

Ctra N340, km. 1136, E-43300 Montroig (Tarragona)

Tel: **977 810 486**. Email: **info@latorredelsol.com**

A pleasant banana tree-lined approach road gives way to avenues of palms as you arrive at Torre del Sol, sister site to Templo del Sol (ES8537N). Torre del Sol is a very large site occupying a good position with direct access to the clean, soft sand beach, complete with a beach bar. Strong features here are 800 metres of clean beach-front with a special Mediterranean type of pitch, and the entertainment that is provided all season. There is a separate area where the 'Happy Camp' team will take your children to camp overnight in the Indian reservation, plus they can amuse them two days a week with other activities. The cinema doubles as a theatre to stage shows all season. A complex of three pools, thoughtfully laid out with grass sunbathing areas and palms has a lifeguard. There is good shade on a high proportion of the 1,500 individual, numbered pitches. All have electricity and are mostly of about 70-80 sq.m. There is wireless internet access throughout the site. There is usually space for odd nights but for good places between 10/7-16/8 it is best to reserve (only taken for a stay of seven nights or more). Part of the site is between the railway and the sea so there is train noise. We were impressed with the provision of season-long entertainment and to give parents a break whilst children were in the safe hands of the animation team who ensure they enjoy the novel 'Happy Camp' and various workshops.

Facilities

Four very well maintained, fully equipped, toilet blocks include units for disabled people and babies. Washing machines. Large supermarket. Shops. Full restaurant. Takeaway. Bar with large terrace where entertainment held daily all season. Beach bar. Coffee bar and ice cream bar. Pizzeria. Open roof cinema; 3 TV lounges. Well sound-proofed disco. Swimming pools (two heated). Solarium. Sauna. Jacuzzi. Tennis. Squash. Minigolf. Sub-aqua diving. Bicycle hire. Fishing. Windsurfing school; sailboards and pedaloes for hire. Playground, crèche and Happy Camp. Fridge hire. Library. Hairdressers. Business centre with IT equipment. Car repair and car wash. No animals permitted. No jet skis. Off site: Golf 4 km.

Open: 15 March - 20 October.

Directions

Entrance is off main N340 road by 1136 km. marker, about 30 km. from Tarragona towards Valencia. From motorway take Cambrils exit and turn west on N340. GPS: N41:02 E00:58.49

Charges 2007

Per unit incl. 2 adults and electricity	€ 19,70 - € 58,80
extra person	€ 3,25 - € 9,00
child (0-10 yrs)	free - € 7,15

All plus 7% VAT. Discounts in low season for longer stays.

Camping Cheques accepted.

Check real time availability and at-the-gate prices...

www.**alanrogers**.com

ES8537 Camping Naturista El Templo del Sol

E-43890 Hospitalet del Infante (Tarragona)

Tel: **977 823 434**. Email: **info@eltemplodelsol.com**

El Templo del Sol is a large, luxurious terraced naturist site with a distinctly Arabesque style and superb buildings in Moorish style. The owner has designed the magnificent main turreted building at the entrance with fountains and elaborate Moorish arches. The site has over 400 pitches of two different sizes, some with car parking alongside and 85 with full services. There is some shade and the pitches are on terraces giving rewarding views over the sea. Attractive steps give ready access to the sandy beach. There is some daytime rail noise especially in the lower areas of the site where the larger pitches are located.

Facilities

The sanitary blocks are amongst the best providing everything you could require. Extensive facilities for disabled campers. Washing machines. Well stocked supermarket. Health shop. Souvenir shop. Bars. Restaurant and snack bar (1/4-10/10). Swimming pools (20/3-15/10). Jacuzzi. Cinema. Games area. Boules. Separate round children's pool and play area. Miniclub. Doctor available. Library. Safety deposit boxes. Entertainment. Hairdresser. Bicycle hire. ATM. Dogs are not accepted. No jet skis. Off site: Fishing 100 m. Golf 2 km. (night time only). Bicycle hire and boat launching 3 km. Riding 7 km. Theme parks.

Open: 20 March - 20 October.

Directions

From N340 south of Tarragona, exit at km. 1123 towards L'Hopitalet and follow signs. GPS: N40:58 W00:54.05

Charges 2006

Per unit incl. 2 persons and electricity	€ 18,70 - € 38,55
extra person	€ 3,30 - € 8,00
child (under 10 yrs)	free - € 5,70
small tent	€ 2,75 - € 4,65

Plus 7% VAT.
Discounts for longer stays.

ES8555 Camping Eucaliptus

Platja Eucaliptus s/n, E-43870 Amposta (Tarragona)

Tel: **977 479 046**. Email: **eucaliptus@campingeucaliptus.com**

In the Delta del Ebro national park, a unique area of wetland (320 square kilometre) and close to the golden sands of Platja Eucaliptus, this site's location is wonderful. Arriving at Camping Eucaliptus is like finding an oasis after the extraordinary drive through miles of flat marshland and rice fields. The 264 grass pitches are level and have plenty of shade, all with easy access to electricity and water. The site is very well maintained and three modern buildings near the entrance house the reception, toilet block, shop, bar and restaurant. The terrace overlooks the pleasant pool area with lawned gardens for sunbathing and the campsite's own lagoon.

Facilities

The single toilet block is kept very clean and includes open style washbasins and good sized shower cubicles. Baby bath. Good facilities for disabled people. Laundry facilities. Dog shower. Well stocked shop. Gas supplies. Large bar with satellite TV. Good restaurant and snack bar with takeaway (all year). Large terrace. Play area. Swimming pool with paddling pool (1/6-15/9). Bicycle hire. Attractive barbecue area with covered seating.

Open: All year.

Directions

From N340 take Els Montels exit (at 1083 km. marker). Follow signs to Els Montels taking the TV3405 through the Delta del Ebro. At the end of this long straight road there are signs for Platjas Eucaliptus. Site is on right just before the large expanse of beach.

Charges 2006

Per person	€ 3,65 - € 4,50
pitch	€ 5,20 - € 5,60
electricity (5A)	€ 3,60

BARCELONA IS THE CAPITAL OF THE CATALUNYA REGION OF NORTHEAST OF SPAIN ON THE MEDITERRANEAN COAST, BORDERING FRANCE AND ANDORRA IN THE NORTH. IT IS AN HISTORIC AND VIBRANT CITY, BOASTING AN ARRAY OF SUPERB MUSEUMS, IMPRESSIVE ARCHITECTURAL BUILDINGS, AND NUMEROUS BEACHES – NO-ONE SHOULD VISIT SPAIN WITHOUT GOING TO BARCELONA!

Our advice on driving in Barcelona is quite simple – don't even think about it! Leave your car or motorcaravan somewhere outside the city and catch the train into the centre. The services are plentiful, usually run on time and fares are cheap by comparison with the UK. There are several stations in the centre of Barcelona, including the Placa de Catalunya.

Spend a few hours wandering around the maze of little streets that comprise the tree-lined Ramblas which leads down through the medieval heart of the city (the Barrio Gotico) towards the port area. Stop off at one of the many bistros and cafés that abound here; or maybe take in a visit to the Picasso Museum. A word of warning though, do stay alert for pick-pockets as it is also apparently a happy hunting ground for petty thieves.

Barelona's metro system is excellent and provides an easy way of getting around; a targeta (ticket strip) offers ten journeys at a discounted price. An alternative is to use the tourist buses which run from Catalonia Square. Complete with multi-lingual commentary, these offer unlimited travel on two different routes for an all-in price of around €12 for the day or €15 for two days. You will also receive a book of vouchers with your tickets giving discounts on entry fees to many of the city's main attractions and to some restaurants. The services operate half-hourly most of the year and you can get on and off as you please.

The buses pass numerous famous buildings, including those designed by Gaudi: the world-famous, but still unfinished Temple Expiatori de la Sagrada Familia (Church of the Holy Family), his apartment block Casa Milã in the Passeig de Grãcia and the magnificent Palau Guell, the first modern building to be declared a World Heritage building by UNESCO. Also of interest en-route is the stadium, pool and sailing harbour used during the 1992 Olympic Games, the home of FC Barcelona, the old Bull Ring and the National Palace, now home to the Art Museum. The bus also stops by the funicular railway, which offers excellent views across the city.

If your time in Barcelona is limited, a day using the tourist buses, taking you from one point of interest to another, is time well spent and provides at least something of an insight into this fascinating city.

MAP 3

This Mediterranean region is famous for its magnificent orange groves and beautiful long, sandy beaches. Centuries of Moorish presence have resulted in a profound Hispano-Moorish heritage.

Comunidad Valenciana

VALENCIANA IS MADE UP OF THE PROVINCES OF CASTELLON, VALENCIA AND ALICANTE

THE CAPITAL OF THE REGION IS VALENCIA

La Costa del Azahar (Orange-blossom Coast) stretches from Vinaros to Almanzora, with the great port of Valencia in the centre. Orange groves grow right down to the coast, particularly in the northern section. Good beaches can be found around Benicassim and Peñíscola. South of Valencia, the Costa Blanca derives its name from its 170 miles or so of silvery-white beaches – some of the best beaches are to be found on this coast, especially between Gandía and Benidorm. As a result, it is one of the most popular tourist areas in Spain. The capital city of Valencia boasts a great nightlife and plays host to numerous festivals held throughout the year, including the unique fiesta of Las Fallas de Saint Joseph, when enormous papiermâché sculptures are set ablaze. Throughout it all are bullfights, music and fireworks. Alicante, the capital of the province of the same name, is dominated by the great Moorish castle of Santa Barbara, which offers marvellous views of the entire city. It also has several beaches in and around the town.

Places of interest

Castellón de la Plana: Santa Maria cathedral.

El Puig: monastery, Museum of Print and Graphics (world's smallest book).

La Albufera: vast lagoon, home to 250 species of bird.

Morella: medieval fortress town, dinosaur museum.

Oropesa: 16th century Tower of the King.

Peñíscola: medieval castle.

Cuisine of the region

Rice is the dominant ingredient, grown locally in paddy fields; the most famous dish is the *Paella Valenciana*. Soups and stews known locally as *ollas* are popular and seafood is readily available. Tiger nut milk is a soft drink exclusive to this region, usually accompanied by *fartons* (local pastries).

Arnadi: dessert with pumpkin and sweet potato.

Arroz al horno: rice, baked with chickpeas.

Arroz con costra: meat-based paella topped with baked egg crust.

Arroz negro: rice cooked with squid.

Bajoques farcides: stuffed peppers.

Olla recapte: with potatoes and pork.

Turrón: made of nuts and honey, either soft and flaky or hard like nougat.

CASTILLA-LA MANCHA

8558
8559
8560
8570
8580

CASTELLON
DE LA PLANA

8590

A7

8625

✳ VALENCIA

A3

VALENCIANA

✳ ALBACETE

8620
8615
8612

8645   8675   8754

8755

8687
8683
8685

8689

8690   8681

✳ ALICANTE

A7

MURCIA ✳

8742
8743

ES8558 Camping Vinaros

Ctra N340 km 1054, E-12500 Vinaros (Castelló)
Tel: **964 402424**. Email: **info@campingvinaros.com**

Taking its name from the seaside town nearby, this pleasant site has 239 flat numbered pitches of average size on flat ground. Mature trees provide shade and neat hedges separate the pitches, all of which have an individual sink. A newer area has little shade as yet. The site entrance is directly off the N340, with an impressive restaurant outside the main boundary. There is a spacious entrance with lots of outside parking, but there is traffic noise. A small swimming pool has a sunbathing area and a paddling pool (May-Sept). The pleasant snack bar serves snacks all year.

Facilities

Two exceptionally clean, fully equipped toilet blocks use marble and tiling to create a light environment enhanced by potted shrubs. Some washbasins are in cabins. Facilities for disabled campers. Laundry facilities. Motorcaravan services. Milk and bread delivered daily. Restaurant, snack bar and bar (all year). Play area. Swimming pool (1/4-30/10). Petanque. Musical and other entertainment in season. Large aviary and terrapin pool. Children's club (high season) and artistic activities for adults (all year). Off site: Beach and fishing 800 m. Bus service 500 m. Rail station close by. Vinaros 500 m. with extensive choice of bars and restaurants. Golf 7 km.

Open: All year.

Directions

Take exit 43 (Ulldecona) from the A7. Switch to the N340 and head towards Barcelona. Site is at 1054 km. marker directly off N340.

Charges guide

Per unit, all incl.	€ 13,40

All plus 7% VAT.
Stay over 7 days in low season € 7.20 + 7% VAT.

ES8580 Bonterra Park

Avenida de Barcelona 47, E-12560 Benicasim (Castelló)

Tel: **964 300 007**. Email: **info@bonterrapark.com**

If you are looking for a town site which is not too crowded and has very good facilities, this one may be for you, as there are few quality sites in the local area and this is open all year. It is a 300 metre walk to a good, shady beach – and parking is not too difficult. The site has 331 pitches (70-90 sq.m), all with electricity (6/10A) and a variety of bungalows. Bonterra has a clean and neat appearance with reddish soil, palms, grass and a number of trees which give good shade. There is a little road and rail noise. The site has an attractive pool complex including a covered pool for the winter months. The beach is good for scuba diving or snorkelling – hire facilities are available at Benicasim. This is a well run, Mediterranean style site useful for visiting local attractions such as the Carmelite monastery at Desierto de las Palmas, six kilometres distant or the historic town of Castellon.

Facilities

Four attractive, well maintained sanitary blocks provide some private cabins, washbasins with hot water, others with cold. Baby and dog showers. Facilities for disabled campers. Laundry. Motorcaravan services. Restaurant/bar. Shop (all year). Swimming pool, covered pool and children's pool. Playground (some concrete bases). Tennis. Multi-sport court. Gymnasium. Disco. Bicycle hire. Mini-club. Satellite TV. Internet access (WiFi). Off site: Town facilities. Sandy beach and fishing 500 m. Riding 3 km. Boat launching 5 km. Golf 10 km. Nature Park.

Open: All year.

Directions

Site is about 1 km. east of Benicasim village with access off the old main N340 road running parallel with the coast. The road re-numbering here is very confusing but there are many blue signs to the site with the campsite name so it is not difficult to find. Coming from the north, turn left at sign 'Benicasim por la costa'. On the A7 from the north use exit 45, from the south exit 46. GPS: N40:03 W00:04.46

Charges 2007

Per person	€ 3,40 - € 5,00
child (3-9 yrs)	€ 2,85 - € 4,00
pitch acc. to type and season	€ 14,35 - € 34,75

All plus 7% VAT. Less in low season and special long stay rates excl. July/Aug.

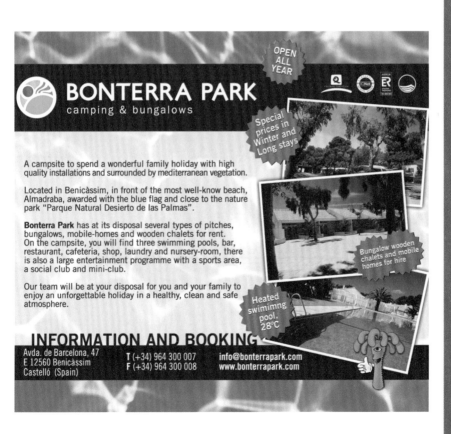

ES8570 Camping Torre La Sal 2

Cami L'Atall, E-12595 Ribera de Cabanes (Castelló)

Tel: **964 319 744**. Email: **camping@torrelasal2.com**

Torre La Sal 2 is a large site divided into two by a road, with a reception on each side with friendly, helpful staff. There are two pool complexes (one can be covered in cooler weather and is heated) which are both on the west side, whilst the beach (of shingle and sand) is on the east. Both sides have a restaurant – the restaurant on the beach side has two air conditioned wooden buildings and a terrace. On the western side are a children's play park, a large disco and sporting facilities including a sports centre, tennis, squash and two football pitches.

Facilities	Directions
Toilet facilities are of a good standard in both sections, four to the west and two to the east, with facilities for disabled campers in both. Baby rooms. Washing machines. Motorcaravan services. Shop, bars, restaurants and takeaway (all year). Swimming pools – one heated and covered. Jacuzzi and sauna (winter). Large play area. Games room. Sports facilities. Bullring. Varied activities and entertainment. WiFI internet access. Off site: Village has a range of shops bars and restaurants. Riding 10 km.	From A7/E15 take exit 45 for Oropesa on N340. Move north to 1,000 km. marker and take road to the coast and town of Camil'atall. Site is well signed from here.

Open: All year.

Charges 2006

Per person	€ 5,85
child (1-9 yrs)	€ 5,25
pitch incl. electricity	€ 19,40
Plus 7% VAT.	

ES8559 Azahar Residencial Camping & Bungalow Park

Ptda. Villarroyos, s/n, E-12598 Peñiscola (Castelló)

Tel: **964 475 480**. Email: **info@campingazahar.com**

Set inland (3 km.) from the busy coastal resort of Peñiscola, Camping Azahar is set amongst the orange groves. The site has 110 level touring pitches, all with access to electricity (6/10A) and accessed by wide, gravel roads. Shade is provided by young trees and three large, barn-type roof structures. The pitches are not separated and those undercover are big enough to suit larger units. Although this is a new site, there are already plans for development. These include an extra toilet block and a spa that will provide saunas, sun beds, jacuzzi, hydrotherapy pool and massage rooms.

Facilities	Directions
One modern toilet block in the centre of the site includes open style washbasins. Washing machine. Shop. Bar/restaurant with small terrace (all year). Outdoor swimming pool (Easter - Sept). Play area. Minigolf. Bicycle hire. Internet access. Animals not accepted July/Aug. Off site: Costa Azahar shopping and entertainment complex 1 km. Irta mountains 3 km. Peñiscola 3 km. Fishing and golf 5 km. Beach, and sailing 5 km.	From A7 (Barcelona - Valencia) take exit 43 and N340 towards Peñiscola which will direct you onto the Cv141. Approaching outskirts of the town turn left signed Camping Azahar and follow signs.

Open: All year.

Charges 2006

Per unit incl. 2 persons, 3A electricity	€ 12,00 - € 15,00
extra person	€ 2,50 - € 4,20
child (3-10 yrs)	€ 1,80 - € 3,00

ES8620 Camping L'Alqueria

E-46730 Gandia (Valencia)

Tel: **96 284 0470**

Camping L'Aqueria is situated on the main Gandia to Gau road and, although in an urban location, it is near (2 km.) the beaches of Gandia. The 137 touring pitches are of a good size and on level ground, all with 6/10A electricity and easy access to one of many water points. Some are separated by dividing hedges and there is plenty of shade from mature trees. An orchard area to the rear of the site is designated for casual camping and is adjacent to the football pitch.

Facilities	Directions
Four toilet blocks, three with British style toilets, placed evenly around the site. Mostly combined shower and washbasin cubicles. Laundry facilities (key from reception). Motorcaravan service point. Shop and snack bar (1/4-15/10). Covered swimming pool (all season) and outdoor paddling pool (1/6-15/10). Steam room and spa facilities. Fridge hire. Off site: Fishing, golf, bicycle hire, riding and boat launching 1 km. Beach 2 km. Shops, restaurant etc. within 1 km.	From A7 (Valencia - Alicante) take exit 60 and follow signs to Gandia on the N332. Through the town follow signs for Gau and Platjas Gandia. Site is northwest of Gandia.

Open: All year.

Charges 2006

Per person	€ 3,26 - € 4,27
child	€ 2,62 - € 3,60
pitch	€ 8,45 - € 12,20

ES8560 Camping Playa Tropicana

Playa Tropicana, E-12579 Alcossebre (Castelló)

Tel: **964 412 463**. Email: **info@playatropicana.com**

Playa Tropicana is a unique site which will strike visitors immediately as being very different. It has been given a tropical theme with scores of 'Romanesque' white statues around the site including in the sanitary blocks. The site has 300 marked pitches separated by lines of flowering bushes under mature trees. The pitches vary in size (50-100 sq.m), most are shaded and there are electricity connections throughout (some need long leads). 50 pitches have water and drainage. It has a delightful position away from the main hub of tourism, alongside a good sandy beach which shelves gently into the clean waters. To gain access to this it is necessary to cross a pretty promenade in front of the site, which also has statues. It is in a quiet position and it is a drive rather than a walk to the centre of the village resort. The theme extends into an excellent restaurant where, in high season, you may dine on the upper terrace with uninterrupted sea views. A variety of entertainment is provided and there is also a children's club and social room with films and soft drinks bar in high season. The site has several large water features by the high quality restaurant (some are very cheeky!). Aviaries are housed in a corner of the site.

Facilities

Three sanitary blocks delightfully decorated, fully equipped and of excellent standard, include washbasins in private cabins. Baby baths and facilities for disabled people. Washing machine. Motorcaravan services. Gas supplies. Large supermarket. Superb restaurant, a little expensive. (Easter - late Sept). Swimming pool (18 x 11 m.) and children's pool. Playground. Bicycle hire. Children's club. Fishing. Torches necessary in some areas. No TVs allowed in July/Aug. Dogs are not accepted. Off site: Fishing and watersports on the beaches. Riding and boat launching 3 km. Golf 25 km.

Open: All year.

Directions

Alcoceber (or Alcossebre) is between Peniscola and Oropesa. Turn off N340 at 1018 km. marker towards Alcossebre on CV142. Just before entering town proceed through the traffic lights to main road. At next junction, turn right and follow coast road to site in 2.5 km. The sliding gate is on the coast road and a bell is on the right side.

Charges 2007

Per unit incl 2 persons	
and electricity	€ 18,00 - € 60,00
extra person	€ 3,50 - € 7,00
child (1-10 yrs)	€ 2,50 - € 6,00

Electricity and VAT included.
Many discount schemes out of season.
Camping Cheques accepted.

ES8625 Kiko Park Rural

Ctra Embalse Contreras, km. 3, E-46317 Villargordo del Cabriel (Valencia)

Tel: **962 139 082**. Email: **kikoparkrural@kikopark.com**

Approaching Kiko Park Rural, you will see a small hilltop village appearing in a landscape of mountains, vines and a jewel-like lake. Kiko was a small village and farm and the village now forms the campsite and accommodation. Amenities are contained within the architecturally authentic buildings, some old and some new. The 103 pitches (with 6A electricity and water) all have stunning views, as do the swimming and paddling pools. Generous hedge plantings have been made which already afford some privacy. Hundreds of trees planted in 2003 are yet to provide shade due to their size, although this will soon remedy itself.

Facilities

Three toilet blocks are very well equipped, including excellent facilities for disabled people. Motorcaravan services. Gas. Well stocked shop. Excellent restaurant. Pleasant bar. Swimming and paddling pools. Very good playground. Bicycle hire. Animation in high season. Many adventurous activities can be arranged, including white water rafting, gorging, orienteering, trekking, bungee and riding. Large families and groups catered for. Off site: Fishing, canoeing and windsurfing on the lake. Village 3 km.

Open: All year.

Directions

From autopista A7/E15 on Valencia ring road (near the airport) take A3 to west. Villagordo del Cabriel is 80 km. towards Motilla. Take the village exit and follow signs through village and over a hill – spot the village on a hill 2 km. away. That is the campsite!

Charges 2007

Per person	€ 4,60 - € 5,75
child (up to 10 yrs)	€ 3,50 - € 4,00
pitch	€ 6,30 - € 13,00

Camping Cheques accepted.

ES8590 Camping Monmar

Ctra Serratelles s/n, E-12593 Moncofa (Castelló)

Tel: **964 588 592**. Email: **campingmonmarmoncofa@wanadoo.es**

This purpose built, very neat site is in the small town of Moncofa, just 200 metres from the sea and right beside a water park with pools and slides. There are 170 gravel based pitches arranged in rows off tarmac access roads. All have 6A electricity, water and a drain. Hedges have been planted to separate the pitches but these are still small so there is little shade (canopies can be rented in high season). The site's facilities and amenities are all very modern but small stone reminders of the area's Roman and Arab history are used to decorate corners of the site.

Facilities

Three modern toilet blocks are well placed and provide good, clean facilities. Free hot showers. Facilities and good access for disabled visitors. Laundry with washing machines, dryer and ironing board. Shop (1/7-31/8). Bar and restaurant (weekends and high season). Swimming pool (all year). Good play area. Boules. Dogs and other pets are not accepted. Off site: Water complex. Local amenities within walking distance. Beach 400 m.

Open: All year.

Directions

Turn off N340 Castellon - Valencia road on CV2250 signed Moncofa. Follow sign for tourist information office in town and then signs for site. Pass supermarket and turn left to site in 600 m.

Charges 2006

Per unit incl. 2 persons and electricity	€ 18,00 - € 24,00
extra person	€ 6,00

VAT included. Discounts in low season with this Guide and for longer stays.

ES8615 Kiko Park Oliva

E-46780 Oliva (Valencia)

Tel: 962 850905. Email: kikopark@kikopark.com

Kiko Park is a smart site nestled behind protective sand dunes alongside a 'blue flag' beach. There are sets of attractively tiled steps over the dunes or a long boardwalk near the beach bar (good for prams and wheelchairs) to take you to the fine white sandy beach and the sea. The 180 large pitches all have electricity and the aim is to progressively upgrade all these to serviced 'super' pitches. There are plenty of flowers, hedging and trees adding shade, privacy and colour. A new outdoor pool complex with a spa, whirl pool, solarium, gym and a pool bar was added in 2006. An award-winning restaurant with architecture that reminds one of a ship is near the tropical style beach-bar, both overlooking the marina, beautiful beach and sea. This is an excellent site for watersport enthusiasts, as it is beside a marina for boat launching. A wide variety of entertainment is provided all year and Spanish lessons are taught along with dance class and aerobics during the winter. The site is run by the second generation of a family involved in camping for 30 years and their experience shows. They are brilliantly supported by a friendly, efficient team who speak many languages. The narrow roads leading to the site can be a little challenging for very large units but it is worth the effort.

Facilities

Four modern sanitary blocks are very clean with large showers, washbasins (a few in cabins), British style WCs and excellent facilities for disabled visitors (who will find a large part of this site flat and convenient). Laundry facilities. Motorcaravan services. Gas supplies. Supermarket (all year, excl. Sundays). Restaurant. Bar with TV. Beach-side bar and restaurant (all year). Swimming pools and gym. Playground. Watersports facilities. Diving school in high season (from mid-June). Entertainment for children from mid-June. Petanque. Bicycle hire. Off site: The footpath to the marina leads into the town - about 10 minutes walk. Indoor pool 1 km. Golf 5 km. Riding 7 km.

Open: All year.

Directions

From A7 north of Benidorm take exit 61 to the town and then the beach; site is at the northwest end.

Charges 2006

Per person	€ 2,70 - € 5,50
child (under 10 yrs)	€ 2,20 - € 4,80
pitch acc. to services and season	€ 9,30 - € 29,00
dog	€ 0,60 - € 2,20
electricity (per kWh)	€ 0,30

ES8612 Euro Camping

Playa de Oliva, E-46780 Oliva (Valencia)

Tel: **962 854 098**. Email: **info@eurocamping-es.com**

This English owned site with an intimate and friendly atmosphere is located beside the Playa de Oliva's golden sands. To reach it, you travel through the famous Valencia orange orchards. However be warned the final approach road to the site is very narrow and large units will find it necessary to drive through overhanging foliage. The rectangular site has tarmac and gravel roads. The 315 gravel pitches, all with electricity, are on the small side but are well maintained and eucalyptus trees provide shade for many. The reception staff are helpful and speak excellent English.

Facilities

Two mature sanitary blocks and a third newly built are well maintained. Push-button lighting in toilet blocks – torch required. Toilet facilities for disabled campers. Washing machines and dryer. Motorcaravan services. Well stocked supermarket. Restaurant/bar. Play area. Animation in high season. WiFi internet access. Off site: Golf and riding 1 km. Bicycle hire 5 km.

Open: All year.

Directions

From Alicante - Valencia autopista A7 take exit 61 onto N332 to Oliva. Exit at km. 213 or 210 and follow campsite signs.

Charges 2007

Per person	€ 4,25
child (2-10 yrs)	€ 2,95
pitch incl. electricity	€ 19.95 - € 34,95

Camping Cheques accepted.

ES8645 Camping Mariola

Ctra. Bocairent - Alcoi, km. 9, E-46880 Bocairent (Valencia)

Tel: **962 135160**. Email: **info@campingmariola.com**

Situated high in the Sierra Mariola National Park, in a beautiful rural setting but only 12 km. from the old town of Bocairent, this is a real taste of Spain with hilltop views all around. Used mainly by the Spanish, the site is an undiscovered jewel with 170 slightly sloping pitches. These are well spaced and have shade from a mixture of young and mature trees. An orchard area well away from the main site (with no amenities close by) is used for more casual camping. A traditional, stone built restaurant is slightly elevated with views over the site.

Facilities

Six identical small toilet blocks offer adequate facilities with British style WCs and showers with shared changing area. Open style washbasins. No facilities for disabled persons. Washing machine. Motorcaravan services. Small shop (weekends only). Bar/restaurant (weekends only in low season). Satellite TV. Outdoor pool with separate paddling pool (June - Sept). Two multisport pitches. Play area. Communal barbecue area. Children's club and entertainment (August only). Off site: Riding and golf 12 km.

Open: All year.

Directions

From the CV40 take exit for Ontinyent and follow the CV81. Pass town of Bocairent heading west and in 2 km. look for camping sign (at textiles factory). Turn south on VV2031 to Alcoy. Turn right at first roundabout and straight on at next through small industrial estate. Persevere upwards for 10 km. and site is a turn to left. GPS: N38:45.16 W0:32.53

Charges 2006

Per person	€ 3,25 - € 4,10
pitch incl. electricity	€ 7,80 - € 9.70

Camping Cheques accepted.

ES8675 Camping Vall de Laguar

C/Sant Antonio 24, La Vall de Laguar, E-03791 Campell (Alacant)

Tel: **96 557 74 90**. Email: **info@campinglaguar.com**

Near the pretty mountain-top village of Campell, this new site is perched high on the side of a mountain with breathtaking views of hilltop villages, the surrounding hills and distant sea. With a wholehearted welcome from the owners, the well maintained site promises a real taste of Spain. The pitches, pool, terrace and restaurant all share the views. The 68 average size gravel pitches are on terraces and all have electricity and water. Trees and hedges have been planted and now give ample shade.

Facilities

Two new sanitary blocks have excellent clean facilities including some for disabled campers. Washing machines and dryers. Restaurant with pretty terrace. Bar and pool bar. Swimming pool and small pool bar. Small entertainment programme in high season. Barbecue area with sinks. Torches useful. Off site: Attractive town close by. Golf and beach 18 km.

Open: All year.

Directions

Site is 20 km. west of Xabia/Javea. From A7/E15 exit 62 head to Beniarbeig on minor road. From there to Sanet, Benidoleig and finally Vall de Laguar. Site is well signed from the town and sits above it.

Charges 2006

Per person	€ 3,90
pitch	€ 8,65 - € 9,10
electricity	€ 2,20
Minimum charge Easter and July/August	€ 19.23

ES8681 Camping Villasol

Avenida Bernat de Sarria, E-03503 Benidorm (Alacant)

Tel: **965 850 422**. Email: **camping-villasol@dragonet.es**

Benidorm is increasingly popular for winter stays and Villasol is a genuinely good, purpose built modern site. Many of the 309 well separated pitches are arranged on wide terraces which afford views of the mountains surrounding Benidorm. All pitches (80-85 sq.m.) have electricity and satellite TV connections, with 160 with full services for seasonal use. Shade is mainly artificial. Reservations are only accepted for winter stays of over three months (from 1 Oct). There is a small indoor pool, heated for winter use, and a very attractive, large outdoor pool complex (summer only) overlooked by the bar/restaurant and restaurant terrace.

Facilities

Modern toilet blocks provide free, controllable hot water to showers and washbasins and British WCs. Good facilities for disabled campers. Laundry facilities. Good value restaurant. Bar. Shop. Swimming pools, outdoor and indoor. Playground. Evening entertainment programme. Dogs are not accepted. Off site: Fishing and bicycle hire 1.3 km. Golf 8 km.

Open: All year.

Directions

From autopista exit 65 (Benidorm) and turn left at second set of traffic lights. After 1 km. at another set of lights turn right, then right again at next lights. Site is on right in 400 m. From northern end of N332 bypass follow signs for Benidorm Playa Levante. In 500 m. at traffic lights turn left, then right at next lights. Site is on right after 400 m.

Charges 2006

Per person	€ 5,00 - € 6,50
child (1-9 yrs)	€ 3,80 - € 4,80
pitch incl. electricity	€ 14,00 - € 21,80

All plus 7% VAT.
Good discounts for longer stays in winter.

ES8683 Camping Benisol

Avenida de la Comunidad Valenciana s/n, E-03500 Benidorm (Alacant)

Tel: **965 851 673**. Email: **campingbenisol@yahoo.es**

Camping Benisol is a well developed and peaceful site with lush, green vegetation and a mountain background. Mature hedges and trees afford privacy to each pitch and some artficial shade is provided where necessary. There are 298 pitches of which around 115 are for touring units (60-80 sq.m). All have electrical hook-ups (4/6A) and 75 have drainage. All the connecting roads are now surfaced with tarmac. Some day-time road noise should be expected. The site has an excellent restaurant serving traditional Spanish food at great prices, with a pretty, shaded terrace overlooking the pool with its palms and thatched pool bar.

Facilities

Modern sanitary facilities, heated in winter and kept very clean, have free, solar heated hot water to washbasins, showers and sinks. Laundry facilities. Gas supplies. Restaurant with terrace and bar (all year, closed 1 day a week). Shop. Swimming pool (Easter - Nov). Small, old-style play area. Minigolf. Jogging track. Tennis. Golf driving range. ATM. Off site: Riding 1 km. Bicycle hire 3 km. Fishing (sea) 3 km. Golf 14 km. Bus route.

Open: All year.

Directions

Site is northeast of Benidorm. Exit N332 at 152 km. marker and take turn signed Playa Levant. Site is 100 m. on left off the main road, well signed.

Charges 2006

Per person	€ 4,90 - € 5,25
child (1-10 yrs)	€ 4,00 - € 4,40
pitch incl. electricity	€ 16,05 - € 18,80

All plus 7% VAT. Less 15-60% in low seasons.
No credit cards.

ES8685 Camping Caravaning El Raco

Avenida Doctor Severo Ochoa, s/n, E-03500 Benidorm (Alacant)

Tel: **96 586 8552**. Email: **campingraco@inicia.es**

This purpose built site with good facilities and very competitive prices provides about 1,000 pitches (180 for touring units). There is wide access from the Rincon de Loix road. The site is quietly situated 1.5 km. from the town, Levante beach and promenade. It has wide tarmac roads and pitches of 80 sq.m. or more, separated by low cypress hedging and some trees which provide some shade. Satellite TV connections are provided to each pitch and there are 94 with all services including (10A) electricity. The good value restaurant, bar and elegant pools are all at the entrance, some distance from the touring pitches.

Facilities

Four large toilet blocks are well equipped. Facilities for disabled people. Dishwashing sinks. Laundry facilities. Gas supplies. Motorcaravan services. Restaurant. Bar. Well stocked shop. Busy bar with TV also open to public and good value restaurant. Outdoor swimming pool, no slides or diving board (1/4-31/10). Indoor heated pool (1/11-31/3). Playground. ATM. Off site: Beach 1 km. Bicycle hire 2 km. Golf 6 km. Theme parks.

Open: All year.

Directions

From autopista exit 65 (Benidorm, Levante) at second set of traffic lights turn left on N332 (Altea, Valencia). After 1.5 km. turn right (Levante Playa), then straight on at next lights for 300 m. to site on right. From north on N332 follow signs for Playa Levante (or Benidorm Palace). At lights turn left (Playa Levante).

Charges 2006

Per person	€ 5,00 - € 5,80
child (1-9 yrs)	€ 3,70 - € 4,50
pitch incl. electricity	€ 14,60 - € 18,60

Discounts for longer stays.
VAT included. No credit cards.

ES8687 Camping Cap Blanch

Playa de Cap Blanch 25, E-03590 Altea (Alacant)

Tel: **965 845 946**. Email: **capblanch@ctv.es**

This well run, small site has plenty of character. It is open all year and is very popular for winter stays. Alongside the beach road, it has direct access to the pebble beach and is within a few hundred yards of all Albir's shops and restaurants. The 250 pitches on flat, hard gravel are of a good size and well maintained with 5A electricity. The site tends to be full in winter and is very popular with several nationalities, especially the Dutch. For winter stays, it would pay to get there before Christmas as January and February are the peak months.

Facilities

The refurbished sanitary block can be heated and provides good facilities including some washbasins in cabins, baby facilities and a room for disabled visitors (both these accessed by key). Motorcaravan services. Gas supplies. Laundry. Bar and restaurant. Takeaway. Playground. Tennis. Boules. Fitness centre. Organised entertainment and courses. ATM. Off site: Restaurants, shops and commercial centre close. Golf 0.5 km. Bicycle hire 1 km. Riding 5 km.

Open: All year.

Directions

Site is on the Albir - Altea coast road and can be reached from either end. From N332, north or south, watch for sign Playa del Albir and proceed through Albir to the coast road. Site is on north side of Albir, well signed.

Charges 2006

Per person	€ 3,50 - € 5,50
child (3-12 yrs)	€ 3,00 - € 4,50
pitch incl. car	€ 8,50 - € 24,00
electricity	€ 3,00 - € 4,50

VAT included. Less 10-35% for low season stays 7-30 days, special rates for long stays.

ES8742 Camping Internacional La Marina

Ctra N332 km 76, E-03194 La Marina (Alacant)

Tel: **965 419 200**. Email: **info@campinglamarina.com**

Efficiently run by a friendly Belgian family, La Marina has 370 pitches of seven different types and size ranging from about 50 sq.m. for tents to 100 sq.m. with electricity (10A), TV, water and drainage. Artificial shade is provided and the pitches are extremely well maintained on level, well drained ground with a special area allocated for tents in a small orchard. The lagoon swimming pool complex is absolutely fabulous and has something for everyone (with lifeguards). William Le Metayer, the owner, is passionate about La Marina and it shows in his search for perfection. A magnificent new, modern building houses some superb extra amenities. Member of Leading Campings Group. These include a relaxed business centre with internet access, a tapas bar decorated with amazing ceramics (handmade by the owner's mother) and a quality restaurant with a water fountain feature and great views of the lagoon. There is also a conference centre and an extensive library, with the whole of the lower ground floor dedicated to children with a play area and a 'cyber zone' for teenagers. With a further bar and a soundproofed disco, the building is of an exceptional, eco-friendly standard. A fine fitness centre and covered, heated pool (14 x 7 m) are close by. A pedestrian gate at the rear of the site gives access to the long sandy beach through the coastal pine forest that is a feature of the area. We recommend this site very highly whatever type of holidaying camper you may be.

Facilities

The elegant sanitary blocks offer the very best of modern facilities. Heated in winter, they include private cabins and facilities for disabled visitors. Laundry facilities Motorcaravan services. Gas. Supermarket. Bars. Restaurant (all year). Swimming pools (1/4-15/10). Indoor pool. Fitness centre. Sauna. Play rooms. Extensive activity and entertainment programme. Sports area. Tennis. Huge playground. Hairdresser. Off site: Fishing 800 m. Boat launching 5 km. Golf 7 km. Bicycle hire 8 km. Riding 15 km. Hourly bus service from outside the gate. Theme parks.

Open: All year.

Directions

Site is 2 km. west of La Marina. Leave N332 Guardamara de Segura - Santa Pola road at 75 km. marker if travelling north, or 78 km. marker if travelling south. Site is well signed.

Charges 2006

Per person	€ 5,00 - € 7,20
child (under 10 yrs)	€ 3,50 - € 4,80
pitch incl. electricty,	
acc. to type and season	€ 19,10 - € 37,20
dog	€ 1,00 - € 2,00

Plus 7% VAT. Seven grades of pitch.
Less in low season, plus good discounts
for longer stays 16/9-14/6, excluding Easter.

ES8743 Complejo Ecoturistico Marjal

Ctra N-332, km 73.4, E-03140 Guardamar del Segura (Alacant)

Tel: **966 725 022**. Email: **camping@marjal.com**

Marjal is located beside the estuary of the Segura river, alongside the pine and eucalyptus forests of the Dunas de Guardamar natural park. The fine sandy beach can be reached through the forest (800 m). This is a new site with a huge lagoon-style pool and a superb sports complex. There are 212 pitches on this award winning site, all with water, electricity, drainage and satellite TV points, the ground covered with crushed marble, making the pitches clean and pleasant. There is some shade and the site has an open feel with lots of room for manoeuvring. Reception is housed within a delicately coloured building complete with a towering Mirador, topped by a weather-vane depicting the 'Garza Real' (heron) bird which frequents the local area and forms part of the site logo. The large leased restaurant overlooks the pools and the river that leads to the sea in the near distance. This situation is shared with the taperia (high season) and bar with large terraces fringed by trees, palms and pomegranates. The impressive pool/lagoon complex (1,100 sq.m) has a water cascade, an island bar plus bridge, one part sectioned as a pool for children and a jacuzzi. The extensive sports area is also impressive with qualified instructors who will customise your fitness programme whilst consulting the doctor. No effort has been spared here, the quality heated indoor pool, light-exercise room, sauna, solarium, beauty salon, fully equipped gym and changing rooms, including facilities for disabled visitors, are of the highest quality. Aerobics and physiotherapy are also on offer. All activities are discounted for campers. A programme of entertainment is provided for adults and children in season by a professional animation team.

Facilities

Three excellent heated toilet blocks have free hot water, elegant separators between sinks, spacious showers and some cabins. Each block has high quality facilities for babies and disabled campers, modern laundry and dishwashing rooms. Car wash. Well stocked supermarket. Restaurants. Bar. Large outdoor pool complex (1/6-31/10). Heated indoor pool (low season). Fitness suite. Jacuzzi. Sauna. Solarium. Aerobics and aquarobics. Play room. Minigolf. Floodlit tennis and soccer pitch. Bicycle hire. Games room. TV room. ATM. Business centre. Internet access. Off site: Beach 800 m. Riding or golf 4 km.

Open: All year.

Directions

On N332 40 km. south of Alicante, site is on the sea side between 73 and 74 km. markers.

Charges 2006

Per person	€ 5,00 - € 7,00
child (4-12 yrs)	€ 2,50 - € 4,00
pitch	€ 18,00 - € 30,00
electricity	€ 2,00 - € 3,00
All plus 7% VAT.	

ES8689 Camping Playa del Torres

Partida Torres Norte 11, Apdo. Correus 243, E-03570 Villajoyosa (Alacant)

Tel: **966 810 031**. Email: **into@playadeltonnes.com**

Jacinto and Mercedes have a pretty beachside site with the lower part set under eucalyptus trees. Reception is placed in one of the site's tasteful wooden buildings close to the beach (excellent English is spoken). If you prefer a smaller site away from the 'high rise' and bustle of Benidorm offering high quality this could be for you. The 85 lower pitches, some large, are on flat ground with shade. 10 good pitches are right alongside the beach fence (book early). All have electricity (16A), some are fully serviced and there are ample water fountains around the site along with efficient, modern lighting.

Facilities

The sanitary building is of a high specification, as are the fittings within, including excellent showers. Laundry. Bar. Cafeteria. Shop. Swimming pool. Children's play area. Petanque. Fishing. Barbecues. Freezer. Satellite TV. Reception will assist with all tourist activities. Off site: Riding 100 m. Golf 18 km. Serious or recreational walking and climbing is possible about 20 minutes away from the site. Benidorm is very close.

Open: All year.

Directions

From Villajoyosa on N332, site is 1 km. east of the town. Look for clear site signs towards beach. From Benidorm on N332, site is 3 km. on the left, but a left turn is prohibited. Proceed 400 m. to traffic lights to turn, then proceed as above.

Charges 2006

Per person	€ 4,90
child (4-13 yrs)	€ 3,80
pitch	€ 4,90 - € 35,00
electricity (plus meter)	€ 3,97
Plus 7% VAT. Less 5-50% for low season stays of 7 days or more.	

ES8690 Camping Costa Blanca

Calle Convento, 143, Nacional 332 - km. 120.5, E-03560 El Campello (Alacant)

Tel: **965 630670**. Email: **info@campingcostablanca.com**

This small site has 80 pitches with 60 for tourers, some with views of the distant hills. Bungalows line three sides of the white walled rectangular site with a railway (not too busy) on the final side. Reception is efficient with keen staff members speaking several languages. The flat pitches are on gravel and all have 6A electricity. Some are small (40, 60 or 80 sq.m.) and will be a challenge for large units. There is natural shade from trees and some artificial shade. A pleasant pool is the centre-piece with a bright poolside bar and a restaurant with a patio.

Facilities

Four clean refurbished sanitary units offer a variety of facilities including cabins with toilet and basin, toilet and bidet, washbasins with hot water, others with cold. Two baby baths in cabins. Facilities for disabled campers. Washing machines and dryer. Motorcaravan services at entrance (€ 4 per token). Restaurant/bar (all year). Shop (9/7-15/9). Swimming pool. Basic play area (supervision required). Limited live entertainment in season. Communal barbecue. Off site: Town facilities. Fishing, sailing and watersports 500 m. Riding 8 km. Golf 8 km. Boat launching 500 m. ATM 1 km.

Open: All year.

Directions

From north of Alicante on A7 or N332 take exit for El Campello. Follow signs to town centre and site is signed 1.5 km. on the right before the town. It is a little difficult to see as it is tucked back into a square of housing with a clear untouched area to its front.

Charges 2007

Per person	€ 3,35 - € 4,75
child (1-10 yrs)	€ 2,65 - € 3,80
pitch	€ 8,80 - € 22,25
electricity	€ 3,80

Camping Cheques accepted.

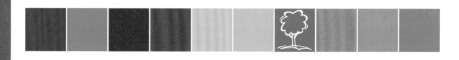

ES8754 Camping Jávea

Ctra Cabo de la Nao, km. 1, E-03730 Jávea (Alacant)

Tel: **965 791 070**. Email: **info@camping-javea.com**

The 200 metre long access road to this site is a little unkempt as it passes some factories, but all changes on the final approach with palms, orange and pine trees, the latter playing host to a colony of parakeets. English is spoken at reception. The boxed hedges and palms surrounding this area with a backdrop of hills dotted with villas presents an attractive setting. Three hectares provides space for 214 numbered pitches with 179 for touring units. Flat, level and rectangular in shape, the pitches vary in size 60-80 sq.m. (not advised for caravans or motorhomes with an overall length exceeding 7 m).

Facilities

Two very clean, fully equipped, sanitary blocks include two children's toilets plus a baby bath. Two washing machines. Fridge hire. Small bar and restaurant where in high season you purchase bread and milk. Large swimming pool with lifeguard and sunbathing lawns. Play area. Boules. Electronic barriers (deposit for card). Caravan storage. Off site: Sandy beach 3 km. Old and New Javea within easy walking distance with supermarkets and shops catering for all needs.

Open: All year.

Directions

Exit N332 for Javea on A134, continue in direction of Port (road number changes to CV 734). At roundabout (Lidl supermarket) turn right signed Arenal Platges and Cabo de la Nao. Straight on at next roundabout to camping sign and slip road in 100 m. If you miss slip road go back from next roundabout.

Charges 2007

Per person	€ 4,50 - € 5,30
child	€ 4,08 - € 4,80
pitch	€ 11,39 - € 13,40
electricity	€ 3,40

ES8755 Camping Caravanning Moraira

Camino Paellero 50, E-03724 Moraira-Teulada (Alacant)

Tel: **965 745 249**. Email: **campingmoraira@campingmoraira.com**

This small hillside site with some views over the town and marina is quietly situated in an urban area amongst old pine trees and just 400 metres from a sheltered bay. Terracing provides shaded pitches of varying size, some really quite small (access to some of the upper pitches may be difficult for larger units). Some pitches have water and drainage and a few have sea views. There are electricity connections. An attractive irregularly shaped pool with paved sunbathing terrace is below the small bar/restaurant and terrace. The pool has observation windows where you can watch the swimmers, and is used for sub-aqua instruction.

Facilities

The high quality toilet block, with polished granite floors and marble fittings, is built to a unique and ultra modern design with extra large free hot showers. Washing machine and dryer. Motorcaravan services. Bar/restaurant and shop (1/7-30/9). Small swimming pool (all year). Sub-aqua with instruction. Tennis. Torches may be required. Off site: Shops, bars and restaurants within walking distance. Beach 1.5 km. Fishing 400 m. Bicycle hire 1 km. Golf 8 km.

Open: All year.

Directions

Site is best approached from Teulada. From A7 exit 63 take N332 and in 3.5 km. turn right (Teulada and Moraira). In Teulada fork right to Moraira. At junction at town entrance turn right signed Calpe and in 1 km. turn right into road to site on bend immediately after Res. Don Julio. Do not take the first right, as the signs seem to indicate, otherwise you will go round in a loop.

Charges 2006

Per person	€ 4,70
child (4-9 yrs)	€ 3,60
pitch incl. car	€ 10,50 - € 12,60
electricity	€ 3,20

All plus 7% VAT. Less 15-60% in low season.

MAP 2

In the province of Murcia you'll find sandy beaches, dunes and unspoilt coves along the coast; inland hills and valleys plus the regional parks of Sierra de Carche, Sierra de la Pila, Sierra de Espuña, and Carrascoy and El Valle.

THE CAPITAL OF THE REGION IS THE CITY OF MURCIA

Murcia, the capital of the region, was founded in the ninth century by the Moors on the banks of the Río Segura. The square of Cardinal Belluga houses two of the town's architectural gems, the Episcopal Palace and the Cathedral, and there is a range of museums and exhibitions to visit. With narrow medieval streets, the characterful town of Cartagena has lots of bars and restaurants plus two nautical museums: the National Museum of Maritime Archaeology and the Naval Museum. Also on a nautical theme, the International Nautical Week is celebrated here in June. Along the coast there are numerous beaches offering a wide range of water sports: sailing, windsurfing, canoeing, water skiing and diving. And the area between the coastal towns of Águilas and Mazarrón is a breeding ground for tortoises and eagles. Inland are the historic towns of Lorca and Caravaca de le Cruz. The former is known as the 'baroque city' with its examples of baroque architecture, seen in the parish churches, convents, and houses; the latter too is home to beautiful churches, including El Santuario de Vera Cruz.

Places of interest

Águilas: seaside town with good beaches.

Moratalla: pretty village, castle offering stunning views of the surrounding countryside and forests.

Puerto de Mazarrón: Enchanted City of Bolnuevo - a small area of eroded rocks, nature reserve and lagoon at La Rambla de Moreras.

San Pedro del Pinatar: seaside resort, La Pagan beach is renowned for its therapeutic mud, which reputedly relieves rheumatism and is good for the skin.

Santiago de la Ribera: upmarket resort with sailing club.

Cuisine of the region

Vegetables are important and found in nearly every dish. Fish is also popular, cooked in a salt crust or *a la espalda* (lightly fried and baked), and usually accompanied by rice. Fig bread is a speciality of the region.

Bizcochos borrachos: sponge soaked in wine and syrup.

Cabello de Ángel: pumpkin strands in syrup.

Caldero: made of rice, fish and the hot ñora pepper.

Caldo con pelotas: stew made of turkey with meatballs.

Chuletas de cordero al ajo cabañil: suckling lamb chops served with a dressing of garlic and vinegar.

Tocino de cielo: dessert made with egg yolks and syrup.

Yemas de Caravaca: cake made with egg yolks.

ES8745 Camping La Fuente

Camino de La Bocamina, E-30626 Banos de Fortuna (Murcia)

Tel: **968 685125**. Email: **info@campingfuente.com**

Located in an area known for its thermal waters since Roman and Moorish times and with just 62 pitches, La Fuente is a gem. The main attraction here is the huge pool complex where the water is constant at 36 degrees all year. The site is in two sections, one where pitches are in standard rows and the other where they are in circles around blocks. The flat pitches are on shingle, have 10A electricity, and unusually all have their own mini-sanitary block. There is accommodation on site but it is separate from the camping area. Unusually winter is high season here.

Facilities

All pitches have their own facilities including a unit for disabled campers. Washing machines and dryers. High quality restaurant shared with accommodation guests. Snack bar by pool. Supermarket. Bicycle hire. Communal barbecues. New jacuzzi. Off site: Spa town, massage therapies, hot pools. Golf and riding 20 km.

Open: All year.

Directions

From A7/E15 Alicante - Murcia road take C3223 to Fortuna then follow signs to Banos de Fortuna. The site with its bright yellow walls can be easily seen from the road and is very well signed in the town. GPS: N38:12.409 W01:06.439

Charges 2006

Per person	€ 3,25
child (3-12 yrs)	€ 1,25
pitch (with private sanitary facilities)	€ 8,00 - € 10,00
dog	€ 1,00
electricity (plus € 0.22 per kWh)	€ 1,50
Pitch prices discounted after five days.	

ES8753 Caravaning La Manga

Autovia Cartagena - La Manga Salida 11, E-30370 La Manga del Mar Menor (Murcia)
Tel: 902 021 352. Email: lamanga@caravaning.es

This is a very large well equipped, 'holiday style' site with its own beach and both indoor and outdoor pools. With a good number of typical Spanish long stay units, the length of the site is impressive (1 km.) and a bicycle is very helpful for getting about. The 1,000 regularly laid out, gravel touring pitches (84 or 110sq. m.) are generally separated by hedges which also provide a degree of shade. Each has 10A electricity supply, water and the possibility of satellite TV reception. This site's excellent facilities are ideally suited for holidays in the winter when the weather is very pleasantly warm. If you are suffering from aches and pains try the famous local mud treatment. Reception will assist with bookings. November daytime temperatures usually exceed 20 degrees. La Manga is a 22 km. long narrow strip of land, bordered by the Mediterranean on one side and by the Mar Menor on the other. There are sandy bathing beaches on both sides and considerable development in terms of hotels, apartments, restaurants, night clubs, etc. in between – a little reminiscent of Miami Beach! The very end of the southern part is great for 'getting away from it all' (take a picnic for the beach and be sure to go over the little bridge for privacy). The campsite is situated on the approach to 'the strip' enjoying the benefit of its own semi-private beach with impressive tall palm trees alongside the Mar Menor which provides shallow warm waters, ideal for families with children. Here you will find a sailing, canoeing and windsurfing school, and an excellent restaurant/bar serving traditional Spanish tapas and meals. In winter, when British occupancy exceeds 90%, typical British meals are available including Sunday roast and full breakfasts.

Facilities

Seven clean toilet blocks of standard design, well spaced around the site, include washbasins (with hot water in five blocks). Laundry. Gas supplies. Large well stocked supermarket. Restaurant. Bar. Snack bar. Swimming pool complex (April - Sept). Indoor pool, gymnasium, sauna, jacuzzi and massage service. Open air cinema (April - Sept). Tennis. Petanque. Minigolf. Play area. Watersports school. Internet café (also WiFi) . Winter Spanish classes. Off site: Bus to Cartagena from outside site. Golf, bicycle hire and riding 5 km.

Open: All year.

Directions

Use exit (Salida) 15 from MU312 dual-carriageway towards Cabo de Palos, signed Playa Honda (site signed also). Cross road bridge and double back on yourself. Site entrance is clearly visible beside dual-carriageway with many flags flying.

Charges 2007

Per pitch incl. 2 persons	
and electricity	€ 20,00 - € 32,50
extra person	€ 3,75 - € 4,80
child	€ 3,20 - € 3,75

All plus 7% VAT. Discounts and special prices for low season and long winter stays.
Camping Cheques accepted.

ES8752 Camping Naturista El Portus

El Portus, E-30393 Cartagena (Murcia)

Tel: **968 553 052**. Email: **elportus@elportus.com**

Set in a secluded south facing bay fringed by mountains, El Portus is a fairly large naturist site enjoying magnificent views and with direct access to a small sand and pebble beach. This part of Spain enjoys almost all year round sunshine. There are some 400 pitches, 300 for tourers, ranging from 60-100 sq.m, all but a few having electricity (6A). They are mostly on fairly level, if somewhat stony and barren ground. El Portus has a reasonable amount of shade from established trees and nearly every pitch has a view. Residential units are situated on the hillside above the site.

Facilities

Five acceptable toilet blocks, all unisex, are of varying styles and fully equipped. Opened as required, they are clean and bright. Showers all with hot water. Unit for disabled visitors, key from reception. Washing machines. Motorcaravan services. Well stocked shop. Bar with TV and libary. Restaurants serve good quality, sensibly priced food. The beach restaurant is closed in low season. Swimming pools. Play area. Tennis. Petanque. Yoga. Scuba-diving club (high season).Windsurfing. Spanish lessons. Small boat moorings. Disco and entertainment (high season). Off site: Fishing from beach. Riding and golf 40 km.

Open: All year.

Directions

Site is on the coast, 10 km. west of Cartagena. Follow signs to Mazarron then take E22 to Canteras. Site is well signed for 4 km. If approaching through Cartagena, exit the town on N332 following signs for Canteras. Site signed on joining the N332.

Charges 2006

Per person	€ 6,00
child (3-9 yrs)	€ 4,40
pitch	€ 13,75
pitch incl. 6A electricity	€ 19,00
dog	€ 4,10

Plus 7% VAT. Special discounts for longer stays and in low season.
Camping Cheques accepted.

ES8748 Camping Los Madriles

Ctra de la Azohia, km. 4.5, E-30868 Isla Plana (Murcia)

Tel: **968 152 151**. Email: **camplosmadriles@terra.es**

An exceptional site with super facilities, Los Madriles is run by a hard working team, with constant improvements being made. Twenty kilometres west of Cartagena, the approach to the site and the surrounding area is fairly unremarkable, but the site is not. A fairly steep access road leads to the 311 flat, good to large size terraced pitches, each having electricity, water and a waste point. Most have shade from large trees with a number benefiting from panoramic views of the sea or behind to the mountains. The site has huge rectangular and lagoon style pools with water sprays and jacuzzis.

Facilities

Four sanitary blocks and one small toilet block provide excellent facilities, including services in one block for disabled campers. Private wash cabins. Washing machines and dryers. Motorcaravan services. Car wash. Restaurant/snack bar. Bar. Supermarket. Swimming pools with jacuzzi. Boules. Play areas. Bicycle hire. ATM. Dogs and other animals are not accepted. Torches useful. Off site: Town close by. Fishing 800 m. (Licence required, purchase in Puerto Mazarron). Boat launching 3 km. Riding 6 km. Golf 20 km. Beach 800 m.

Open: All year.

Directions

From north: From E15/A7 take exit 627 signed MU602, Cartagena and Fuente Alamo. After 5 km. turn right on MU603 signed Mazarron (do not turn into Mazarron). Continue towards Puerto Mazarron and take N332 (Cartagena). On reaching coast continue with N332 (Cartagena and Alicante). Shortly after at roundabout turn right towards Isla Plana and La Azohia. Site is signed and on the left in 5 km. From south: From E15/A7 take exit 617 signed Mazarron (C3315) and on joining MU603 directions as above. GPS: N37:34.761 W01:11.71

Charges 2007

Per person	€ 4,20 - € 5,20
child (1-7 yrs)	€ 4,00 - € 5,00
pitch	€ 12,60 - € 15,60
electricity	€ 3,20

MAP 2

Andalucía

Famous for its sun, its beautiful traditions, its poets, original folklore, age-old history and magnificent heritage left behind by the Moors, Andalucía is one of the most attractive regions in Spain.

THIS COMPRISES EIGHT PROVINCES: ALMERIA, CADIZ, CORDOBA, GRANADA, HUELVA, MALAGA, JAEN AND SEVILLE

THE REGIONAL CAPITAL IS SEVILLE

With the River Guadalquivir running through it, the charming city of Seville is one of the most visited places in the region. The old city, with its great monuments; the Giralda tower, Cathedral and the Alcázar, plus the narrow, winding streets of Santa Cruz, is particularly popular. Also on the Guadalquivir, Cordoba is located northeast of Seville. It too has a picturesque Jewish Quarter along with a rich Moorish heritage. Indeed, the Mezquita is one of the grandest mosques ever built by the Moors in Spain. Located further east on the foothills of the Sierra Nevada mountain range, Granada is home to the impressive Alhambra, a group of distinct buildings including a Royal Palace, splendid gardens, and the fortress of Alcazaba. The Sierra Nevada, Spain's highest range, offers good skiing and trekking. Further south, you'll find the fine beaches and tourist areas of the Costa Tropical and the Costa del Sol, including the developed resort of Malaga. There are more beaches on the west coast plus one of the oldest settlements in Spain, the bustling port of Cádiz.

Places of interest

Almeria: preserved Moorish heritage with greatest purity. Located on a beautiful bay.

Casa-Museo Pablo Ruiz Picasso: art museum including collection of originals by Pablo Picasso.

Jaen: medieval fortress, Renaissance cathedral, 11th century Moorish baths, Santa Catalina castle.

Jerez de la Frontera: birthplace of sherry and Spanish brandy, site of renowned equestrian school.

Mijas: enchanting village, with narrow streets bordered by brilliantly white-washed houses.

Parque Natural de las Sierras de Cazorla y Segura: largest park in Spain with mountains, river gorges, forests and wildlife.

Ronda: beautiful town on the edge of an abrupt rocky precipice.

Cuisine of the region

Andalucía has more tapas bars than anywhere else in Spain. Sea food in abundance, fresh vegetables and fruit: oranges from Cordoba, persimmons, pomegranates, figs, strawberries from Alpujarra; avocados, mangos, guavas, papayas from the coast of Granada and Malaga. Locally produced wine and sherry.

Alboronia: vegetable stew.

Alfajors: almond and nut pastry.

Gazpacho ajoblanco: cold soup with garlic and almond.

Gazpacho salmorejo: much thicker and made with tomatoes only.

Pestiños: honey coated pastries.

Tocinillo de cielo: pudding made with egg yolks and syrup.

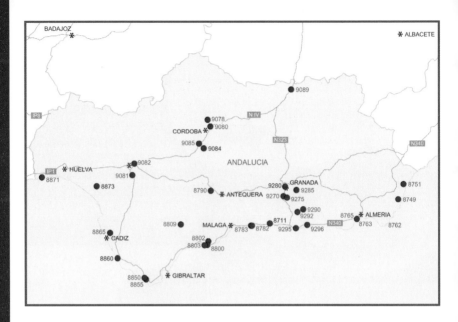

ES8751 Camping Cuevas Mar

Cuevas del Almanzora, E-04618 Palomares (Almeria)

Tel: **950 467 382**. Email: **cuevasmar@arrakis.es**

The popularity of this well established, neat and tidy campsite during the warm winter months has demanded an extension to the site with the number of pitches now 180. The 'new' area already has a mature appearance with the growth of shrubs and trees planted to provide pitch dividers and shade. Some of these places are quite close to the road although a little nearer the beach at 200 metres. All the pitches are flat and are of an acceptable 80-100 sq.m. with a stone chip surface and 6A electricity supply. During the hot summer months overhead shade canopies are erected on several pitches.

Facilities

The well designed sanitary blocks provide sufficient showers and toilets for all. Washing machines and dryer. Water to the taps is to European standard, however a single tap provides high quality water from a nearby mountain spring source (175 m. from some pitches). Daily fresh bread, emergency provisions and gas from reception. Open air unheated swimming pool and jacuzzi (all year). Off site: Many restaurants in the near vicinity. Fishing 200 m. Bicycle hire 3 km. Golf 4 km. Riding 12 km. Beach 600 m.

Open: All year.

Directions

From E15/A7 take exit 537 passing under autovia following signs in general direction of Cuevas Del Almanzora. At T-junction turn right toward Palomares and Vera. In 1 km. on right hand bend turn left towards Palomares. Continue to roundabout, take first exit and site is on left in 2 km. To avoid left turn continue 500 m. to next roundabout and return.

Charges guide

Per person	€ 4,70
child	€ 3,70
pitch incl. car	€ 9,40
electricity	€ 3,15

Generous discounts for longer winter stays.
No credit cards.

ES8749 Camping Sopalmo

Apartado de Correo 761, Sopalmo, E-04638 Mojacar (Almeria)

Tel: **950 478413**

This is a tiny, homely site run by the cheerful Simon and his charming wife Macu (both speaking some English) who are determined that you will enjoy your stay. The site is on three levels (with a slightly steep gravel track to the gates) with space for 32 tents, caravans or medium sized motorcaravans. All the pitches are marked, level and on gravel with electricity (6A). The site is unspoilt and has much rustic charm with the family house providing the focal point. Attractive trees and shrubs around the site include olives, figs, mimosa and cacti.

Facilities

The small sanitary block is very clean and fully equipped. Hot showers assisted by solar power. Facilities for disabled campers. Basic laundry and dishwashing facilities in a pleasant roofed area near reception. Bar. Breakfast available in summer and the baker calls at 10.30 daily. Torch useful. Internet access. Poor to nil mobile phone reception. Off site: Bus to Mojacar from site. Beach 2 km. (naturism permitted). Nearest serious shops 5 km. Riding 6 km. Golf 10 km.

Open: All year.

Directions

Exit from main coast road (N340) at junction 520 (northeast of Almeria). Take the AL152 (formerly A150) to Mojacar Playa and continue south towards Carboneras. Site is 6 km. south of Mojacar Playa, signed off the road

Charges 2007

Per person	€ 4,30
pitch i ncl. electricity	€ 8,00 - € 12,30

Plus 7% VAT. Reductions for low season and longer stays. No credit cards.

ES9089 Camping Despenaperros

Ctra Infanta Elena, E-23213 Santa Elena (Jaén)

Tel: **953 664 192**. Email: **campingdesp@navegalia.com**

This site is on the edge of Santa Elena in a natural park with shade from mature pine trees. This is a good place to stay en-route from Madrid to the Costa del Sol or to just explore the surrounding countryside. The 116 pitches are fully serviced including a satellite TV/internet link. All rubbish must be taken to large bins outside the site gates (a long walk from the other end of the site). The site is run in a very friendly manner where nothing is too much trouble. Reception has a monitor link with tourist information and access to the region's sites of interest.

Facilities

Two traditional, central sanitary blocks have Turkish style WCs and well equipped showers. One washing machine (launderette in town). Shop. Excellent bar (all year) and charming restaurant (12/3-20/10). Swimming pools (15/6-15/9). Tennis. First aid room. Caravan storage. Night security. Off site: Walking, riding and mountain sports nearby. The main road gives good access to Jaen and Valdepenas.

Open: All year.

Directions

Travelling north towards Madrid on A4 (E5) take exit 259 (Santa Elena). Drive through town and site is on right up steep slope (alternative entrance for tall vehicles – ask at reception). Travelling south towards Bailén take exit 257 and as above.

Charges 2006

Per person	€ 3,27 - € 3,50
pitch incl. electricity	€ 8,94 - € 9,35

All plus 7% VAT.

ES8762 Camping Los Escullos

Paraje de los Escullos s/n, E-04118 San Jose-Nijar (Almeria)

Tel: **950 389 811**. Email: **info@losescullossanjose.com**

This gradually sloping, well maintained, medium sized site has a number of bungalows and permanent caravans. Visiting touring units have 100 pitches (60-70 sq.m) divided by hedges and trees and each with a 16A electric supply. Specific taps about the grounds provide drinking water. The months of May and June are very quiet, whilst the site is near full through the winter months with many British visitors enjoying the warm climate. The salinas on the approach to Cabo de Gata are famous for bird life (including flocks of pink flamingo).

Facilities

The main sanitary block is large, clean and fully equipped with hot showers and facilities for disabled campers. Second small block close to reception. Mini supermarket. Bar/restaurant. Takeaway (15/6-15/9). Large outdoor pool. Jacuzzi. Massage. Well equipped gym. Internet access. Multi-sports court. Bicycle hire. Off site: No public transport. Fishing 1 km. Riding 7 km. Golf 25 km. Walking track to the nearest beach (stony) 1 km.

Open: All year.

Directions

From A7/E15 autovia exit at either exit 479 or 471 in direction of San Jose. On approach to San Jose left turn toward Los Escullos. Site is signed.

Charges guide

Per person	€ 3,90 - € 5,25
child (2-14 yrs)	€ 3,30 - € 4,40
pitch	€ 6,50 - € 10,90
electricity	€ 3,00 - € 3,70

ES8763 Camping Cabo de Gata

Ctra Cabo de Gata s/n, Cortijo Ferrón, E-04150 Cabo de Gata (Almeria)

Tel: **950 160 443**. Email: **info@campingcabodegata.com**

Since this medium sized site opened in 1993, it has strived continually to make improvements and today can be regarded as a very pleasant, all year campsite offering facilities to a good standard. Very popular with British visitors through the winter, it is located within the Cabo de Gata-Nijar natural park and set in open farmland, yet is only a 1 km. walk from a fine sandy beach. The 250 gravel pitches are level and of a reasonable size, with 6/16A electricity and limited shade from maturing trees or canopies. There are specific areas for very large units and 7 chalets for rent. A modern, airy reception is adjacent to internet facilities, whilst the nearby irregularly shaped swimming pool in close proximity to the bar/restaurant are both first class. To the west, Salinas de Acosta and the lighthouse at Faro de Gata (fine views). The salinas are reknowned for their bird life and from one of the hides you will see large flocks of pink flamingo and many other species. Almeria has many quality shops and the Alcazaba (955 A.D.), whilst a short drive inland near Tabernas, Mini Hollywood (Clint Eastwood sphagetti western fame) and the white washed village of Nijar noted for its basketry and rugs.

Facilities	Directions
Two, well-maintained, clean toilet blocks provide all the necessary sanitary facilities. including British type WCs, washbasins and free hot showers. Facilities for disabled campers. Restaurant, bar and shop (open all year). Swimming pool. Tennis court. Small playground. Library. Bicycle hire. English spoken. Entertainment programme. Off site: Nearest beach 1 km. Bus 1 km. Fishing 1 km. Golf 10 km. Riding 15 km.	From A7-E15 take exit 460 or 467 and follow signs for Retamar via N344 and for Cabo de Gata. Site is on the right before village of Cabo de Gata. The final stretch of road is in a poor state of repair due to restrictions imposed within the natural park.

Open: All year.

Charges 2006

Per person	€ 5,00
child (3-10 yrs)	€ 4,50
pitch	€ 9,00 - € 10,50
electricity (6-16A)	€ 3,85 - € 4,40
Camping Cheques accepted.	

ES8765 Camping La Garrofa

Ctra Nacional 340 - km 435,4, Direccion a Aguadulce via Litoral, E-04002 Almeria (Almeria)

Tel: **950 235 770**. Email: **info@lagarrofa.com**

One of the earliest sites in Spain (dating back to 1957), La Garoffa nestles in a cove with a virtually private beach accessed only by sea or through the campsite. It is rather dramatic with the tall mountain cliffs behind. Many of the rather small 100 flat and sloping sandy pitches are shaded, with some very close to the beach and sea. An old fortress looks down on the campsite – you can walk to it via a valley at the back of the site and across an old Roman bridge.

Facilities	Directions
Sanitary facilities are mature but clean. Facilities for disabled campers. Restaurant/snack bar. Shop. Play area. Torches useful. Fishing. Off site: Town close by. Walks. Sub aqua diving. Bicycle hire 2 km. Golf 8 km. Excursions (tickets to attractions sold). Bus stop nearby to Almeria or Aguadulce.	Site is west of Almeria. Take 438 exit from the N 340 and follow the camping signs. The site is below the minor road on the beach side.

Open: All year.

Charges 2006

Per person	€ 4,20
child	€ 4,00
motorcaravan	€ 7,10
caravan	€ 4,90
tent	€ 4,70

ES9078 Camping Los Villares

Parque Periurbano, Avenida de l Fuen Santa 8, F-14071 Córdoba (Córdoba)

Tel: **957 330145**

This is a site with a difference. Unusually it is part of one of Spain's natural parks and the environ-mental rules must be strictly followed. For peaceful, simple camping with no frills, there is an area with electricity for 30 units about five minutes walk from a toilet block, restaurant and reception. The 170 tent pitches are delightfully informal. Bountiful pine, olives, gums and other trees provide shade and the setting is absolutely natural. Thoughtfully some natural stone tables and benches are scattered around. The natty little bar and restaurant provide a simple menu and drinks.

Facilities

The single toilet facility is centrally located, provides free hot water and is of good quality. Washing machines. Restaurant/bar. Shop. Five-a-side soccer. Off site: Natural Parque (protected) - walks and wildlife.

Open: All year.

Directions

Site is 7 km. north of Cordoba on the north side of the river which bisects the city. It is simpler to go to the centre to find the small access road to Parque and site. Follow signs for Parador (state run hotel) or Parque Periurbano (small camping sign inside fairly large green edged signs). Pass the municipal camping - then look for a major right turn and follow clear signs out of city. GPS: N37:57.443 W04:48.620

Charges guide

Per person	€ 3,00
pitch incl. electricity	€ 8,50 - € 11,50
No credit cards.	

ES9080 Camping Municipal El Brillante

Avenida del Brillante 50, E-14012 Córdoba (Córdoba)

Tel: **957 403 836**. Email: **elbrillante@campings.net**

For a municipal site this is impressive. Cordoba is one of the hottest places in Europe and the superb pool here is more than welcome. If you really want to stay in the city, then this large site is a good choice. It has 120 neat pitches of gravel and sand, the upper pitches covered by artificial and natural shade but the lower, newer area with little. The site becomes very crowded in high season. The entrance is narrow and may be congested so care must be exercised – there is a lay-by just outside.

Facilities

The toilet blocks have been renovated and an impressive newer block has facilities for babies and disabled people. Motorcaravan services. Gas supplies. Bar and restaurant (1/4-30/9). Shop (all year). Swimming pool (15/6-15/9). Play area. Off site: Bus service to city centre from outside site. Commercial centre 300 m. (left out of site, right at traffic lights).

Open: All year.

Directions

Site is on the north side of the river. From the NIV/E25 road from Madrid, take exit at km. 403 (the middle of three for Cordoba) and follow signs for Mosque/Cathedral into city centre. Pass it (on right) and turn right onto the main avenue. Continue and take right fork following signs for campsite.

Charges 2006

Per unit incl. 2 persons	€ 17,80
extra person (over 10 yrs)	€ 4,50
No credit cards.	

ES9084 Camping La Campiña

Ctra Altea Quintana-Pte Genil, E-14547 Santaella (Córdoba)

Tel: **957 315 303**. Email: **info@campinglacampina.com**

What a charming site – literally amongst the olive trees and set high on a hill to catch cool summer breezes. Everything is immaculately kept and we rarely see sites of this size with such excellent amenities and standards. The 35 pitches are level and most have shade, the surface is gravel and there are views over the olive fields to the surrounding hills. There is a large pool in a garden setting with cool green lawn and the restaurant, with its traditional rustic charm, has a delightful menu of home made food. The 'menu del dia' was delicious and very good value.

Facilities

Two small traditional sanitary blocks have clean services including facilities for disabled campers (key at reception). Washing machines. Restaurant. Snack bar. Shop. Swimming pool. Table tennis. Basketball. Torches useful. Off site: Bus from gate to Cordoba. Town 2 km. Riding 15 km. Golf 40 km.

Open: All year excl. 20 December - 20 January.

Directions

Take exit 441 (La Rambla/Montilla) from the N-IV (E5). Continue past Santaella towards La Victoria. Site is tucked off this road behind high hedging. If approaching from Cordoba, take exit 424 (Aldea-Quintana) towards Santaella for 11.5 km. to the site.

Charges 2006

Per person	€ 4,25
pitch with electricity	€ 5,90

ES9085 Camping Carlos III

Ctra Madrid - Cadiz, km 430, E-14100 La Carlota (Córdoba)

Tel: **957 300 338**. Email: **camping@campingcarlosiii.com**

This rural site lies 25 km. south of Cordoba, just off the main Cordoba – Sevilla road and may be a good alternative to staying in the city. A very large, busy site especially at weekends, it has many supporting facilities including a good swimming pool and a pool, play area and animal corner for children. With the catering services open all year, the site has a more open feel than the bustling municipal site in Cordoba. The touring areas are canopied by trees which offer considerable shade for the 300 separated pitches. On sandy, gently sloping ground, around two-thirds have 5A electricity.

Facilities

Modern toilet blocks provide a mix of British and Turkish WCs, with hot showers in the block near reception. Laundry service. Motorcaravan services. Bar/restaurant, shop (all year). Swimming pools (1/6-15/9). Aviary. Table tennis. Boules. Minigolf, Play area. Hairdressers. Off site: Bus service outside site. Riding 500 m. Village 2 km.

Open: All year.

Directions

From N-IV Cordoba-Seville motorway take La Carlota exit (at km. 429 point northbound or exit 432 southbound). Site is 500 m. and well signed.

Charges 2006

Per person	€ 4,80
child (3-12 yrs)	€ 3,60
pitch incl. electricity	€ 12,40 - € 14,40

Plus 7% VAT. Discounts after 7 days.

ES9270 Camping Suspiro del Moro

Ctra Bailén - Motril, km 144., Puerto Suspiro del Moro, E-18630 Granada (Granada)

Tel: **958 555 411**. Email: **campingsuspirodelmoro@yahoo.es**

Suspiro Del Moro is 11 kilometres south of Granada just off the Motril road and can also be approached on the scenic mountain road from Almunecar. Based high in the Sierra Nevada mountain range, the area offers spectacular views from just outside the site. The site is small and rectangular with a cool and peaceful atmosphere (there may be road noise). Family run, it is well kept with gravel paths leading to the flat, grass pitches which benefit from the shade of the mature trees.

Facilities

Clean and tidy, small toilet blocks are situated around the camping area with British style WCs and free hot showers. Laundry and dishwashing facilities. Small basic shop. Small simple restaurant/bar (high season). Small play area on gravel. Off site: Swimming pool and restaurant adjacent. Sierra Nevada and Granada within reasonable distance to explore.

Open: All year.

Directions

Leave Granada to Motril road (E902/A44) at junction 144 (from south) or 139 (from north) and follow un-named campsite signs. At roundabout go towards Suspiro, then left (signed after turn). Site is about 600 m. on right on A4050 beside large restaurant. GPS: N37:04.092 W03:39.118

Charges 2006

Per person	€ 3,60 - € 4,80
pitch incl. electricity	€ 10,10 - € 12,50

ES9275 Camping Los Avellanos de Sierra Nevada

Ctra de la Fábrica s/n, E-18152 Dilar (Granada)

Tel: **958 596016**. Email: **Avellano@Teleline.es**

This is a fascinating tiny business with a philosophy of peace and tranquillity, a world apart from other sites in southern Spain. This has been achieved by Pilar and her brother Idvier. The site is also called Camping Cortijo, which loosely translates the Spanish as a 'big house in grounds with animals, birds and produce where people work towards people'. There is a fabulous old house and 20 beautifully terraced pitches (mainly for tents) with amazing views enjoying the sound of water tinkling through the ancient irrigation channels on its way to the crops (cars are parked separately).

Facilities

Toilet facilities are modern and clean. Pretty bar/restaurant serves typical local fare and sells basic supplies (very limited in low season). Kitchen for hire. Restaurant/bar. Swimming pool (high season only). Table tennis. Darts. Bicycle hire. Riding. Fishing in river Dilar. Details of walks from reception. Torches essential. Excellent rooms to let. Off site: Tours of Granada (20 minutes away), especially the Alhambra, organised. Site also useful for skiing in Sierra Nevada in season.

Open: All year.

Directions

Heading south from Granada on (E902) A44 exit 139 (Otura). Heading north exit 144. Head towards Otura on GR 5025. Proceed through town and right at roundabout (Dilar/Rio Dilar) on through village. In 2 km. site on right, very steep climb. Not suitable for American RVs.

Charges guide

Per person	€ 3,16
pitch	€ 6,75

Electricity and larger units - price on application. All plus 7% VAT. No credit cards.

ES9280 Camping Sierra Nevada

Avenida Madrid 107, E-18014 Granada (Granada)

Tel: **958 150 062**. Email: **campingmotel@terra.es**

This is a good site either for a night stop or for a stay of a few days while visiting Granada and for a city site it is surprisingly pleasant. Quite large, it has an open feeling and, to encourage you to stay a little longer, an irregular shape pool with a smaller children's pool open in high season. There is some traffic noise around the pool as it is on the road boundary. With 148 pitches for touring units, the site is in two connected parts with more mature trees and facilities to the northern end.

Facilities

Two very modern sanitary blocks, with excellent facilities, including cabins, very good facilities for disabled people and babies. Washing machines. Motorcaravan services. Gas supplies. Shop (15/3-15/10). Swimming pools with lifeguards and charge of € 1.50 (15/6-15/9). Bar/restaurant by pool. Tennis. Table tennis. Petanque. Large playground. Doctor lives on site. Off site: Fishing 10 km. Golf 12 km. Bus station 50 m. from site gate.

Open: 1 March - 31 October.

Directions

Site is just outside the city to north, on road to Jaén and Madrid. From autopista, take Granada North - Almanjayar exit 123 (close to central bus station). Follow road back towards Granada and site is on the right, well signed. From other roads join the motorway to access the correct exit. GPS: N37:12.241 W03:37.022

Charges 2006

Per person	€ 5,25
pitch incl. electricity	€ 15,60
VAT included.	

ES9292 Camping Puerta de La Alpujarra

Ctra Lanjarón- Orgiva (Las Barreras), E-18400 Orgiva (Granada)

Tel: **958 784450**. Email: **puertalapujarra@yahoo.es**

You will receive a warm welcome from the family who run this site and nothing is too much trouble. The site overlooks the Sierra Nevada with lovely panoramic views. There are 77 pitches, terraced and with plenty of shade (43 with electricity connections). This is an area that is becoming more popular with tourists and is an ideal spot from which to explore the mountain villages. Orgiva, steeped in history, is just 1.5 km. from the site and there are many interesting walks from here.

Facilities

Three central sanitary blocks are clean and provide open washbasins and roomy shower cubicles. Toilet for disabled visitors (no shower). Laundry. Shop. Bar, restaurant and takeaway (all season, closed Wed). Outdoor swimming pool (mid June-mid Oct). Play area. Torches useful. Off site: Orgiva 1.5 km. Pampaneria, Bubion and Capileira (steep and winding so care should be taken).

Open: All year.

Directions

Head south from Granada on A44 (E902) and exit 164 signed Lanjaron onto A348. Alpujarra is signed with Orgiva. Site is on right on outskirts of Orgiva (signed).

Charges 2006

Per person	€ 4,20
child	€ 2,90
pitch incl. electricity	€ 11,40

ES9295 Camping Don Cactus

CN 340 km 343, E-18730 Carchuna-Motril (Granada)

Tel: **958 623 109**. Email: **camping@doncactus.com**

Situated between the main N340 and the beach, this family run campsite is pleasantly surprising with clever planning and ongoing improvements. It is a comfortable site of 320 pitches. The flat pitches vary in size with electricity (5/12A), some providing water and satellite TV connections, and are arranged along avenues with eucalyptus trees (which keep the mosquitoes away apparently) for shade. This quieter section of the coast is beautiful with coves and access to larger towns if wished. The friendly reception staff are very helpful with tourist advice and can arrange trips if needed.

Facilities

The large toilet block provides British style WCs, showers and plenty of washbasins. Laundry facilities. Beach showers. Well stocked shop. Bar, restaurant and takeaway (all year). Swimming pool (in high season € 1.50 per day). Tennis. Play area. Summer activities for children. Pets corner. ATM. Internet point. Dogs are not accepted in July/Aug. Barbecues only in special area. Caravan storage. Off site: Bus service 500 m.

Open: All year.

Directions

From Motril - Carucha road (N340/E15) turn towards the sea at km 343. (site signed, but look at roof level for large green tent on the top of the building!). Travel about 600 m. then turn east to site on left.

Charges 2006

Per person	€ 5,00
child (4-10 yrs)	€ 4,75
pitch incl. electricity	€ 14,50
Low season discounts for longer stays.	
Camping Cheques accepted.	

93

ES9285 Camping Las Lomas

Ctra de Sierra Nevada, E-18160 Güejar-Sierra (Granada)

Tel: **958 484 742**. Email: **laslomas@campings.net**

This site is high in the Güéjar Sierra and looks down on the Patano de Canales reservoir. After a wonderful drive to Güéjar-Sierra, you are rewarded with a site boasting excellent facilities. It is set on a slope but the pitches have been levelled and are quite private, with high separating hedges and many mature trees giving good shade (some pitches are fully serviced, with sinks and most have electricity). The large bar/restaurant complex and pools have wonderful views over the lake and a grassed sunbathing area runs down to the fence (safe) looking over the long drop below. A new feature is luxury rooms for rent, including one with a superb spa which is for hire by the hour. Any infirm visitors will need a car to get around as the inclines are extreme.

Facilities

Pretty sanitary blocks (heated in winter) provide clean facilities. First class facilities for disabled campers and well equipped baby room (key at reception). Spa for hire. Motorcaravan services. Good supermarket. Restaurant/bar. Swimming pool. Play area. Table tennis. Minigolf. Basketball. Many other activities including parascending. Barbecue. Internet access. Torches useful. Off site: Buses to village and Granada (15 km). Tours of the Alhambra organised. Useful site for winter skiing.

Open: All year.

Directions

Heading south towards Granada on A44 (E902 Jaén - Motril) take exit 132 onto A395 (Alhamba/Sierra Nevada). After 4 km. marker, exit 5B (Sierra Nevada). At 7 km marker, exit right onto slip road. At junction turn left (Cenes de la Vega/Güéjar-Sierra). In 200 m. turn right on A4026. In 1.6 km. turn left (Güéjar-Sierra). Drive uphill, past dam and site is on right in 2.8 km.

Charges 2006

Per person	€ 4,00 - € 5,00
child (2-10 yrs)	€ 3,00 - € 4,00
pitch	€ 10,00 - € 12,00
VAT included.	

ES9290 Camping El Balcon de Pitres

E-18414 Pitres (Granada)

Tel: **958 766111**. Email: **info@balcondepitres.com**

A simple country site perched high in the mountains of the Alpujarras, on the south side of the Sierra Nevada, El Balcon de Pitres has its own rustic charm. Many thousands of trees planted around the site provide shade. There are stunning views from some of the 175 level grassy pitches (large units may find pitch access difficult). The garden is kept green by spring waters, which you can hear and sometimes see, tinkling away in places. The Lopez family, have built this site from barren mountain top to cool oasis in the mountains in just fifteen years. It is a wonderful relaxing place to cool down, away from the heat of the coast. On Saturday evenings in summer there is a wide variety of live entertainment around an exotic Morrocan tent, which serves as a bar and which is far enough away from the pitches not to disturb sleeping campers. Local visitors often add to the 'hot August night' ambience. The pool is very popular in summer with locals as well as campers. The area is famous for its mineral water and there are many local artisans working in the mountains. There are wonderful walks and lots of attractions including mountaineering sports such as canyoning, parascending, and trekking in the area.

Facilities

Two toilet blocks provide adequate facilities but the steeply sloping site is unsuitable for disabled campers and thus there are no facilities for them. Snack bar. Bar. Shop (closed Tuesdays). Swimming pools (extra charge, € 2.40 adult € 1.50 child). Bicycle hire. Torches useful. Off site: Fishing. Canyoning. Trekking. Parascending. Quad bikes. Sports centre for football.

Open: All year.

Directions

Site is about 30 km. northeast of Motril. Heading south on A44 (E902) exit 164 (Lanjaron) onto E348 towards Orgiva. Fork left at sign (A4132) Pampaneira 8 km. Continue to Pitres (7 km). Site signed. (Steep and winding roads) GPS: N36:55.911 W03:19.961

Charges 2006

Per person	€ 5,00
child	€ 4,50
pitch incl. car	€ 7,00 - € 10,50
electricity (2A)	€ 3,00

ES9296 Camping Castillo de Banos

Ctra 340 km 360, La Mamola, E-18750 Granada (Granada)

Tel: **958 82 95 28**. Email: **info@campingcastillo.com**

This is a smaller sister site to Don Cactus (ES9295). It is located right on the beach (the side gate leads straight onto a small pebble beach). Many pitches run along the sea with a bamboo fence which provides some shade and from many pitches you can see and hear the sea. It is a peaceful and wonderful setting. There are 240 pitches of various sizes (mostly medium) shaded by a variety of trees. About 20% in one area are taken by static units. This is a good choice for those looking for a quieter site to just relax.

Facilities

One toilet block provides basic stainless steel double sink facilities with only cold water for dishwashing and laundry. British WCs and good showers. Small shop. Restaurant/bar (15/6-1/9).Internet in reception. Special barbecue area with sink. Off site: Bus stop 200 m. The main road gives access to main tourist areas. Alpujarras, Almeria, Granada, Motril are all over an hour's drive.

Open: All year.

Directions

From N340 Motril - Adra road turn south at km 360 (towards sea). At roundabout take second turn (small camping sign) and site is about 50 m. on the right, Head for building with large green tent on top.

Charges 2006

Per person	€ 4,90
child (4-10 yrs)	€ 4,70
pitch incl. electricity	€ 12,00
Camping Cheques accepted.	

ES8711 Nerja Camping

Ctra N340, km 297, E-29787 Maro (Málaga)

Tel: **952 529 714**. Email: **nerjacampimg5@hotmail.com**

This site is set on the lower slopes of the Sierra Almijara, some five kilometres from Nerja and two kilometres from the excellent beaches. Nerja Camping is a small, slightly jaded site of 55 pitches (30 with 15A electricity and no statics) with impressive views of the surrounding mountains and the Mediterranean. The pitches are on the small side and set on slopes with some terracing along with some artificial shade. The roads, although sloping, should present few problems for siting units. A new motorway will be close, bur extensive sound barriers are being intalled.

Facilities

The single sanitary block has adequate facilities and a solar energy hot water system. There are some free hot showers, washbasins (1 only with hot water) and laundry facilities. Small swimming pool (March - Sept). Small restaurant/bar (March - Sept). Essentials from the bar. Off site: Fishing 3 km. Bicycle hire or riding 5 km. Sub-aqua diving, parascending and watersports. Day trips to Granada or Gibraltar.

Open: All year excl. October.

Directions

Site signed from main N340 coast road about 5 km. east of Nerja after 296 km. marker. If coming from Nerja, go 500 m. past site entrance (opposite radio masts) to cross very busy main road.
GPS: N36:45.630 W03:50.085

Charges 2006

Per person	€ 4,75
child (2-10 yrs)	€ 3,75
pitch incl. car	€ 9,50 - € 12,75

ES8782 Camping Caravaning Laguna Playa

Prolongacion Paseo Maritimo, E-29740 Torre del Mar (Málaga)

Tel: **952 540 631**. Email: **info@lagunaplaya.com**

Laguna Playa is a pleasant and peaceful site run by a father and son team (the son speaks excellent English) and they give a personal service, alongside one of the Costa del Sol beaches. Trips are organised to the famous Alhambra Mosque in Granada on a weekly basis and the site is well placed for visits to Malaga and Nerja. The pitches are flat, of average size and with good artificial shade supplementing that provided by the many established trees on site. All pitches have electricity (5/10A). The busy restaurant with a terrace offers good value for money and many locals use it.

Facilities

Two well equipped, modern, sanitary blocks, both recently refurbished, include baby baths and good facilities for disabled campers. Laundry facilities. Supermarket. Bar and busy restaurant also used by locals (closed in low season). Swimming pools (high season). Play area. Children's entertainment. Off site: Beach promenade 200 m. Bicycle hire 500 m. Regular bus service 700 m. outside site. Golf 1.5 km. Riding 2 km.

Open: All year.

Directions

Site is on the sea front west of the town of Torre del Mar, off the main N340 Malaga - Nerja road. Follow signs and take care not to enter the first site you meet on the beach as this is inferior and will be demolished in new development in the near future.

Charges 2007

Per person	€ 4,60
child (2-10 yrs)	€ 3,70
pitch	€ 9,80
electricity	€ 3,50

ES8783 Camping Naturista Almanat

Carril de la Torre Alta s/n, E-29749 Almayate (Málaga)

Tel: 952 556 462. Email: almanat@arrakis.es

With direct access to a one kilometre grey sand and shingle naturist beach, this established all year naturist site, set amongst agricultural land with mountain backdrop, is proving a firm favourite with many British seeking winter sun. The facilities on site are to a very high standard. The entire 2-hectare site is flat with a fine shingle surface. A large number of trees planted when the site opened in 1998 have now matured, providing much needed shade in the summer. The 160 touring pitches vary in size and shape with the majority demanding physical manoeuvring of a touring caravan.

Facilities

The large, unisex toilet is fully equipped, regularly cleaned and all under cover. Good facilities for disabled campers near reception. Small shop. Bar/restaurant with terrace overlooking the sea. Large unheated swimming pool. Play area. Sauna and gym. Cinema (56 seats) showing VHS tapes or DVD. Weather permitting, one is expected to be nude which is obligatory in the pool area and bar during the day. Off site: Torre del Mar is 2 km. Regular bus service 1 km. Fishing, riding nearby.

Open: All year.

Directions

Exit the N340 autovia at junction 265 signed Costa 340a. Take the Costa direction and on reaching the coast turn left onto 340a toward Torre del Mar. Site well signed in 4 km. on right.
GPS: N36:43.607 W04:06.796

Charges 2006

Per person	€ 4,40
child (2-10 yrs)	€ 3,50
pitch incl. electricity (16A)	€ 6,80 - € 11,60

All plus 7% VAT. No credit cards.

ES8790 Camping La Laguna

Ctra La Rábita s/n, E-29620 Fuente de Piedra (Málaga)

Tel: 952 73 52 94. Email: info@camping-rural.com

In a remote area of Andalucia, this tiny campsite of just 30 pitches looks over the salty lakes and marshes of the Laguna de Fuente. The average size pitches are on a sloping, terraced hillside, with views of the lake. With a gravel surface and little shade, many pitches slope so chocks would be useful. There is a separate grassy area for tents near the pool and bungalows (cars are not permitted here). Unusually for a site of this size there is a pool and an excellent bar, snack bar and huge restaurant which serves beautiful Spanish food. Try the excellent, inexpensive 'menu del dia'.

Facilities

One neat block has clean facilities including for disabled campers. Washing machines. Restaurant. Bar with TV. Snack bar. Shop. Swimming pool. Pool bar. Electronic games. Bicycle hire. Torches useful. Off site: Lake with flamingos. Bicycle hire 1 km. Fishing 5 km. Riding 10 km. Golf 40 km. Excursions.

Open: All year.

Directions

Site is 20 km. northwest of Antequera. From Antequera take A92 and exit at 132 km. point and follow road to the town. Site is well signed, but the signs are small and there are two sites. This one is on the northeast corner of the lake.

Charges guide

Per person	€ 4,53 - € 4,96
child (0-12 yrs)	€ 2,94 - € 3,21
pitch incl. electricity	€ 6,42 - € 8,83

ES8800 Camping Marbella Playa

Ctra N-340, km. 192,800, E-29600 Marbella (Málaga)

Tel: 952 833 998. Email: recepcion@campingmarbella.com

This large site is 12 kilometres east of the internationally famous resort of Marbella with public transport available to the town centre and local attractions. A sandy beach is about 150 metres away with direct access. There are 430 individual pitches of up to 70 sq.m. with natural shade (additional artificial shade is provided to some), and electricity (10/20A) available throughout. The site is busy throughout the high season but the high staff/customer ratio and the friendly staff approach ensures a comfortable stay. A large pool complex with a restaurant/bar provides a very attractive feature.

Facilities

Four sanitary blocks of mixed ages, are fully equipped and well maintained. Three modern units for disabled visitors. Large supermarket with butcher and fresh vegetable counter. Bar, restaurant and café (all open all year). Supervised swimming pool (free - April/Sept). Playground (on gritty sand). Torches necessary in beach areas. Off site: Bus service 150 m. Fishing 100 m. Golf and bicycle hire 5 km. Riding 10 km. Beach 200 m.

Open: All year.

Directions

Site is 12 km. east of Marbella with access close to the 193 km. point on the main N340 road.
GPS: N36:29.476 W04:45.795

Charges guide

Per person	€ 2,80 - € 4,65
child (1-10 yrs)	€ 3,90
pitch incl. electricity	€ 15,75 - € 25,55

All plus 7% VAT. Reductions (up to 50%) for long stays and senior citizens outside 16/6-31/8.

ES8803 Camping La Buganvilla

Ctra N340, km 188.8, E-29600 Marbella (Málaga)

Tel: **952 831 973**. Email: **info@campingbuganvilla.com**

This site has a grand total of 1,000 pitches, of which 300 are for touring units. They are mostly on terraces so there are some views across to the mountains and hinterland of this coastal area. La Buganvilla is a large, uncomplicated site with mature trees providing shade to some pitches. The terrain is a little rugged in places and the buildings are older in style but all were clean when we visited. A pool near the bar and restaurant is ideal for cooling off after a day's sightseeing. The restaurant offers barbecue style meals.

Facilities

Three painted sanitary blocks are clean and adequate with laundry facilities. Large bar/restaurant with terrace overlooking the pool area. Extremely well stocked mini supermarket. Play area. Basketball and tennis in high season. Dogs are not accepted in July/Aug. Off site: Bus service close to site entrance. Fishing and watersports 400 m. Bicycle and scooter hire 1 km. Golf 5 km. Resort type entertainment close.

Open: All year.

Directions

Site is between Marbella and Fuengirola off the N340. Access at 188.8 km. can only be achieved if travelling in a westerly direction, (Fuengirola towards Marbella). From the opposite direction, continue to 'cambio de sentido' signed Elviria.

Charges 2006

Per person	€ 5,00 - € 6,00
child (under 10 yrs)	€ 2,50 - € 4,00
pitch incl. car	€ 10,00 - € 13,00

All plus 7% VAT. Discounts in low season.
Camping Cheques accepted.

ES8802 Camping Cabopino

Ctra N340, km 194.7, E-29600 Marbella (Málaga)

Tel: **952 834 373**. Email: **info@campingcabopino.com**

This large mature site is alongside the main N340 Costa del Sol coast road, 12 km. east of Marbella and 15 km. from Fuengirola. The Costa del Sol is also known as the Costa del Golf and fittingly there is a major golf course alongside the site. The site is set amongst tall pine trees which provide shade for the sandy pitches (there are some huge areas for large units). The 400 touring pitches, a mix of level and sloping, all have electricity. There is an area on the western side for groups of youngsters.

Facilities

Four mature but very clean sanitary blocks provide hot water throughout (may be under pressure at peak times). Washing machines. Bar/restaurant and takeaway. Shop. Swimming pools (one open all year). Play area. Some evening entertainment. Excursions can be booked. ATM. Torches necessary in the more remote parts of the site. Off site: Beach 600 m. Fishing, bicycle hire and riding within 1 km. Golf 7 km.

Open: All year.

Directions

Site is 12 km. from Marbella. Approaching Marbella from the east, leave the N340 at the 194 km. marker (signed Cabopino). Site is off the roundabout at the top of the slip road.

Charges 2006

Per unit incl. 2 persons and electricity	€ 17,10 - € 28,70
extra person	€ 3,45 - € 5,75

Plus 7% VAT.
Camping Cheques accepted.

ES8809 Camping El Sur

Ctra Ronda - Algeciras, km 1,5, Apdo de Correos 127, E-29400 Ronda (Málaga)

Tel: **952 875 939**. Email: **info@campingelsur.com**

The delightfully decorated entrance and generous manoeuvring area at this site are a promise of something different which is fulfilled in all respects. The very friendly family who run the site have worked hard for many years combining innovative thinking with excellent service. The 114 terraced pitches have electricity (5A) and water, and are partially shaded by olive and almond trees. Most have relaxing views of the surrounding mountains but at an elevation of 850 m. the upper pitches (the very top 45 pitches are for tents only) allow a clear view of the fascinating town of Ronda.

Facilities

The immaculate sanitary block is fully equipped (toilet paper purchased from reception). Laundry facilities in little separate blocks. Gas supplies. Bar and large, high quality restaurant (closed 7-15/1). Kidney shaped pool (1/6-30/9). Playground and adventure play area. Minigolf. Off road bicycle hire. Internet terminal. Off site: Riding 1.5 km. Bicycle hire 2.5 km. The coast is an hour's drive (50 km).

Open: All year.

Directions

Site is on the A369 Ronda - Algerciras road at the 3 km. point south of Ronda (which now has a ring road). GPS: N36:43.276 W05:10.319

Charges 2007

Per person	€ 4,50
pitch incl. electricity	€ 8,00 - € 18,50

Plus 7% VAT. Less 40% in low season.
No credit cards.

Check real time availability and at-the-gate prices...

www.**alanrogers**.com

ES8850 Camping Paloma

Ctra Cadiz-Malaga, km. 70, E-11380 Tarifa (Cádiz)

Tel: **956 684 203**

This spacious, neat and tidy, family orientated site is popular with Spanish families and young people of all nations in high season. Paloma is well established and the many tall palms around the site remind one of how close Africa and the romance of Tangier is. The site has 353 pitches on mostly flat ground, although the westerly pitches are sloping. They are of average size with some places for extra large units, some are separated by hedges and most are shaded by mature trees; around 200 pitches have electrical connections (10A).

Facilities

Two sanitary blocks, one of a good size, although a long walk from the southern end of the site. The other block is smaller and open plan. British style WCs with some Turkish, washbasins have cold water. Facilities for disabled visitors in the smaller block. Washing machine. Gas supplies. Shop. Busy bar and good restaurant. Swimming pool with adjacent bar (high season only). Play area. Excursions (June-Sept). Off site: Beach 700 m. Bicycle hire 5 km. Riding 10 km. Tarifa 12 km. Golf 25 km.

Open: All year.

Directions

Site is signed off N340 Cadiz road at Punta Paloma, about 10 km. northwest of Tarifa, just west of km. 74 marker. Watch carefully for the site sign - no advance notice. Be sure to use the slip road to turn left if coming from Tarifa. Follow signs down a sandy road for 300 m.

Charges 2006

Per person	€ 3,00 - € 5,00
child	€ 2,40 - € 4,00
pitch	€ 4,80
tent or caravan and car	€ 2,10 - € 3,50
motorcaravan	€ 3,00 - € 5,10

ES8855 Camping Tarifa

Ctra N340, km 78.87, E-11380 Tarifa (Cádiz)

Tel: **956 684 778**. Email: camping-tarifa@camping-tarifa.com

The long, golden sandy beach adjacent to this site is a good feature being ideal for windsurfing and also clean and safe for swimming. The site has a pleasant, open feel and is reasonably sheltered from road noise. It has been thoughtfully landscaped and planted out with an amazing variety of shrubs and flowers and is remarkably clean. The 265 level pitches are of varying sizes and are surrounded by pine trees which provide ample shade. All have electricity (5/10A) and there are adequate water points. There is a smart, modern reception area with an attractive water feature close by.

Facilities

Two modern, fully equipped sanitary blocks include facilities for campers with disabilities and baby room. All spotless when seen. Motorcaravan services. Gas supplies. Supermarket and excellent bar/restaurant - fast food only, all open all year with patio. Swimming pool complex with bar. Large play area. Dogs are not allowed.
Off site: Fishing 100 m. Riding 300 m. Bicycle hire 5 km. Excursions.

Open: All year.

Directions

Site is on main N340 Cadiz road at 78.87 km. marker, 7.5 km. northwest of Tarifa. Large modern signs well ahead of the site with a deceleration lane if approaching from the Tarifa direction.

Charges 2006

Per person	€ 4,81
child (under 10 yrs)	€ 4,50
pitch with electricity	€ 9,50
high season minimum price	€ 17,00
Camping Cheques accepted.	

ES8860 Camping Fuente del Gallo

Apto. 48, E-11149 Conil de la Frontera (Cádiz)

Tel: **956 440 137**. Email: **camping@campingfuentedelgallo.com**

Fuente del Gallo extends a warm welcome to British visitors, particularly as one half of the ownership is Irish. The attractive pool, restaurant and bar complex with its large, shaded terace, are very welcoming in the height of summer. The site is well maintained with 221 pitches allocated to touring units. Each pitch has 10A electricity and a number of trees create shade to some pitches. Although the actual pitch areas are generally a good size, the majority are long and narrow. This could, in some cases, prevent the erection of an awning and your neighbour may feel close. In low season it is generally accepted to make additional use of an adjoining pitch. Good beaches are relatively near at 300 m. with access gained by steps through new houses with palm-lined roads.

Facilities

Two modernised and very clean sanitary blocks include excellent services for babies and disabled visitors and hot water at all facilities. Laundry room with two washing machines. Motorcaravan services. Gas supplies. Well-stocked shop. Attractive bar and restaurant (breakfast served). TV and games rooms. Swimming pool (all season, lifeguard in high season when there is a small charge) with paddling pool. Play area. Safety deposit boxes. Excursions. Torches useful. Off site: Watersports on beach. Fishing 300 m. Riding 1 km. Bicycle and motor scooter hire 2 km. Golf 5 km.

Open: Easter - 3 September.

Directions

From Cadiz-Algeciras road (N340) at km. 23.00, follow signs to Conil de la Frontera town centre, then shortly right to Fuente del Gallo and 'playas', following signs. GPS: N36:17.776 W06:06.611

Charges 2006

Per person	€ 5,40
child (3-10 yrs)	€ 4,40
pitch	€ 8,80 - € 9,50
electricity	€ 4,50

All plus 7% VAT. Less 11-30% for longer stays (except Jul/Aug).

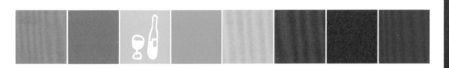

ES8865 Camping Playa Las Dunas de San Anton

P Maritimo de la Puntilla s/n, E-11500 El Puerto de Santa Maria (Cádiz)

Tel: **956 872 210**. Email: **info@lasdunascamping.com**

This site lies within the Parque Natural Bahia de Les Dunes and is adjacent to the long and gently sloping golden sands of Puntilla beach. This is a pleasant and peaceful site (though very busy in August) with some 400 separate marked pitches, 140 for tourers, with much natural shade and ample electrical connections (5/10A). Motorcaravans park in an area called the Oasis which is very pretty. Tent and caravan pitches, under mature trees, are terraced and separated by low walls. A spacious site with a tranquil setting, it is popular with people who wish to 'winter over' in peace.

Facilities

Immaculate modern sanitary facilities with separate facilities for disabled campers and a baby room. Laundry facilities are excellent. Gas supplies. Bar/restaurant (all year). Supermarket (high season). Very large swimming pool (supervised) and toddlers pool (high season). Play areas. Night security all year. Off site: Fishing 500 m. Riding and golf 2 km. Municipal sports centre close by offers all manner of sporting activities and the beach provides additional free sports facilities such as volleyball. Local buses for town and cities visits and a ferry to Cadiz.

Open: All year.

Directions

Site is 5 km. north of Cadiz off N1V route. Take road to Puerto Santa Maria, site is very well signed throughout the town (small yellow signs high on posts).

Charges 2006

Per person	€ 3,79 - € 4,21
child	€ 3,24 - € 3,60
pitch	€ 3,79 - € 6,05
electricity (5A)	€ 4,80

ES9081 Camping Villsom

Ctra Sevilla - Cadiz, km 554.8, E-41700 Sevilla (Sevilla)

Tel: **954 720 828**

This city site was one of the first to open in Spain and it is still owned by the same pleasant family. The administrative building consists of a peaceful and attractive bar with patio and satellite TV (where breakfast is served) and there is a pleasant, small reception area. It is a good site for visiting Seville with a frequent bus service to the centre. Camping Villsom has around 180 pitches which are level and shaded. A huge variety of trees and palms are to be seen around the site and in summer the bright colours of the flowers are very pleasing.

Facilities

Sanitary facilities require modernisation in some areas. Some washbasins have cold water only. Laundry facilities. Small shop selling basic provisions. Bar with satellite TV (open July/Aug). Swimming pool (June-Sept). Putting. Table tennis. Drinks machine. Off site: Bus stop close. Most town facilities including restaurant, supermarket, cinema and theatre.

Open: All year.

Directions

On main Seville - Cadiz NIV road travelling from Seville take exit at km. 553 signed Dos Hermanos - Isla Menor. Go under road bridge and turn immediately right (Isla Mentor) to site 80 m. on right. From Cadiz take same signed exit and at roundabout take fourth exit to go over main road and then down a slip road to go under bridge, then as above.
GPS: N37:16.641 W05:56.210

Charges guide

Per person	€ 3,60
child	€ 3,20
pitch incl. car	€ 5,00 - € 7,65
electricity	€ 2,40
All plus 7% VAT.	

ES9082 Camping Sevilla

Ctra N-IV, km. 534, E-41007 Sevilla (Sevilla)

Tel: **954 514 379**

This site is ideal for visiting the fascinating city of Seville. It is just south of the perimeter of Seville airfield, by day with your ear defenders, you can practise your plane-spotting, but thankfully the usual mandatory respite exists at night, although you are fairly close to the main Seville - Madrid road. With a pretty entrance, this is a flat, sandy site with 85 pitches of varying size for motorcaravans and caravans, plus 450 for tents. Electricity (6/10A) is available. Trees provide some pitches with shade, others have artificial shade. There is the constant change-over bustle of all nationalities coming to visit Seville.

Facilities

Buildings housing the sanitary and supporting facilities are round in shape and a happy yellow colour. Half of the showers are cold water only, the remainder providing free very hot water, but only cold for all other washing functions. Blocks are kept very clean. Two excellent motorcaravan service points. Supermarket, bar and restaurant (high season). Small bar/snack area (low season). Swimming pools (June - Sept; charged). Internet access. Drinks machines. Off site: Bus service 600 m. 'Magic Island' theme park 3 km.

Open: All year.

Directions

From any route follow signs to the airport (very easy) and you will pick up signs for the campsite from any direction. Be sure to follow signs carefully. If you miss the turn the quickest way to cross the motorway is to go through the airport.
GPS: N37:24.994 W05:55.048

Charges guide

Per person	€ 3,25
child (3-11 yrs)	€ 2,75
pitch	€ 4,50 - € 6,50
electricity	€ 2,25
Plus 7% VAT. No credit cards.	

Check real time availability and at-the-gate prices...
www.**alanrogers**.com

ES8871 Camping Giralda

Ctra Provincial 4117, E-21410 Isla Cristina (Huelva)

Tel: **959 343 318**. Email: **campinggiralda@infonegocio.com**

The fountains at the entrance and the circular 'thatched' reception building set the tone for this very large site. The 587 pitches are quite spacious on sand, most benefiting from the attractive mature trees which abound on the site. Most pitches have electricity (142 are for tents). Access to the excellent beach is gained by a short stroll, crossing the minor road alongside the site and passing through attractive pine trees. This is a quiet site out of the main tourist areas, with good leisure and adventure facilities. The many additional activities are listed below.

Facilities

Four large, modern, semi-circular 'thatched' sanitary blocks are clean and fully equipped. Laundry. Shop and bar (all year). Restaurant and snacks (June - Sept). Swimming pools. Archery. Petanque. Mountain biking. Beach games. Table tennis. Watersports school. Play area. Organised activity area for groups low season. Excursions booked. Off site: Beach and fishing 200 m. Bicycle hire 1.5 km. Golf 4 km. Riding 7 km.

Open: All year.

Directions

Leave E1/A49 at exit 113 signed Lepe on N444. Turn right on N431, use Lepe bypass, then left to Le Antilla and then on to Isla Cristina. Site is on right (signed) just as you reach Isla Christina (this route avoids Pozo del Camino and many speed bumps). GPS: N37:11.999 W07:18.052

Charges 2007

Per person	€ 5,80
child (2-10 yrs)	€ 4,20
caravan and car	€ 10,95
motorcaravan	€ 9,00
electricity	€ 5,25

Plus 7% VAT. Winter discounts.

ES8873 Camping La Aldea

El Rocio, E-21750 Almonte (Huelva)

Tel: **95944 2677**. Email: **info@campinglaaldea.com**

This impressive site lies just on the edge of the Parque Nacional de Donana, southwest of Sevilla on the outskirts of El Rocio. The town hosts a fiesta at the end of May with over one million people attending the local shrine. They travel for days in processions with cow drawn or motorized vehicles to attend. If you want to stay this weekend book well in advance! The well planned, modern site is well set out and the 246 pitches have natural shade from trees or artificial shade and 10A electricity. There are 52 serviced pitches with water and sewerage. There are also pitches for tents and bungalows for rent. The facilities are new, large and very clean. A beautiful waiter service restaurant (where the Spanish eat) provides lovely local food. The staff are welcoming and helpful with plenty of tourist information to hand. Expeditions on horseback or by 4x4 vehicle can be arranged in the national park.

Facilities

Two sanitary blocks provide excellent facilities including provision for disabled visitors. Motorcaravan service point. Swimming pool (May – Oct). Restaurant and bar in separate new complex. Shop. Internet connection. Playground. Off site: Bus stop 5 minutes walk. Huelva and Sevilla are about an hour's drive. Beach 15 km.

Open: All year excl. 25 December - 5 January.

Directions

From main Huelva - Sevilla road E1/A49 take exit 48 and drive south through Almonte to outskirts of El Rocio. Site is on left just past 25 km. marker. Go down to the roundabout and back up to be on the right side of the road to turn in.

Charges 2006

Per person	€ 4,00 - € 5,00
child	€ 3,00 - € 4,00
pitch incl. car	€ 7,00 - € 11,00
electricity	€ 4,00

Less 10-15% for low season stays over 3 days.

MAP 3

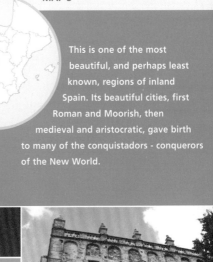

This is one of the most beautiful, and perhaps least known, regions of inland Spain. Its beautiful cities, first Roman and Moorish, then medieval and aristocratic, gave birth to many of the conquistadors - conquerors of the New World.

EXTREMADURA HAS TWO PROVINCES: BADAJOZ AND CÁCERES

Extremadura is a large and sparsely populated region in the west of Spain, bordering central Portugal and consisting of two provinces, both of which bear the name of their main town. Cáceres, to the north, has a fascinating old quarter, ringed by old Moorish walls and superb watchtowers. Nearby Plasencia is home to a splendid Gothic cathedral, old medieval walls and beautiful Baroque and Renaissance palaces. And the attractive town of Trujillo, birthplace of Pizzaro, the conqueror of Peru, has palaces, churches and a bustling town square. To the south is Badajoz, the second province and the largest in Spain. With its fortified main town and Alcazaba (citadel), the city of Badajoz is located on the Vía de la Plata (Silver Route), an old pilgrimage route to Santiago de Compostela used during the Middle Ages. Located on this route, Mérida is one of the best preserved archaeological sites in Spain. Indeed, the city boasts more Roman remains than any other city, including a Roman theatre and amphitheatre, a Roman bridge spanning over 800 metres long, with 60 arches, Roman villas and a Museum of Roman Art.

Places of interest

Alcántara: six-arched Roman bridge, castle, mansions.

Corio: quiet old town enclosed by 4th century Roman walls, cathedral.

Cuacos de Yuste: town with 15th century Jeronimos Monastery.

Guadalupe: old pilgrimage centre, church and monastery.

Jerez de los Caballeros: birthplace of various conquistadores.

Olivenza: town with strong Portuguese influence, castle, ethnographic museum, 17th century church.

Pedroso de Acim: Convento del Palancar – said to be the smallest monastery in the world.

Cuisine of the region

Local cuisine includes the Iberian cured ham and a variety of cheeses; *Torta del Casar, La Serena, Ibores, Gata* and *Cabra del Tietar*. Game abounds in this region (partridge, pigeon, turtledove, rabbit, hare, wild boar, deer) served with wild mushrooms, truffles or wild asparagus. Honey, thyme, heather, rosemary, lavender, lime and eucalyptus are used to prepare a great variety of desserts.

Alfeñiques: caramel dessert.

Nuégados: egg yolk and orange buns.

Perrunillas: small round cakes.

Rosquillas: ring-shaped biscuits.

Técula-mécula: cinnamon, almond and tea.

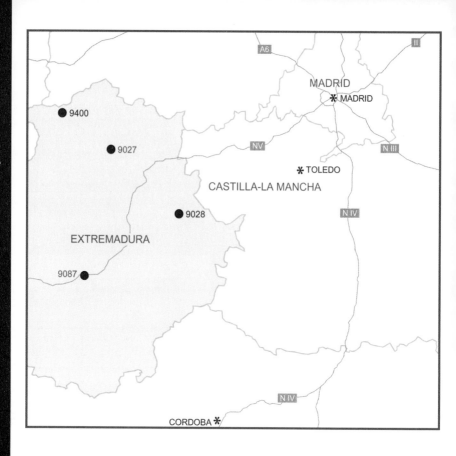

ES9400 Camping Sierra de Gata

Ctra Ex-109 a Gata, km. 4,100, E-10860 Gata (Cáceres)

Tel: **927 672168**. Email: sierradegata@campingsonline.com

For a taste of the real, rural Spain this very Spanish site (no English was spoken when we visited) is situated just before the tiny village of Sierra de Gata, south of Ciudad Rodrigo and northwest of Plasencia. Situated in beautiful countryside with a small stream alongside the site, the pitches are on grass with plenty of shade from trees. This site is undergoing refurbishment with the addition of 12 beautiful new bungalows to sleep 4-6 people. A special area with huts for groups of children to stay is positioned in one corner of the site.

Facilities

Two toilet blocks with British style toilets also include child size toilets, a laundry room and dishwashing facilities. Medium sized shop for necessities in summer. Smart restaurant/bar complex provides good food. Two swimming pools. Tennis. Play area. Fishing. Riding. Bicycle hire. Off site: Restaurant near campsite entrance.

Open: 18 March - 3 November.

Directions

Approach ONLY from the southwest from the 109 Ciudad Rodrico - Coria road. Where the 205 meets the 109 take turn 20-30 m. north signed Gata 10. Travel along this road until km. 4. Turn left (near restaurant and small bridge) and site is ahead through gate. GPS: N40:12.728 W06:38.526

Charges guide

Per person	€ 2,82
child (3-12 yrs)	€ 2,52
pitch	€ 7,81
electricity	€ 2,28

ES9027 Camping Parque Natural de Monfrague

Ctra Plasencia-Trujillo km 10, E-10680 Malpartida de Plasencia (Cáceres)

Tel: **927 459 233**

Situated on the edge of the Monfrague National Park, this well managed site owned by the Barrado family, has fine views to the Sierra de Mirabel and delightful surrounding countryside. Many of the 130 good-sized pitches are grassed on slightly sloping terraced ground. Scattered trees offer a degree of shade, there are numerous water points and electricity is rated at 10A. It would prove difficult to find a more suitable location for those that savour peace, quiet, study of yesteryear, flora and fauna. On rare occasions a goods train travels along the nearby railway line. Used by locals, the air-conditioned restaurant provides good quality food at very acceptable prices. An evening meal on the veranda as the sun sets will provide fond memories of a rewarding holiday. Created as a National Park in 1979, Monfrague is now recognised as one of the best locations in Europe for anyone with any degree of interest in birdwatching. During our visit we saw Spanish Imperial Eagle, Eagle Owl, Griffon, Black and Egyptian Vultures, Black and Red Kites, Azure-winged Magpies, Purple Gallinule, Purple Heron, Black-eared Wheatear, Bee-eater, Blue Rock Thrush and the more rare Black Stork to name but a few. Nearby Plasencia has a medieval aqueduct, fine cathedral (14th C.) and the town's original twin ring of walls containing 68 towers. To the south, the classic historical towns of Merida, Caceres and Trujillo.

Facilities

Large modern toilet blocks, fully equipped, are very clean. Facilities for disabled campers and baby baths. Laundry. Motorcaravan service point. Supermarket/shop. Restaurant, bar and coffee shop. TV room with recreational facilities. Swimming and paddling pools (June - Sept). Play area. Tennis. Bicycle hire. Riding. Animation for children in season. Barbecue areas. Guided safaris into the Park for birdwatching at an acceptable price. Off site: Large supermarket at Plasencia.

Open: All year.

Directions

On the N630, from the north take EX-208 (previously C524) Plasencia - Trujillo; site on left in 6 km. From the south turn right just south of Plasencia on the EX-108 (previously C511) in direction of Malpartida de Plasencia. Right at main junction onto EX-208 to site.

Charges 2006

Per person	€ 3,70
child (3-12 yrs)	€ 3,20
tent or caravan	€ 3,70
car	€ 3,20
motorcaravan	€ 6,20
VAT included.	
Camping Cheques accepted.	

ES9087 Camping Mérida

Ctra NV Madrid-Port, km. 336.6, E-06800 Mérida (Badajoz)

Tel: **924 303 453**. Email: **proexcam@jet.es**

Camping Mérida is situated alongside the main N-V road to Madrid, the restaurant, café and pool complex separating the camping site area from the road where there is considerable noise. The site has 80 good sized pitches, most with some shade and on sloping ground, with ample electricity connections (long leads may be needed) and hedges with imaginative topiary. No English is spoken, but try out your Spanish. Reception is open until midnight. Camping Mérida is ideally located to serve both as a base to tour the local area or as an overnight stop en route when travelling either north/south or east/west.

Facilities

The central sanitary facility includes hot and cold showers, British style WCs. Gas supplies. Small shop for essentials. Busy restaurant/cafeteria and bar, also open to the public. Medium sized swimming and paddling pools (May-Sept). Bicycle hire. Play area (unfenced and near road). Caravan storage. Torches useful. Off site: Town 5 km.

Open: All year.

Directions

Site is alongside NV road (Madrid-Lisbon), 5 km. east of Mérida, at km. 336.6. From east take exit 334 and follow camping signs (doubling back). Site is actually on the 630 road that runs alongside the new motorway. GPS: N38:56.143 W06:18.306

Charges 2006

Per person	€ 3,15
child	€ 2,70
pitch incl. car	€ 6,30
electricity	€ 3,00
All plus VAT.	

ES9028 Camping Las Villuercas

Ctra Villanueva, E-10140 Guadalupe (Cáceres)

Tel: 927 367 139

This rural site nestles in an attractive valley northwest of Guadalupe. The 50 pitches (25 with 10A electricity) are level and of a reasonable size; although large units may experience difficulty in getting into the more central pitches. With an abundance of mature trees most pitches offer some degree of shade. A river runs alongside the site and the ground can be muddy in very wet periods. The site is co-located with hostel accommodation. The restaurant provides excellent food at low prices and leads to a pretty patio with overhead vines and potted plants allowing elevated views of the pools.

Facilities

The single toilet block is older in but very clean, one area for women and one for men, providing British type WCs, washbasins and showers (hot water is from a 40 litre immersion heater which could be overwhelmed in busy periods). Facilities for disabled visitors. Laundry facilities. Restaurant. Bar. Swimming pools. Shop. Tennis. Small playground. Barbecue area. Safe deposit. Medical post. No English spoken. Off site: Riding 2 km. Fishing 3 km.

Open: 1 March - 30 November.

Directions

From NV/E90 Madrid - Mérida exit at Navelmoral de la Mata. Follow south to Guadalupe on the CC713 (83 km). Site is 2 km. from Guadalupe (near Monastery). From further southwest take exit 102 off main E90/NV (northeast of Merida). Follow signs (Guadalupe). Go through a few villages and near the 72 km. marker turn left to site, 100 m. on right.

Charges 2006

Per person	€ 3,00
child (2-12 yrs)	€ 2,50
pitch	€ 5,00 - € 5,50
electricity	€ 2,50

No credit cards.

ES9086 Cáceres Camping

Ctra N630, km. 549.5, E-10005 Cáceres (Cáceres)

Tel: **927 233 100**. Email: **info@campingcaceres.com**

Recommended by our agent in Spain, we plan to conduct a full inspection of this all-year site in 2007. Cáceres Camping is quite a small site, located to the west of the interesting city of Cáceres, a World Heritage site. There are 130 pitches here, and, unusually, each has a chalet providing a shower, washbasin and toilet. The pitches are of a reasonable size (80 sq.m.) and are well shaded. A range of leisure facilities is provided, including a swimming pool and a separate children's pool. Cáceres is a city with much interest, and a fascinating history – cave paintings on the city outskirts date back 30,000 years! The city is capital of High Extremadura and close by, the Montanchez mountain range offers many opportunities for walking and cycling.

Facilities

Individual wash blocks. Bar, restaurant, cafeteria and takeaway meals. Supermarket. Swimming pool, children's pool. Playground. Entertainment programme in high season. Sports pitch planned for 2007. Chalets and apartments for rent. Off site: City centre 2 km. Golf, walking and cycling opportunities.

Open: All year.

Directions

From the east (E90 motorway) take the N521 to Cáceres. Continue on this road to the west of the city. At the large roundabout, 'Campo de Futbol Principe Felipe', the site is signed to the right.

Charges 2006

Per person	€ 3,70
child	€ 3,20
pitch	€ 10,00
electricity	€ 3,00

MAP 3

This region is located south of Madrid and occupies what was the southern part of the ancient kingdom of Castille, including the area known as La Mancha, universally famous as the setting for Miguel de Cervantes great novel 'Don Quijote de la Mancha'.

CASTILLA-LA MANCHA HAS FIVE PROVINCES: ALBACETE, CIUDAD REAL, CUENCA, GUADALAJARA AND TOLEDO

THE CAPITAL OF THE REGION IS TOLEDO

The terrain can be divided into two distinct parts: the plateau, an extensive, flat land with very few mountains, and the mountainous areas, which encircle the plateau around the region's borders, including the foothills along the massifs of the Central mountain range, the Iberian mountain range and the Sierra Morena. Toledo is crammed with monuments and nearly all the different stages of Spanish art are represented with Moorish-Mudejar-Jewish buildings; Gothic structures, such as the splendid cathedral; and Renaissance buildings. Toledo was also home to El Greco and many of his paintings are displayed in the Museum of El Greco. The region of Cuenca is surrounded by mountainous, craggy countryside, with the city itself home to extraordinary houses which hang over the cliff tops of the deep gorges. One of these has been converted into the Museum of Abstract Art. In the heartland of La Mancha, through the region of Ciudad Real, you can follow the Ruta de Don Quixote and see the famous windmills at Campo de Criptana.

Places of interest

Almagro: home of international theatre festival.

Albacete: renowned for its knife-making industry, 16th century cathedral.

Guadalajara: preserved Moorish walls, 10th century bridge, Santa Maria la Mayor, 15th century Duque del Infantado Palace.

Cuisine of the region

Local produce features heavily: aubergines, garlic, peppers, tomatoes, olive oil, meat, including both game and farm animals. Wine from La Mancha, Valdepeñas, Méntrida, Almansa, Dominio de Valdepusa and Finca de Elez.

Alajú: an almond and nut pastry.

Bizcochás de Alcázar: a tart soaked in milk with sugar, vanilla and cinnamon.

Caldereta manchega: lamb stew.

Morteruelo: paté made of pork and game birds.

Pisto manchego: a type of ratatouille with tomatoes, red and green peppers, courgettes, served either hot or cold.

Tiznao: filleted cod which is flame-grilled in an earthenware dish with pepper, tomatoes, onions and garlic.

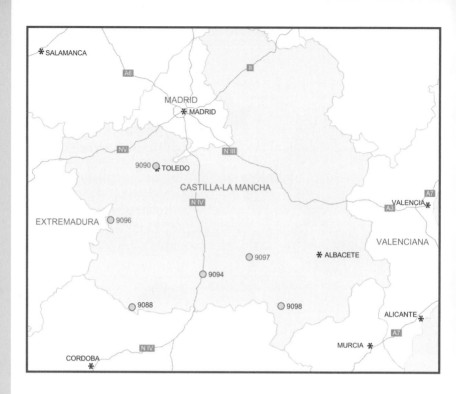

ES9097 Camping Los Batanes

Ctra Lagunas de Ruidera, km. 8, E-02611 Ossa de Montiel (Albacete)

Tel: **926 699 076**. Email: **camping@losbatanes.com**

This large campsite is in a lovely setting at the side of one of the many lakes in this area. The route to get here is beautiful and it is well worth the trip, but careful driving was necessary in parts with our large motorhome. A smaller, older part of the campsite houses reception, a small shop and a bar and restaurant. Here are medium sized pitches, shaded by pine trees with a small river running through. Over a wooden bridge is the main newer, part of the site with over 200 level, gravel and sand pitches of mixed size, shaded again by pine trees.

Facilities

One old toilet block (a slight smell) and a newer, more spacious, better one just finished. If cleaning is maintained they should cope in high season. Small shop. Simple restaurant, snacks and bar (high season). Swimming pools (19 June - Sept). Play area. Children's activities.
Off site: Beautiful walks and many lakes to explore. Watersports in summer. Tourist information either at reception or 9 km. at nearest village. Bus stop in village.

Open: All year.

Directions

On E5/NIV Cordoba - Madrid road (south of Madrid) take 430 road towards Ibacete. Coming into Ruidera turn right (just after lake on the right) signed Lagunas de Ruideria. Drive 8 km. along this country road to site on right.

Charges guide

Per person	€ 3,90 - € 4,80
child (1-13 yrs)	€ 3,25 - € 3,90
pitch	€ 8,50 - € 13,00
electricity (5A)	€ 2,90

Camping Cheques accepted.

ES9088 Camping de Fuencaliente

N420 Cordoba - Tarragona, km. 105, E-13130 Fuencaliente (Ciudad Real)

Tel: **926 698 170**

This quiet site nestles in an attractive valley between the Sierra Modrona and the Sierra Morena. It is a site for getting away from it all and sampling the peaceful mountain beauty. It could be a useful stopover if crossing Spain coast to coast or if you wish to visit the fascinating historic town of Toledo. With very few other desirable sites in this region of Castilla - La Mancha, this one is spacious with 91 generously sized pitches (over 100 sq.m.) all with electricity (6A) and water. There is both artificial shade and natural shade from pine trees and the beautiful, restful views.

Facilities

The large, modern toilet block has excellent facilities. Laundry sinks. Swimming pool (1/6-15/9; free). Restaurant/bar. Supermarket Playground. Barbecue area with table and benches overlooking the countryside. Off site: Fuencaliente 5 km.

Open: 2 April - 9 September.

Directions

From the N420 road (Cuidad Real - Cordoba) turn by 105 km. marker (about 5 km. north of Fuencaliente) onto unmade road signed Camping San Isidro to site.

Charges guide

Per person	€ 3,61
child	€ 3,31
pitch incl. car	€ 5,71 - € 7,81

Electricity included. Plus 7% VAT.

ES9094 Camping La Aguzadera

Ctra N-IV, km. 197.5, E-13300 Valdepeñas (Ciudad Real)

Tel: **926 310 769**. Email: **la-aguzadera@manchanet.es**

This is a small, unassuming site which will be useful to travellers, primarily a transit site but useful if you are following the Valdepeñas wine route. There are few other campsites open all year in this area. With pleasant views of the mountains, the site is part of a huge sports complex where there is lots of activity, although the site is quite separate with lots of room to manoeuvre. The 66 pitches are of average size and are on sloping sand with a few trees providing a little shade. There is some road noise as the site is just off the N4.

Facilities

The central sanitary block is average, unheated, but clean. Washbasins have cold water only. Restaurant and bar. Essentials from bar. Swimming and paddling pools (high season only). Play area. Tennis. Large sports complex alongside (charges apply). Dogs are not accepted. Torches required.

Open: 1 June - 30 September.

Directions

Site is directly off N4 Madrid - Cadiz at 197 km. marker at Valdepeñas exit. Look for the 'Angel of Peace' statue – the site is directly opposite and is well signed.

Charges guide

Per person	€ 4,08
child	€ 2,98
pitch incl car	€ 8,82
motorcaravan	€ 6,79

ES9098 Camping Rio Mundo

Ctra Comarcal 412, km. 205, Mesones, E-02449 Molinicos (Albacete)

Tel: **967 433230**. Email: **riomundo@campingriomundo.com**

This typically Spanish site is situated in the Sierra de Alcaraz (south of Albacete), just off the scenic route 412 between Elche de la Sierra and Valdepeñas. The drive to this site is through beautiful scenery (well worth the drive) and although from the west the main road is winding in some places, it should cause no problems if driven carefully. Shade is provided either by trees or by artificial means for the 100 pitches and electricity is supplied to the centre ones. It is a beautiful setting with majestic mountains and wonderful countryside which begs to be explored.

Facilities

One toilet block provides clean modern facilities. Basic toilet facilities for disabled people. Washing machine. Small shop for basics. Outside bar serving snacks with covered seating area. Another bar by the swimming pool. Playground. Petanque. Barbecue area.

Open: 18 March - 12 October.

Directions

Site is just off the 412 road which runs west to east, between the A30 and 322 roads south of Albacete. Turn at km. 205 on the 412, 5 km. east of village of Riopar and west of Elche de la Sierra. Follow signs to site. The road narrows to one lane for a few hundred yards but keep straight on for 1-2 km. to site.

Charges 2006

per person	€ 3,45 - € 4,45
child	€ 2,40 - € 3,00
pitch incl. electricity	€ 10,60 - € 12,85

ES9090 Camping El Greco

Ctra CM-4000 km. 0,7, Puebla de Montalban, E-45004 Toledo (Toledo)

Tel: **925 220 090**

Toledo was the home of the Grecian painter and the site that bears his name boasts a beautiful view of the ancient city from the restaurant, bar and superb pool. The friendly, family owners make you welcome and are proud of their site which is the only one in Toledo (it can get crowded). The 150 pitches are of 80 sq.m. with electricity and shade from strategically planted trees. Most have separating hedges that give privacy, with others in herring bone layouts that make for interesting parking in some areas. The river Tagus streches alongside the site which is fenced for safety.

Facilities

Two sanitary blocks, both modernised include facilities for disabled campers and everything is of the highest standard and kept very clean. Laundry. Motorcaravan services. Swimming pool (15/6-15/9; charged). Restaurant/bar (1/4-30/9) with good menu and fair prices. Small shop in reception. Playgrounds. Ice machine. Off site: Fishing in river. Golf 10 km. Riding 15 km. An hourly air-conditioned bus service runs from the gates to the city centre, touring the outside of the walls first.

Open: All year.

Directions

Site is on C4000 road on the edge of the town, signed towards Puebla de Montelban; site signs also in city centre. From Madrid on N401, turn off right towards Toledo city centre but turn right again at the roundabout at the gates to the old city. Site is signed from the next right turn.

Charges 2006

Per person	€ 5,56
child (3-10 yrs)	€ 4,81
tent or caravan and car	€ 5,35
motorcaravan	€ 10,48
electricity (6A)	€ 3,75
Plus 7% VAT.	

ES9096 Camping El Mirador de Cabaneros

Canada Real Segoviana, s/n, E-13110 Horcajo de Los Montes (Ciudad Real)

Tel: **926 775439**

With panoramic views all around of the Sierra de Valdefuertes mountains, Camping El Mirador is set in the Cabaneros National Park. This is a well cared for, landscaped site with 80 terraced pitches on gravel and all with electricity. Although level once sited, the approach is via a steep slope which may cause difficulties for larger units. Run by a very helpful and friendly family, this site is in a peaceful location where you can just sit and relax or visit the many attractions that the National Park has to offer. It is an ideal base for walking and birdwatching.

Facilities

One spotlessly clean central toilet block with solar heating includes open washbasins and cubicled showers. Facilities for disabled visitors and babies. Laundry and dishwashing facilities. Motorcaravan services. No shop but bread and gas from reception. Bar and restaurant (mid June - mid Sept, weekends out of season). Outdoor swimming pool. Games room. Basic (unfenced) play area. Tourist information from reception. Off site: Village of Horcajo de los Montes 200 m.

Open: All year.

Directions

From north head towards Toledo (southwest from Madrid). At Toledo, take CM4013 to Cuerva and pick up CM403 to El Molinillo. Turn right onto CM4017 to Horcajo de los Montes. Through village onto CM4016 towards Alcoba de los Montes, past garage and up hill for 2 km. Site on left (narrow approach).

Charges 2006

Per person	€ 3,40 - € 3,80
child	€ 2,30 - € 2,50
pitch	€ 3,40 - € 5,40
electricity	€ 2,60

MAP 3

Madrid

The region of Madrid lies right in the middle of the Spanish mainland bordering Castilla-La Mancha and Castilla and Leon. At the centre lies the city of Madrid, which since the 16th century has been the country's capital.

THE REGION OF MADRID IS A ONE PROVINCE AUTONOMY, ALSO CALLED MADRID

The mountainous region of Madrid can be divided into two areas: the Sierra, in the north and west of the region, which includes part of Somosierra and Guadarrama; and the central and southern parts, where the area is flatter and forms part of the plateau of La Mancha and La Alcarria. Founded by the Moors in the 9th Century, Madrid is now a modern, vibrant city offering innumerable attractions to the visitor. Its architectural heritage is immense. Some of the oldest parts of Madrid lie around the Puerta del Sol; a good starting place for exploring the city. Full of outdoor resturants and bars, Plaza Mayor is considered to be one of the finest in Spain, and in summer becomes an outdoor theatre and music stage. The city also has a large number of parks and gardens, among them el Retiro, the Botanical Gardens, the Parque del Oeste and the Casa de Campo; and numerous museums and art galleries. Outside the capital, the Sierra de Madrid is ideal for winter sports and the beautiful town of Aranjuez, home to the Royal Palace and glorious gardens, is a popular retreat from the city.

Places of interest

Alcala de Henares: university town, birthplace of Cervantes, author of Don Quixote, Cervantes House Museum, Archepiscopal Palace Cathedral.

Chinchón: 15th century castle, beautiful medieval square, 19th century church with painting by Goya, home of Alchoholera de Chinchón – aniseed liqueur!

Parque Natural de la Cumbre: moutain park, highest mountains in the Madrid region.

San Lorenzo de El Escorial: town in heart of Guadarrama Mountains, Monastery of El Escorial, Royal Pantheon.

Cuisine of the region

Tapas is popular with typical dishes including seafood: steamed mussels, anchovies in vinegar and pickled bonito plus croquettes and mini-casseroles. Sea bream and cod is used a lot. Local produce includes beef from the Guadarrama Mountains, olives from Campo Real, aniseed from Chinchón and asparagus from Aranjuez. Madrid is also a good place to experience every regional style of Spanish cooking.

Buñuelos: a type of fritter which is filled with custard, chocolate and cream.

Cocido: meat, potato and chickpea stew.

Con gabardina: prawns cooked in beer.

Torrijas: bread pudding.

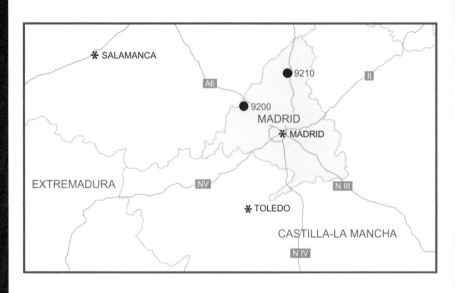

ES9210 Camping Pico de la Miel

Ctra NI Madrid - France, km. 58, E-28751 La Cabrera (Madrid)

Tel: **918 688 082**. Email: pico-miel@picodelamiel.com

Pico de la Miel is a very large site 60 kilometres north of Madrid. Mainly a long-stay site for Madrid, there is a huge number of very well established, fairly old statics. There is a small separate area with its own toilet block for touring units. The 60 pitches are on rather poor, sandy grass, some with artificial shade. Others, not so level, are under sparse pine trees and there are yet more pitches for tents (the ground could be hard for pegs). The noise level from the many Spanish customers is high and you will have a chance to practice your Spanish! Electricity connections are available. Tall hedges abound and with the trees, make it resemble a giant maze. No internal signs are provided and the long walk to the pool can be a challenge. The site is well signed and easy to find, two or three kilometres southwest off the main N1 road, with an amazing mountain backdrop.

Facilities

Dated but clean tiled toilet block, with some washbasins in cabins. It can be heated. En-suite unit with ramp for disabled visitors. Motorcaravan services. Gas supplies. Shop. Restaurant/ Bar (all year). Excellent swimming pool complex (15/6-15/9). Tennis. Playground. Off site: Bicycle hire and riding 200 m. Fishing 8 km.

Open: All year.

Directions

Site is well signed from the N1. Going south use exit 60, going north exit 57 or 60, and follow site signs. GPS: N40:51.547 W03:37.034

Charges 2006

Per person	€ 5,40
child (2-9 yrs)	€ 4,70
caravan or tent	€ 5,20 - € 5,40
car	€ 5,20
motorcaravan	€ 8,60

All plus 7% VAT. Less 10-25% for longer stays.

ES9200 Caravanning El Escorial

Apdo. Correos 8, Ctra M600, km. 3.5, E-28280 El Escorial (Madrid)

Tel: **918 902 412**. Email: **info@campingelescorial.com**

There is a shortage of good sites in the central regions of Spain, but this is one (albeit rather expensive). El Escorial is very large, there are 1,358 individual pitches of which about 600 are for touring, with the remainder used for permanent or seasonal units, but situated to one side of the site. The pitches are shaded (ask for a pitch without a low tree canopy if you have a 3 metre high motorcaravan). There are another 250 pseudo 'wild' spaces for tourists on open fields, with good shade from mature trees (long cables may be necessary for electricity). The general amenities are good and include three swimming pools (unheated), plus a paddling pool in a central area with a bar/restaurant with terrace and plenty of grassy sitting out areas. At weekends in high season the site can be noisy. It is well situated for sightseeing visits especially to the magnificent El Escorial monastery (5 km). Also, the enormous civil war monument of the Valle de los Caidos is very close plus Madrid and Segovia both at 50 km.

Facilities

One large toilet block for the touring pitches, plus two smart, small blocks for the 'wild' camping area, are all fully equipped with some washbasins in cabins. Baby baths. Facilities for disabled campers. The blocks can be heated. Large supermarket (1/3-31/10). Restaurant/bar and snack bar (1/3-31/10). Disco-bar. Swimming pools. Three tennis courts. Two well equipped playgrounds on sand. ATM. Off site: Town 3 km. Riding or golf 7 km.

Open: All year.

Directions

From the south go through town of El Escorial, and follow M600 Guadarrama road. Site is between the 2 and 3 km. markers north of the town on the right. From the north use A6 autopista and exit 47 to M600 towards El Escorial town. Site is on the left.

Charges 2006

Per person	€ 5,35
child (3-10 yrs)	€ 5,20
caravan or tent and car	€ 10,55
motorcaravan	€ 9,20
electricity	€ 3,75

VAT included. No credit cards.

LIFE IN THIS SINGLE PROVINCE REGION THAT OCCUPIES THE GEOGRAPHICAL CENTRE OF THE IBERIAN PENINSULA REVOLVES AROUND THE CITY OF MADRID, WHICH SINCE THE 16TH CENTURY HAS BEEN THE COUNTRY'S CAPITAL.

Founded by the Moors in the 9th Century, Madrid today is something of an enigma. On one hand it is a modern, active city, whilst in the centre the streets are crowded with ancient buildings which reveal much about the development of the city over many centuries. The medieval village has been preserved around the Plaza de la Paja, and the quarter known as 'Madrid of the Austrian' (it was the Habsburg capital in the 16th century) near the traditional city centre, Puerta del Sol, was built in the Golden Age. Located in this area is the Plaza de la Villa, with its beautiful city hall building, and the Plaza Mayor, which is colonaded and considered to be one of the finest in Spain; both are Baroque in style and date from the 17th century.

Another popular attraction is the Royal Palace, a magnificent example of 18th century palatial art, which is surrounded by gardens that are now partially open to the public. Elsewhere, the city also has many interesting treasures from the 19th and 20th centuries and a large number of parks and gardens. Among these are El Retiro, the botanical gardens crafted by royal decree in the 17th Century, the Parque del Oeste and the Casa de Campo.

The city suffered major damage during the Civil War but in the 25 years since Franco's death, thanks to the late mayor, Tierno Galvin, much has been restored. Very much part of the city's modern day life are its two football clubs, Real Madrid and Madrid Atletico. England's David Beckham now wears the white shirt of Real and helps entertain the citizens of Madrid in the famous Santiago Bernabéu stadium.

The Madrid of the 21st century is a vibrant, lively city offering a wide range of events and cultural performances. There are more than thirty theatres, one hundred cinemas, fifty live-music venues, and dozens of galleries and exhibition halls throughout the city. A permanent season of classical music, opera and zarzuela (Spanish operetta) is held in the Auditorio Nacional, the Teatro Real and the Teatro de la Zarzuela. Among Madrid's many museums and art galleries is the Prado Museum, housing one of the oldest collections of art in the world; the archaeological museum, with collections representing practically all the different cultures that have flourished in Spain; and the Reina Sofia Art Centre, which proudly displays Picasso's greatest picture, 'Guernica'.

UnityPlus CARD

Unique Discounts
for Campers
and Caravanners

www.unity-plus.com

NEW

Whether you have a caravan, a motorhome or a tent, the UnityPlus Card is for you. It's not a club but it offers great benefits and it's free! Quite simply, it offers unique discounts for campers and caravanners on a range of products including cheap ferry deals, discounted holidays, camping accessories, specialist insurance and more.

Full details at www.unity-plus.com

Request your UnityPlus Card today!

Paying too much for your
mobile home holiday?

MAP 4

The large region of Castilla y León is located inland, bordering Portugal to the west. It has a rich legacy dating back to the Romans, with an extraordinary wealth of castles, cathedrals and mansions, historic cities and towns.

THE REGION IS MADE UP OF THE FOLLOWING PROVINCES: AVILA, BURGOS, LEON, PALENCIA, SALAMANCA, VALLADOLID, ZAMORA, SEGOVIA AND SORIA

Steeped in history and architectural sights, the major towns and cities of the provinces all have something to offer. In the south, the town of Ávila is set on a high plain, surrounded by 11th century walls; and the graceful city of Salamanca was once home to one of the most prestigious universities in the world. Its grand Plaza Mayor is the finest in Spain. In the east, Segovia is well known for its magnificent Roman aqueduct, with 163 arches and 29 metres at its highest point; the cathedral; and the fairy-tale Alcazár, complete with turrets and narrow towers. And the attractive city of Soria still retains a Romanesque legacy in its network of medieval streets. Burgos in the north, is the birthplace of El Cid and has a Gothic cathedral of exceptional quality. The lively university city of Leon boasts a Royal Pantheon, decorated by Romanesque wall paintings, and also an impressive Gothic cathedral. There too is a Gothic cathedral in Palencia plus an archaeology museum. South of Leon, the old walled quarters of Zamora have a retained medieval appearance, with a dozen Romanesque churches. And in the centre of the region, Valladolid is famous for its extravagant and solemn processions during the Holy Week celebrations.

Places of interest

Astorga: city of Roman origin, chocolate museum, cathedral.

Ciudad Rodrigo: Renaissance mansions, cathedral, 12th century walls.

Coca: impressive Mudejar castle, birthplace of the famous Roman emperor Theodosius the Great.

Pantano de Burgomillodo: reservoir, great for bird-watchers.

Parque Natural del Cañón del Río Lobos: park created around the canyon of the River Lobos with rock formations, cave and good walking tracks.

Parque Natural del Lago de Sanabria y alrededores: mountainous area with deep valleys and glacier lagoons, variety of flora and fauna including 76 types of birds and 17 large mammals.

Cuisine of the region

The region is best known for its roast pork and lamb which has earned it the nickname *España del Asado* (Spain of the Roast). Other local products include trout from Leon and Zamora, and a variety of pulses: white, red and black beans, Castilian and *Pedrosillano* chickpeas, and various types of lentils. Soups feature a lot in winter: trout soup, typical of Órbigo de Leon; garlic soup; Zamora soup, a garlic soup with ripe tomatoes and hot chilli peppers.

Bizcochos de San Lorenzo: sponge cakes.

Farinatos: sausages made from breadcrumbs, pork fat and spices.

Hornazos: sausage and egg tarts.

Judias del barco con chorizo: haricot beans with sausage.

Yemas: a sweet made with egg yolks and sugar.

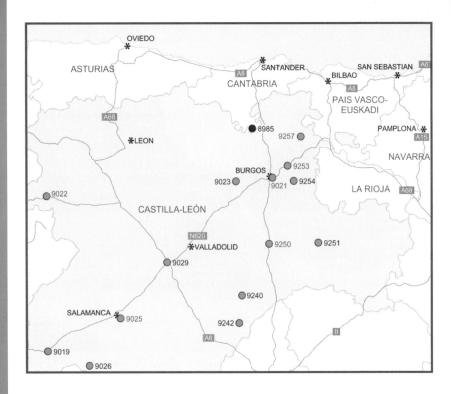

ES9019 Camping La Pesquera

Ctra de Caceres - Arrabal, E-37500 Ciudad Rodrigo (Salamanca)
Tel: **923 481 348**

This modest little site has just 54 pitches and is located near the Rio Agueda looking up to the magnificent fortress ramparts of Ciudad Rodrigo. Entry to the site is through a municipal park with a large play area. Whilst the site is small, it can take even the largest units, the centrally located facilities have all been refurbished to a high standard, the pitches are flat and grassy and the roads are well maintained gravel. The pitches are shaded by trees by day and there is site lighting at night although you may find torches useful due to the tree canopy.

Facilities

Attractive ochre stone sanitary building with British WCs and free hot showers. Facilities for disabled campers. Washing machine. Basics sold from bar in high season. Bar/snacks (April - Sept). Playground outside gates. Barbecue outside gate. Torches useful. Off site: River fishing 1 km. Riding 5 km. Superb walking area.

Open: 25 April - 30 September.

Directions

Site is southwest of Salamancar close to Ciudad Rodrigo. From the E80 N260, any direction, take the 526 to Coria. Site is alongside river directly off the road and well signed.

Charges 2006

Per person	€ 3,20
child (up to 12 yrs)	€ 3,00
tent/caravan and car	€ 3,20
motorcaravan	€ 6,40
electricity	€ 3,00

ES9025 Camping Regio

Ctra de Madrid, km. 4, E-37900 Santa Marta de Tormes (Salamanca)

Tel: 923 138 888. Email: recepcion@campingregio.com

Salamanca is one of Europe's oldest university cities, and this beautiful old sandstone city has to be visited. This is also a useful staging post en-route to the south of Spain or central Portugal. The site is 7 km. outside the city on the old road to Madrid, behind the Hôtel Regio where campers can take advantage of the hotel facilities. The pitches (with a large area for tents) are clearly marked on slightly sloping ground, with some shade in parts and plentiful electricity points (10A). Access to those not on the wide central road can be difficult for caravans. The hotel facilities include a quality restaurant, a somewhat cheaper cafeteria (discounts for campers), and an excellent swimming pool and children's pool (small charge). There is a pool bar and a shaded patio. The site itself has a small bar and restaurant. Visit the city and find the famous frog which is hidden in the fabulous University facade and discover what unusual Spanish fortune will be granted you! Alternatively just enjoy the wonderfully accessible Salamantine architecture and myriad bars around the Plaza Mayor.

Facilities

Very large, fully equipped sanitary block is very clean. Good facilities for disabled campers. Washing machines. Gas supplies. Motorcaravan services. Bar. Supermarket (1/4-30/9). The hotel restaurant, café and swimming pool may be used by campers (discounts at the café and restaurant). Play area. Tennis. English is spoken. Off site: Bus to town terminates at hotel car-park. Fishing 2km. Bicycle hire 4 km. Town centre and golf 7 km.

Open: All year.

Directions

Take the main N501 route from Salamanca towards Avila, then to St Marta de Tormes 7 km east of the city. Hôtel Regio is on the right just outside the town at the 90 km. marker. There are yellow camping signs through the city and on the roads to the east.

Charges 2006

Per person	€ 2,89 - € 3,42
child	€ 2,57 - € 3,00
pitch incl. electricity	€ 12,52 - € 14,66

CAMPING **Regio** 1ᵃ C ★★★★ **BUNGALOWS**

SA 300 · N 630 · SALAMANCA · C 517 · MADRID ➡ · N 501 · N 620 · N 630 · Sta. Marta de Tormes

OPEN THROUGHOUT THE YEAR

Bus to centre of town (4 km)

Next to Hotel REGIO
www.campingregio.com
recepcion@campingregio.com

Tel.: (34) 923 13 88 88
Fax: (34) 923 13 80 44

ES9026 Camping El Burro Blanco

Camino de las Norias s/n, E-37660 Miranda del Castañar (Salamanca)

Tel: 923 161 100. Email: elburroblanco@internet-rural.com

Set on a hill top, within the Sierra Peña de Francia is the romantic walled village of Miranda del Castañar with its charming, crumbling castle. This site has been developed by a Dutch team including husband and wife Jeff and Yvonne and their friend Paul. You are welcomed at the gate and are walked around the facilities. The number of pitches has been reduced to 30 (all now 80 to 120 sq.m.), mostly level with some terracing and 25 with electricity. The pitches are beautifully set in 3.5 hectares of the most attractive woodland.

Facilities

One central modern sanitary facility, fully equipped includes a baby bath. Two washbasins have hot water. Out of season part of the unit is closed and therefore facilities are unisex. Launderette. Gas supplies. Library with book swap and small bar. Off site: Restaurants, bars, shops and ATM in village 600 m. Municipal swimming pool nearby, river swimming and fishing 1.5 km.

Open: 1 April - 1 October.

Directions

From north - south direction take Salamanca - Coria road southwest for about 70 km. through Vecinos, Linares de Rio Frio towards Coria. The road to Miranda is 7 km. northeast of village of Cepeda. Turn off main road and after 1.2 km. turn left on concrete road. Follow for 1.1 km. (a short stretch unmade) to site. GPS: N40:28.488 W05:59.931

Charges 2007

Per person	€ 4,80
pitch incl. electricity	€ 10,50
Plus 7% VAT. No credit cards.	

119

ES9022 Camping El Folgoso

E-49361 Vigo de Sanabria (Zamora)

Tel: **980 626774**

After a pleasant drive through the Sanabria National Park you reach this unspoilt site alongside a beautiful lake. It has green hills to the west and a lake of glacial origin to the east. It is a large site with the majority of the pitches given over to tents, as the terrain is rugged and strewn with enormous rocks, whilst being sheltered by fine dense oaks. The pitches are informal and tents are placed anywhere on terraces or the lower levels. Pitches for caravans and motorcaravans are in more formal lines at the far end of the site with (5A) electricity available.

Facilities

Three sanitary blocks, two refurbished and one newer unit close to the restaurant, provide pre-set showers (on payment), facilities for disabled campers and a variety of washing facilities but all with cold water. Shop. Bar with snacks (all year). Self-service and full restaurants (April - Oct). Bicycle hire. Barbecue area. Torches essential. Off site: Supermarket (April - Oct) just outside site. Playground very close. Gate at rear of site leads to lake 50 m. to fish, swim or enjoy the watersports.

Open: All year.

Directions

From N525 Orense/Ourense - Benavente autovia or the parallel A525, take any exit for Puebla de Sanabria and follow signs for Sanabria National Park. This will place you on the ZA 104 heading north. Pass through of El Puente, Cubelo and Galende to 11 km. marker and site is signed to the right.

Charges 2006

Per person	€ 3,70
child (under 10 yrs)	€ 2,80
pitch incl. electricity	€ 6,30 - € 8,30

ES9021 Camping Municipal Fuentes Blancas

Ctra Cartuja - Miraflores, km. 3,5, E-09193 Burgos (Burgos)

Tel: **947 486 016**. Email: **info@campingburgos.com**

Fuentes Blancas is a comfortable municipal site on the edge of the historical town of Burgos and within easy reach of the Santander ferries. There are around 350 marked pitches of 70 sq.m. on flat ground, 250 with electrical connections (6A) and there is good shade in parts. A small shop caters for most needs, the typically Spanish bar serves snacks and in the evening a restaurant is open offering basic, inexpensive meals. The site has a fair amount of transit trade and reservations are not possible for August, so arrive early.

Facilities

Clean, modern, fully equipped sanitary facilities in five blocks with controllable showers and hot and cold water to sinks (not all are always open). Facilities for babies. Washing machine. Chemical disposal and fresh water hoses for motorcaravans in Block 3. Small shop (all season). Bar/snack bar and restaurant (all season). Swimming pool (1/7-30/8). Playground. English is spoken. Off site: Fishing and river beach 200 m. Bus service to city or a fairly shaded walk. Golf 30 km.

Open: All year.

Directions

From the N623 go through the city centre to km 0. Follow signs for E5/A1 Madrid. After crossing river take slip road for N120/A231 Leon but then turn left towards Fuentes Blancas and Cartuja de Miraflores for 3 km. Site is well signed on left. GPS: N42:20.453 W03:39.469

Charges 2006

Per person	€ 4,15
pitch incl. electricity	€ 11,80
Plus 7% VAT.	

ES9023 Camping Camino de Santiago

Casco Urbano, E-09110 Castrojeriz (Burgos)

Tel: **947 377 255**. Email: **campingcastro@eresmas.com**

This tranquil site lies to the west of Burgos on the outskirts of Castrojeriz, a small unspoilt Spanish rural town. In a superb location, almost in the shadow of the ruined castle high on the hillside, it will appeal to those who like peace and a true touring campsite without all the modern trimmings, and at a reasonable cost. The 50 marked pitches are level, grassy and divided by hedges, with electricity (5A) and drainage available to all. There is also a number of permanent pitches. Mature trees provide shade and there is a pretty orchard in one corner of the site.

Facilities

Adequate sanitary facilities with showers, British and Turkish style WCs, and washbasins with cold water only. These facilities are in older style, but are well maintained and clean. Washing machine. Bar (serving coffee and soft drinks). Games room. Tennis. Play area. Bicycle hire. Barbecue area. Note: the present owner is looking to sell the site so things may change.

Open: 1 March - 30 November.

Directions

From N120/A231 (Leon - Burgos), turn on BU404 (Villasandino, Castrojeriz). Turn left at crossroads on southwest side of town, then left at site sign. GPS: N42:17.484 W04:07.899

Charges 2006

Per person	€ 3,75
pitch incl. electricity	€ 6,50 - € 8,00
All plus 7% VAT.	

ES9250 Camping Costajan

A1-ES-KM164-165, E-09400 Aranda de Duero (Burgos)

Tel: 947 502 070. Email: campingcostajan@telefonica.net

This site is well placed as an en-route stop for the ferries, being 80 km. south of Burgos. This is the capital of the Ribera del Duero wine region that produces many fine wines competing with the great Riojas. With 225 unmarked pitches, all with electricity available, there are around 100 for all types of tourer. Large units may find access to the 225 unmarked, variably sized pitches a bit tricky among dense olive and pine trees and on the slightly undulating sandy ground but the trees provide good shade. There are 115 electricity connections.

Facilities

Good, heated, modern sanitary facilities have hot and cold water. Facilites for disabled people. Washing machine. Gas supplies. Shop with essentials (all year). Bar serving simple meals (all year). Free access to adjacent large swimming pool (June - Sept). Tennis. Minigolf. Torch useful. Reception opens 08.00-14.00 and 18.00-22.00 (if unmanned, choose a pitch and book in later). Off site: Riding 2 km. Fishing and river beach 3 km.

Open: All year.

Directions

From A1/E5 take exit at 164,5 km. and turn south on N1 towards Aranda de Duero. The site is on the right at the 162 km. mark. GPS: N41:42.120 W03:41.282

Charges 2006

Per person	€ 4,00 - € 4,20
child	€ 3,85 - € 4,00
pitch	€ 4,20 - € 15,00
electricity	€ 4,00

ES9253 Camping Picon del Conde

Ctra NI, km 263, E-09292 Monasterio de Rodilla (Burgos)

Tel: 947 594 355

This all year site is unusual, in that it has been amazingly decorated by the owner, Pedro Fasseler Sagredo who is lively and friendly, as are his family. The experience begins as you drive under an art nouveau style entry arch. The 60 level, grass pitches, all with electricity (5A), are of a reasonable size with separating hedges giving some privacy and trees offering shade. Long cables may be needed on some pitches. There is some traffic noise from the busy N1 alongside and from the nearby motorway. This site is a good stopover if heading for the ferry or for exploring the area.

Facilities

Modern, attractively tiled toilet block with controllable showers but cold water to basins and sinks. Dishwashing is up 12 steps and toilets and showers a further 12! Good facilities at ground level for disabled campers. Motorcaravan service point. Restaurant and friendly bar. Attractive swimming pool (15/6-1/9). Play area. Tennis and fronton. Off site: Fishing 2 km. Riding and golf 18 km. Burgos 25 km. Skiing 40 km.

Open: All year.

Directions

Monasterio de Rodilla is 25 km. northeast of Burgos From A1 (Burgos - Vitoria) motorway, join N1 at exit 2 (heading northeast) or exit 3 (southwest) Site is on the N1 at the 263 km. marker (behind motel). GPS: N42:27.619 W03:27.481

Charges 2006

Per person	€ 3,20
child	€ 2,90
pitch	€ 4,90 - € 7,00
electricity	€ 3,30

ES9254 Camping Puerta de la Demanda

Ctra de Pineda, km. 2, E-09199 Villasur de Herreros (Burgos)

Tel: 983 796819

This recently built site is being improved and shows great promise. On flat ground, it is overlooked on three sides by the hills and mountains of the Sierra de la Demanda which give the site its name. There is little shade over 50 well marked large pitches all of which have electricity (5A) and drainage. The modern buildings are of local stone and wood in sympathy with the quiet surroundings, yet providing an excellent set of facilities. Just 300 m. away is a dam which may provide non-powered water sports and a river is very close for swimming and fishing.

Facilities

Attractive new sanitary building with British WCs and free hot showers. Washing machine, dishwashing (H&C) and laundry (C) sinks. Facilities for disabled campers. Bar serving meals and selling basics (all season). Torches useful. Off site: River fishing 1 km. Sailing on nearby reservoir. Shop, restaurants and bars in attractive village 1 km. Superb walking area.

Open: 1 February - 30 November.

Directions

From the N120 (Burgos - Logroño), turn east at Ibeas de Juarros (about 13 km. east of Burgos) on Bu-P8101/Bu820 through Arlanzon to Villasur de Herreros. Site is beyond village after km 13.

Charges 2006

Per person	€ 3,11
child (up to 12 yrs)	€ 2,46
pitch incl. car	€ 5,24 - € 6,02
electricity	€ 2,46
Plus 7% VAT.	

ES9257 Camping Frias

E-09211 Ciudad de Frias (Burgos)

Tel: **947 357198**. Email: **camfrias@burgos.net**

Located in a natural park northeast of Burgos, on the edge of the old, small Spanish town of Frias, much of this site is taken up with static units. However, an area at the end is reserved for touring caravans and motorcaravans. A beautiful river runs alongside, about 20 feet below the campsite but with access to fishing, and the level, numbered pitches have views across the really beautiful scenery surrounding the campsite. A little shade is provided from a few trees. This is very Spanish site (no English was spoken when we visited).

Facilities

One toilet block provides basic facilities with British style WCs, washbasins with cold water only and coin operated showers. Two washing machines. Shop with good range of produce (all year). Bar and restaurant. Two swimming pools (22/6-15/9). Off site: Transport would be needed to visit any interesting places.

Open: All year.

Directions

Site is on the north side of Frias – approach only from this side. From A1 exit 5 onto A2122 (Quintana Martin Galindez), with a few tunnels but spectacular scenery (turn right on 625 then left to Quintana). After 16 km. turn left to Frias. Site is 3 km. on right.

Charges 2006

Per person	€ 2,95
pitch incl. electricity	€ 11,00

Less 10% in low season. Plus 7% VAT.

ES9242 Camping El Acueducto

Avenida D. Juan de Borbón, 49, Ctra CL601, km. 112, E-40004 Segovia (Segovia)

Tel: **921 425 000**. Email: **campingsg@navegalia.com**

Located right on the edge of the interesting city of Segovia with lovely views across the open plain with mountains in the background, this is a family run, typically Spanish site. The grass pitches are mostly of medium size, although a few pitches near the gate would have room for larger motor-caravans. Reception is small but the owner is helpful and speaks good English. El Acueducto is well positioned for discovering Segovia. About three miles away, Segovia is deeply and haughtily Castilian, with plenty of squares and mansions from its days of Golden Age grandeur, when it was a royal resort.

Facilities

Two traditional style toilet blocks provide basic facilities, a laundry room and dishwashing sinks, all of which are clean. Small shop for basics. Bar. Two swimming pools. Table tennis. Large play area. Off site: Large restaurant a few yards along the road providing good food. Bus service into city centre. Madrid is within driving distance.

Open: 1 April - 30 September.

Directions

From the north on N1 (Burgos - Madrid) take exit 99 on N110 towards Segovia. On outskirts of city take third exit on N603 signed Madrid. Pass one exit to Segovia and take second signed Segovia and La Granja. At roundabout turn right towards Segovia. Site is 500 yards on right.

Charges 2006

Per person	€ 4,50 - € 5,00
pitch	€ 14,00 - € 15,50

ES9240 Camping El Cantosal

Ctra de Santiuste, km. 2, E-40480 Coca (Segovia)

Tel: **627 445906**. Email: **info@asecal.net**

On the 'Ruta de Mudejar' (Mudejar castles and buildings), near the nature reserve 'Hoces del Duraton' is this tiny campsite of 46 pitches, all with 5A electricity. The setting has a fairy tale air about it – the magnificent fifteenth century Castillo de Coca can be seen from most of the site. The grass and sand pitches are flat and partly shaded by tall trees in the daytime, and lit by pretty post lights at night. Designed in sympathy with the surroundings, the recently built stone buildings and all the facilities are of the highest quality. The bar serves snacks and excellent coffee.

Facilities

The huge, modern toilet block has British style WCs and free showers. Washing machine, dishwashing (H&C) and laundry sinks under cover. Facilities for disabled campers. Bar. Large playground just outside the site. Off site: Village with shops bars and restaurants. Swimming pool (discount). Fishing 2 km. Golf 20 km. Village of Coca with superb castle with attractive flowered gardens and bull ring 2 km.

Open: 15 June - 15 September.

Directions

Coca is 65 km. SSE of Valladoid. From N601 (Madrid - Valladoid) at Olmedo turn southeast on Vp1105 to Coca. At T-junction marked Coca 2 km. Santuiste 7 km, turn into site road through stone pillars on the left and signed Zona De Picnic El Cantosal.
GPS: N41:12.447 W04:02.097

Charges 2006

Per person	€ 3,06
pitch incl. electricity	€ 5,84

ES9251 Camping Cañon del Rio Lobos

Ctra Burgos de Osma - San Leonardo, E-42317 Ucero (Soria)

Tel: **975 363565**

This is a delightful site with vast amounts of flowers, set among attractive limestone cliffs of the Burgos canyons. The site is pricey but facilities are excellent and there are few others in the area. Reception is purpose built and control of the security barrier is from within – everything here is very organised. The camp logo depicts a bird of prey and many of these wheel above the site. The very attractive swimming pool is within a secure walled area, which again has many flowers and shrubs and is private from the road that runs alongside the site (some road noise).

Facilities

Two fully equipped toilet blocks (only one opened when site is quiet). Bar serving a 'menú del dia' and smart restaurant. Basic shopping from bar. Swimming pool (extra charge). Two excellent tennis courts (extra charge). Play area. Bicycle hire. Fishing. Torch useful. Off site: Local bus service 1 km. on Wed./Sat.for town. Walking, climbing, caving, fishing in nearby 'Parque Natural'. Riding 10 km. Golf 35 km.

Open: Easter - 30 September.

Directions

Ucero is 60 km. west of Soria. From N234 (Burgos - Soria) turn south in San Leonado de Yagüe on So690. Turn left after village on So920 signed El Burgo de Osma. Site is on left in 18 km. just before Ucero. From N122/A11 (Valladolid - Soria) turn north in El Burgo de Osma on So920 signed San Leonardo, 16 km. to Ucero. Site is on right after village.

Charges 2007

Per person	€ 5,00
child	€ 4,00
pitch incl. electricity	€ 17,60 - € 18,60
All plus 7% VAT.	

ES9029 Camping El Astral

Camino de Pollos 8, E-47100 Tordesillas (Valladolid)

Tel: **983 770 953**. Email: **info@campingelastral.es**

The site is in a prime position alongside the wide River Duero (safely fenced). It is homely and run by a charming man, Eduardo Gutierrez, who has excellent English and is ably assisted by brother Gustavo and sister Lola. The site is generally flat with 154 pitches separated by thin hedges. They vary in size from 60 - 80 sq.m. with mature trees providing shade. There is an electricity pylon tucked in one corner of the site but this is hardly noticeable. This is a friendly site ideal for exploring the area as you move through Spain.

Facilities

One attractive sanitary block including two cabins with WC, bidet and washbasin. Some facilities for disabled campers, including ramps. Baby room in ladies' area. Washing machines. Motorcaravan services. Supermarket. Bar. Restaurant fequented by locals. Swimming and paddling pools (1/6-15/9). Playground. Tennis (high season). Minigolf. English speaking staff. Local bus service. Animation daily in high season. Torches are useful.

Open: 1 April - 30 September.

Directions

Tordesillas is 28 km. southwest of Valladolid. From all directions, leave the main road towards Tordesillas and follow signs to campsite or 'Parador' (a hotel opposite the site). GPS: N41:29.779 W05:00.312

Charges 2007

Per person	€ 4,20 - € 6,00
child (0-12 yrs)	€ 3,30 - € 5,00
caravan or tent	€ 4,20 - € 6,00
car or motorcycle	€ 3,60 - € 5,00
electricity (5A)	€ 3,50
Plus 7% VAT. Discounts in low season and for longer stays.	

MAP 4

With a coastline of inlets and wide, rocky estuaries sheltering traditional old fishing villages and fine beaches, Galicia is perhaps best known for Santiago de Compostela, the place where the famous pilgrim route comes to an end.

THIS REGION IS MADE UP OF FOUR PROVINCES: OURENSE, LUGO, A CORUÑA AND PONTEVEDRA

The obvious highlight in the region has to be the beautiful medieval city of Santiago de Compostela, capital of Galicia and world famous centre of the old European pilgrimage. Now a World Heritage Site, the city boasts an impressive Romanesque cathedral with more churches, convents and monasteries dotted around. One of the best times to go to Santiago de Compostela is during the Festival of St James on 25 July, which has also been designated Galicia Day. Following the route into the city, are the towns of Portomarín and Samos. Near Samos, the Lóuzara valley and the Sierra do Oribio are ideal for those interested in hiking and wildlife. The Galician coastline is characterized by high cliffs and estuaries collectively known as the Rías Atlas and Rías Baixas with the Costa da Morte or Coast of Death separating them; so called because of the hundreds of shipwrecks that litter the cliffs and rocks. It was also once considered by the pilgrimages to be the 'end of the world'. Along the coast are medieval towns and villages including Noia, Muros, A Coruña and Finisterre. Corcubión, Camariñas and Corme-Laxe are other rias with fishing villages and home to some of the best barnacles in the region.

Places of interest

A Coruña: medieval quarters, Romanesque churches, Roman lighthouse.

Baiona: one of the region's best resorts.

Camariñas: town on the 'end of the world', good barnacle hunting ground, lacemaking traditions.

Lugo: town completely enclosed within preserved Roman walls, along which are 85 towers.

Malpica: seaside harbour, jumping off point for nearby islands.

Pontevedra: picturesque old town with lively atmosphere.

Vigo: fishing port, beaches.

Viveiro: beaches, old town surrounded by Renaissance walls.

Cuisine of the region

Local cuisine features heavily in fiestas and throughout the region are numerous markets. Good quality seafood is found in abundance; *percebes* (barnacles) are a favourite. *Pulpo* (octopus) is also popular and special *pulperías* will cook it in the traditional way. Vegetable dishes include the Galician broth, made with green beans, cabbage, parsnip, potatoes and haricot beans. *Aguardiente gallego*, a regional liqueur, is used to make the traditional mulled drink known as *queimada*, where fruit, sugar and coffee grains are added and then set alight.

Caldeirada: fish soup.

Caldo gallego: thick stew of potato cabbage.

Empanada: light-crusted pastries often filled with pork, beef, tuna or cod.

Lacon con grelos: ham boiled with turnip greens.

ES8942 Camping Los Manzanos

Ctra Santa Cruz - Meiras, km. 0,7, E-15179 Santa Cruz (A Coruña)
Tel: **981 614 825**. Email: **info@camping-losmanzanos.com**

Los Manzanos has a steep access drive to the main buildings and is divided by a stream into two sections linked by a bridge. Pitches for larger units are marked and numbered, 85 with electricity (12A) and, in one section, there is a fairly large, unmarked field for tents. Some aircraft noise should be expected as the site is under the flight path to La Coruña (but no aircraft at night). The site impressed us as being very clean, even when full, which it tends to be in high season. Some huge interesting stone sculptures create focal points and conversation pieces. This site is to the east of the historic port of La Coruña, not far from some ria (lagoon) beaches and with good communications to both central and north Galicia – it is only an hour and a half drive from Santiago de la Compostela, for example.

Facilities

One good toilet block provides modern facilities including free hot showers. Small shop with fresh produce daily (limited outside July/Aug). High quality restaurant/bar (July/Aug). Swimming pool with lifeguard, free to campers (15/6-15/9). Playground. Barbecue area. Bungalows for rent. Off site: Bus service at end of entrance drive. Beach and fishing 800 m. Bicycle hire 2 km. Golf and riding 8 km.

Open: Easter - 15 September.

Directions

The nearest large city is La Coruña. From A9/E1 going south, take exit 7 for 'O Burgo'. Site is north of Oleiras, in Santa Cruz on the road to Meiras heading out of town, and is well signed from there.

Charges 2006

Per person	€ 5,00
child	€ 3,80
pitch incl. car	€ 10,00 - € 10,60
electricity	€ 3,20

All plus 7% VAT.

ES9024 Camping As Cancelas

Rue do 25 de Xullo 35, E-15704 Santiago de Compostela (A Coruña)

Tel: **981 580 476**. Email: **info@campingascancelas.com**

The beautiful city of Santiago has been the destination for European Christian pilgrims for centuries and they now follow ancient routes to this unique city, the whole of which is a national monument. The As Cancelas campsite is excellent for sharing the experiences of these pilgrims in the city and around the magnificent cathedral. It has 156 marked pitches (30-70 sq.m), arranged in terraces and divided by trees and shrubs. On a hillside overlooking the city, the views are very pleasant, but the site has a steep approach road and access to most of the pitches can be a challenge for large units. Electrical hook-ups (5A) are available, the site is lit at night and a security guard patrols. There are many legendary festivals and processions here, the main one being on July 25th, especially in holy years (when the Saint's birthday falls on a Sunday). Examine for yourself the credibility of the fascinating story of the arrival of the bones of St James at Compostela (Compostela translates as 'field of stars'), and also discover why the pilgrims dutifully carry a scallop shell on their long journey. There are many pilgrims' routes, including one commencing from Fowey in Cornwall.

Facilities

Two very modern toilet blocks are fully equipped, with ramped access for disabled campers. The quality and cleanliness of the fittings and tiling is good. Laundry with service wash for a small fee. Small mini market (open July/Aug.). Restaurant. Bar with TV. (main season). Well kept, unsupervised swimming pool and children's pool. Small playground. Off site: Regular bus service runs into the city from near football ground 200 m. from site. Huge commercial centre (open late and handy for off season use) 20 minutes walk downhill (uphill on the return!).

Open: All year.

Directions

From motorway AP9-E1 take exit 67 and follow signs for 'Casco Historico' and 'Centro Ciudad' then follow site signs.

Charges 2007

Per person	€ 4,00 - € 5,25
child (up to 12 yrs)	€ 2,50 - € 4,00
pitch	€ 8,00 - € 11,00
electricity	€ 3,30
All plus VAT.	

MAP 4

Asturias

Like its neighbouring province, Cantabria, Asturias also has a beautiful coastline, albeit more rugged and wild, with the Picos range separating them. In the south the Cantabrian mountains form a natural border between Asturias and Castilla-León.

THIS IS A ONE PROVINCE REGION

THE CAPITAL IS OVIEDO

Situated between the foothills of the Picos mountains and the coast is the seaside town of Llanes, in the east. It has several good beaches, beautiful coves and given its location, is a good base for exploring the Picos del Europa. Along the coast towards Gijón are more seaside resorts including Ribadesella, with its fishing harbour and fine beach. The cities of Gijón and, in particular, Avilés are renowned for their Carnival festivities, a national event which takes place in late February. This week-long party involves dancing, live music, fireworks and locals who dress up in elaborate fancy-dress costumes. South of here towards the centre of the province is the capital, Oviedo. The city boasts a pedestrian old quarter with numerous squares and narrow streets, a cathedral, palaces, a Fine Arts Museum, Archaeological Museum plus various remarkable churches that date from the 9th century. There are also plenty of sidrerías (cider houses).The west coast of Asturias is more rugged. One of the most attractive towns along here is Luarca, built around a cove surrounded by sheer cliffs. With a fishing harbour and an array of good restaurants and bars, the town's traditional character is reflected in its chigres – old Asturian taverns – where visitors can learn the art of drinking cider.

Places of interest

Avilés: 14th and 15th century churches and palaces.

Cuillero: small, charming fishing port.

Gijón: 18th century palace, beaches, museums.

Villahormes: seaside town with excellent swimming coves.

Villaviciosa: atmospheric old town, 13th church, cider factory.

Cuisine of the region

Local specialities include *fabada,* a type of stew made with haricot beans called *fabes, potes* (soups) and of course cider, which can be drunk in *sidrerías*. The customary way to serve cider is to pour it from a great height, a practice know as *escanciar,* into a wide-mouthed glass only just covering the *culín* or bottom. Rice pudding is the traditional dessert and *frixuelos* (crepe), *huesos de santo* (made from marzipan) and *tocinillo de cielo* (syrup pudding) are eaten during festivals.

Brazo de gitano: a type of Swiss roll.

Carne gobernada: beef in white wine with bacon, eggs, peppers and olives.

Fabada asturiana: haricot beans, chorizo, cabbage, cured pork shoulder and potatoes.

Pastel carbayón: almond pastry.

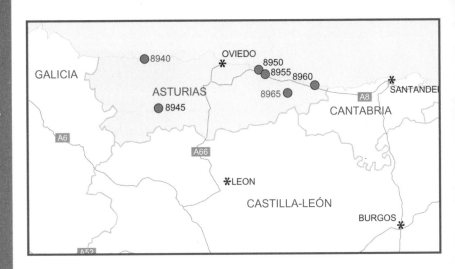

ES8945 Camping Lagos de Somiedo

Valle de Lago, E-33840 Somiedo (Asturias)

Tel: **985 763 776**

This is a most unusual gem of a small site in the Parque Natural de Somieda. Winding narrow roads with challenging rock overhangs, hairpin bends and breathtaking views (for 8 km.) finally bring you to the lake and campsite at an elevation of 1,200 m. This is a site for 4x4s, powerful small camper-vans and cars – not for medium or large motorhomes, and caravans are not accepted. It is not an approach for the faint hearted! The friendly Lana family make you welcome at their unique site, which is tailored for those who wish to explore the natural and cultural values of the Park without the 'normal' campsite amenities.

Facilities

There are British style toilets and free hot water to clean hot showers and washbasin. Facilities for babies and children. Washing machine. Combined reception, small restaurant, bar and reference section. Shop for bread, milk and other essentials, plus local produce and crafts. Horses for hire, trekking. Lectures on flora, fauna, history and culture. Fishing (licence required). Barbecue area. Small play area. Gas supplies. Off site: The very small village is 500 m. and it maintains the Spanish customs and traditions of this area.

Open: Easter - 15 October.

Directions

From N634 via Oviedo turn left at 442 km. marker on AS-15 signed Parque Natural de Somiedo. At 9 km. marker past village of Longoria, turn left on AS-227. At 38 km. marker, turn left into Pol de Somiedo, signed Centro Urbano. Follow signs for Valle de Lago and El Valle; 8 km. of hairpin bends from Pola, passing Urria on the left, brings you to the valley. Site is signed on the right.

Charges 2006

Per person	€ 4,50
child	€ 3,50
pitch incl. car	€ 7,00
electricity (motorcaravan only)	€ 2,50
All plus 7% VAT.	

ES8940 Camping Los Cantiles

Ctra N634, km. 502,7, E-33700 Luarca (Asturias)

Tel: **985 640 938**. Email: **cantiles@campingloscantiles.com**

Luarca is a picturesque little place with a pretty inner harbour and two sandy beaches, and Los Cantiles is two kilometres to the east of town on a cliff top that juts out into the sea, giving excellent views from some pitches and the sound of the waves to soothe you to sleep. The site is well maintained and is a pleasant place to stop along this under-developed coastline. The 150 pitches, 99 with electricity, are mostly on level grass, divided by huge hedges of hydrangeas and bushes. Some pitches have gravel surfaces. There is a separate area for late arrivals in high season.

Facilities

Two modern, fully equipped sanitary blocks (one in low season which is heated in winter) are kept very clean. Facilities for disabled people and babies. Laundry. Freezer service. Gas supplies. Small shop (July-Sept). Bar with hot snacks (1/7-15/9). Day room for backpackers with tables, chairs and cooking facilities (own gas). Bicycle hire. Torches helpful after midnight. English is spoken. Off site: Indoor swimming pool, sauna and fitness centre, plus a bar/restaurant and shop 300 m. Luarca 2 km. Beach and fishing 700 m. Riding 4 km.

Open: All year.

Directions

Luarca is 85 km. west of Gijon. From N632 Gijon - La Coru–a road turn south at 154 km. marker onto N634 for Luarca. After km. 502 marker east of Luarca, site is well signed to the left through an estate. GPS: N43:32.953 W06:31.459

Charges 2007

Per person	€ 4,00
child (4-10 yrs)	€ 3,50
pitch incl. electricity	€ 8,95 - € 10,95

Plus 7% VAT. No credit cards.

ES8960 Camping La Paz

Ctra N-634 Irun - Coruna, km. 292, E-33597 Vidiago-Llanes (Asturias)

Tel: **985 411 235**. Email: **delfin@campinglapaz.com**

This site occupies a spectacular location. The reception building is opposite a solid rock face and many hundred feet below the site and the climb to the upper part of the site is quite daunting but staff will place your caravan for you, although motorcaravan drivers will have an exciting drive to the top, especially to the loftier pitches. Once there, the views are absolutely outstanding, both along the coast and inland to the Picos de Europa mountains. There is also a lower section in a shaded valley to which access is easier, if rather tight in places.

Facilities

Four good, modern toilet blocks are well equipped and include controllable hot showers. They are kept very clean even at peak times. Baby bath. Full laundry facilities. Motorcaravan services. Restaurant and bar/snack bar with small shop (all season). Watersports. Games room. Fishing. Torches useful in some areas. English spoken. Off site: Shop, bar and restaurant in nearby village. Golf, riding, sailing and boat-launching all 8 km.

Open: Easter - 12 October.

Directions

Vidiago is 85 km. west of Santander. Site is signed from A8/N634 Santander - Oviedo/Gijón road near km. 292 marker (on non-motorway section).

Charges guide

Per person	€ 4,50
child	€ 4,15
pitch	€ 9,25 - € 10,75
electricity	€ 2,75

All plus 7% VAT.

ES8950 Camping Costa Verde

Playa de la Griega, E-33320 Colunga (Asturias)

Tel: **985 856 373**

This coastal site with a marked Spanish flavour is just 1.5 km. from the town of Colunga. Although little English is spoken, the cheerful owner and his helpful staff will make sure you get a warm welcome. The great advantage for many is that, 200 metres from the gate, is a spacious beach with a low tide lagoon, ideal for younger children. Some of the 200 pitches are occupied on a seasonal basis, but there are 155 for tourers. These are flat but with little shade and electricity (6A) is available (long leads needed in places). The site gets very busy in high season.

Facilities

The single toilet block is of a high standard with a mixture of British and Turkish style toilets (all British for ladies), large showers and free hot water throughout. Laundry. Well stocked shop. Bar/restaurant is traditional and friendly. Play area. Torches needed. Off site: Nearby towns of Ribadesella, Gijón and Oviedo. Excellent beaches. Fishing in river alongside site. Bicycle hire 2 km. Sailing 4 km. Golf and riding 18 km.

Open: Easter - 1 October.

Directions

Colunga is 45 km. east of Gijón. Leave the A8 Santander - Oviedo motorway at km. 345 exit and take N632 towards Colunga. In village, turn right on As257 towards Lastres; site is on right after 1 km.

Charges 2006

Per person	€ 4,20
pitch incl. electricity	€ 6,90 - € 10,30

VAT included.

ES8955 Camping Caravaning Arenal de Moris

A8 Salida 337, E-33344 Caravia Alta (Asturias)

Tel: **985 853 097**. Email: **camoris@teleline.es**

This smart, well run site is close to three fine sandy beaches so gets very busy at peak times. It has a backdrop of the mountains in the nature reserve known as the Sueve which is important for a breed of short Asturian horses, the 'Asturcone'. The site has 330 grass pitches (269 for touring units) of 40-70 sq.m. and with 200 electricity connections available (5A). With little shade, some pitches are terraced with others on an open, slightly sloping field with views of the sea. The restaurant with a terrace serves local dishes and overlooks the pool with hills and woods beyond.

Facilities

Three sanitary blocks provide comfortable, controllable showers (no dividers) and vanity style washbasins, laundry facilities and external dishwashing (cold water). Supermarket. Bar/restaurant. Swimming pool. Tennis. Play area in lemon orchard. English is spoken. Off site: Fishing 200 m. Golf 5 km. Riding, bicycle hire and sailing 10 km. Bar and restaurants in village 2 km. Beach 200 m.

Open: 1 June - 17 September.

Directions

Caravia Alta is 50 km. east of Gijón, Leave A8 Santander - Oviedo motorway at km. 337 exit, turn left on N632 towards Colunga and site is signed to right in village, near 16 km. marker.
GPS: N43:28.349 W05:10.999

Charges 2006

Per person	€ 5,00
child	€ 4,22
pitch incl. car	€ 7,60 - € 10,87
electricity	€ 3,20

ES8965 Camping Picos de Europa

E-33556 Avin-Onis (Asturias)

Tel: **985 844 070**. Email: **info@picos-europa.com**

This delightful site is, as its name suggests, an ideal spot from which to explore these dramatic limestone mountains on foot, by bicycle or on horseback. The site itself is newly developed and the dynamic owner, José or his nephew who helps out when he is away are both very pleasant and nothing is too much trouble. The site is in a valley beside a pleasant, fast flowing river. The 140 marked pitches are of varying sizes and have been developed in three avenues, on level grass backing on to hedging and with 6A electricity to all.

Facilities

Toilet facilities are in two separate buildings. Showers and some toilets are at the end of the reception building. Washing machine and dryer. The main toilets, plus more showers, baby bath, etc are near the pool. Shop and swimming pool (July - Sept). Bar and cafeteria style restaurant (all year) serves a good value 'menu del dia' and snacks. Fishing. Torches necessary. Off site: Riding 12 km. Golf 25 km. Coast at Llanes 25 km.

Open: All year.

Directions

Avin is 15 km. east of Cangas de Onison As114 road to Panes and is probably best approached from this direction especially if towing. From A8 (Santander - Oviedo) use km. 326 exit and N634 northwest to Arriondas. Turn southeast on N625 to Cangas and join As114 (Covodonga/Panes) by-passing Cangas. Site is just beyond Avin after 16 km. marker.
GPS: N43:20.178 W04:56.699

Charges 2006

Per person	€ 4,82
child (under 14 yrs)	€ 3,75
pitch	€ 5,00 - € 6,42
electricity	€ 3,21
All plus 7% VAT.	

MAP 4

The region of Cantabria in the north of Spain offers the best of both worlds. On the one hand there is the glorious coastline with beautiful beaches and pretty fishing villages; while inland there are a number of national parks including the mountainous, Picos de Europa.

CANTABRIA IS A ONE PROVINCE REGION

THE CAPITAL IS SANTANDER

The capital, Santander, is an elegant city which extends over a wide bay with views of the Cantabrian Sea. Its historic quarter is situated against a backdrop of sea and mountains, although the town is best known for its beaches; the Playa de la Magdalena, which has a summer windsurfing school, and the popular El Sardinero beach. There is also a Maritime Museum and Museum of Prehistory and Archaeology, plus a small zoo housed in the gardens of the old royal palace. A short distance from the city is the pretty medieval village of Santillana del Mar and the prehistoric caves of Altamira. Despite being closed indefinitely for restoration work, the adjacent Altamira Museum houses a replica of these caves and their impressive prehistoric drawings. Also on the outskirts of the capital is the Cabárceno Nature Park with more protected areas scattered around the region, including those at Oyambre, Peña Cabarga and Saja-Besaya. The largest is the mountain range of Picos de Europa, a national park which shares its territory with Asturias and Castilla-León. With river gorges, valleys, woodlands and an abundance of wildlife, it is popular with walkers, trekkers and climbers.

Places of interest

Castro Urdiales: beaches, Gothic church, Roman bridge, old quarter.

Comillas: rural town, beaches, Gaudí-designed villa.

Laredo: lively seaside resort, 13th church, 5 km. long sandy beach.

Lierganes: 17th and 18th architecture, spa.

Potes: on east side of Picos de Europa, mountain bike hire, paragliding available.

San Vicente de la Barquera: picturesque fishing port.

Cuisine of the region

Seafood is used a lot, including fresh shellfish, sardines, *rabas* (fried squid), *bocartes rebozados* (breaded whitebait). Cheese is produced throughout the region; *queso de nata* (cream cheese), *picón* from Treviso Bejes, and smoked cheeses from Áliva or Pido. A typical dish of the region is the Cantabrian stew, which contains haricot beans, cabbage, rice and sausage. Desserts include the traditional cheesecakes of the Pas Valley and pastries. The local tipple is *orujo*, a strong liquor.

Maganos encebollados: squid with onion.

Quesada: cheesecake.

Sobaos pasiegos: sponge cakes.

Sorropotún: type of fish stew.

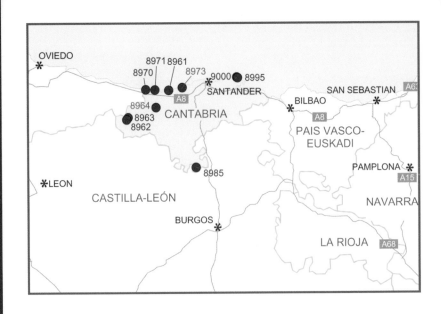

ES8961 Camping El Helguero

Ctra Santillana-Comillas, E-39527 Ruiloba (Cantabria)

Tel: 942 722 124. Email: reservas@campingelhelguero.com

This site, in a peaceful location surrounded by tall trees and impressive towering rock formations, caters for 240 units (of which 100 are seasonal) on slightly sloping ground. There are many marked pitches on different levels, all with access to electricity (5A), but with varying amounts of shade. There are also attractive tent and small camper sections set close in to the rocks and some site owned chalets. The site gets very crowded in high season, so it is best to arrive early if you haven't booked. The reasonably sized swimming pool and children's pool have access lifts for disabled campers.

Facilities

Three well placed toilet blocks, although old, are clean and all include controllable showers and hot and cold water to all basins. Facilities for children and disabled visitors. Washing machines and dryers. Motorcaravan services. Small supermarket (July/Aug). Bar/snack bar plus separate more formal restaurant. Swimming pool (caps compulsory). Playground. Activities and entertainment (high season). ATM. Torches useful in some places. Off site: Bus service 500 m. Bar/restaurants in village (walking distance). Beach, fishing, sailing, golf and riding, all 3 km. Santillana del Mar 12 km.

Open: 1 April - 30 September.

Directions

Site is 45 km. west of Santander. From A8 (Santander - Oviedo) take km. 249 exit (Cabezón and Comillas) and turn north on Ca135 towards Comillas, At km. 7 turn right on Ca359 to Ruilobuca and Barrio la Iglesia. After village turn right up hill on Ca358 to site on right (note: signs refer to 'Camping Ruiloba'). GPS: N43:22.973 W04:14.880

Charges 2007

Per person	€ 3,80 - € 4,50
child (4-10 yrs)	€ 3,30 - € 3,80
caravan or tent	€ 3,80 - € 4,50
motorcaravan	€ 7,60 - € 9,00
electricity	€ 3,45

Camping Cheques accepted.

Check real time availability and at-the-gate prices...

www.alanrogers.com

ES8962 Camping La Isla Picos de Europa

Picos de Europa, E-39570 Potes-Turieno (Cantabria)

Tel: **942 730 896**. Email: **campicoseuropa@terra.es**

La Isla is beside the road from Potes to Fuente Dé, with many mature trees giving good shade and glimpses of the mountains above. Established for over 25 years, a warm welcome awaits you from the owners (who speak good English) and a most relaxed and peaceful atmosphere exists in the site. The 121 unmarked pitches are arranged around an oval gravel track under a variety of fruit and ornamental trees. Electricity (6A) is available to all pitches, although some need long leads. A small bar and restaurant are located under dense trees by the small river which runs through the site.

Facilities

Single, clean and smart sanitary block retains the style of the site. It includes washbasins with cold water. Washing machine. Gas supplies. Freezer service. Small shop and restaurant/bar (all season). Small swimming pool (caps compulsory; 1/5-30/9). Play area. Barbecue area. Fishing. Bicycle hire. Riding. Off site: Shops, bars and restaurants plus Monday morning market in Potes 4 km. Fuente Dé and its spectcular cable-car ride 18 km.

Open: 1 April - 30 October.

Directions

Potes is 110 km. southwest of Santander. From A8/N634 (Santander - Oviedo) take km. 272 exit for Unquera. Take N621 south to Panes and travel up spectacular gorge (care needed if towing) to Potes. Site is on right of N621, 4 km. beyond Potes.

Charges guide

Per person	€ 3,30 - € 3,60
pitch incl. electricity	€ 8,90 - € 12,20

All plus VAT. Low season reductions.

ES8963 Camping La Viorna

Ctra Santa Toribio, E-39570 Potes (Cantabria)

Tel: **942 732 021**. Email: **campinglaviorna@hotmail.com**

The wonderful views of the valley below from the open terraces of this site with its spectacular backdrop of mountains make it an attractive base from which to tour this region or to relax by the excellent swimming pool. It is popular with both families and couples. There are beds of flowers and the trees are maturing, providing shade on many pitches. Access is good for all sizes of unit to the 115 pitches of around 70 sq.m, all of which have electricity (3 or 6A). In high season, however, tents may be placed on less accessible, steeply sloping areas.

Facilities

Single, neat sanitary block of high standard, clean and modern. Washbasins have cold water only. Facilities for disabled visitors double as unit for babies (key). Laundry facilities. Shop. Restaurant/bar with terrace (all season). Swimming pool (23 x 13 m) and children's pool (15/5-30/9; caps compulsory). Play area. Games room. Many sporting activities arranged such as parascending, mountain biking, trekking, rafting and canoeing. Off site: Potes with shops, restaurants and bars 1.5 km. Bicycle hire 1 km. Fishing and riding 1.5 km.

Open: Easter/1 April - 30 October.

Directions

Potes is 110 km. southwest of Santander. From A8/N634 (Santander - Oviedo) take km. 272 exit for Unquera (end of motorway section). Take N621 south to Panes and up spectacular gorge (care needed if towing) to Potes. After town take left fork signed Toribio de Liébana and site is on right after 800 m. GPS: N43:09.261 W04:38.609

Charges guide

Per person	€ 3,20 - € 3,50
pitch incl. electricity	€ 10,70 - € 11,80

All plus VAT.

ES8964 Camping El Molino de Cabuerniga

Sopeña de Cabuérniga, Ctra C625, km 42, E-39510 Cabuérniga (Cantabria)

Tel: **942 706 259**. Email: **cmcabuernigа@campingcabuerniga.com**

Located in a peaceful valley with magnificent views of the mountains, beside the Saja river and only a short walk from the picturesque and unspoiled village of Sopeña, this gem of a site is on an open, level, grassy meadow with trees. Wonderful stone buildings and artefacts are a feature of this unique site. There are 102 marked pitches, all with electricity (3/6A), although long leads may be needed in places. This comfortable site is very good value and ideal for a few nights (or you may well choose to stay longer once there) whilst you explore the Cabuérniga Valley.

Facilities

A single, modern sanitary block provides spacious, controllable showers. Washing machines. Unit for disabled campers. Baby and toddler room. Bar serving breakfasts and 'bocadillos' (sandwiches) includes small shop section. Wonderful playground in rustic setting – supervision recommended. Fishing. Bicycle hire. Off site: Bus service 500 m. Restaurant in village 1 km. Riding and bicycle hire 3 km. Golf 20 km. Beach 20 km. Skiing 50 km.

Open: All year.

Directions

From A8 (Santander - Oviedo) take km. 249 exit and join N634 to Cabezón de la Sal. Turn southwest on Ca180 towards Reinosa for 11 km. to Sopeña (site signed to left). Turn into village (watch for low gutters) bearing right following small site signs.

Charges 2006

Per person	€ 4,00
pitch incl. electricity	€ 11,50

All plus VAT.

ES8970 Camping Las Arenas-Pechon

Ctra Pechon - Unquera, km. 2, E-39594 Pechon (Cantabria)

Tel: **942 717 188**. Email: **lasarenas@ctv.es**

This site is in a very quiet, but rather spectacular location bordering the sea and the Tina Mayor estuary, with views to the mountains and access to an attractive little beach. Otherwise, enjoy the pleasant kidney shaped pool that also shares the views. Taking 350 units, half the site has grassy pitches (60 sq.m) in bays or on terraces with stunning sea and mountain views. There are some quite steep slopes to tackle – reception is at the top, as are the bar and restaurant (the latter has a terrace with fantastic views of the estuary and of the mountains beyond).

Facilities

Clean, well tiled sanitary facilities are in the older, simple style. Various blocks include showers (no divider; add hot water to the cold by pushing a switch). Washing machines. Well stocked supermarket. Restaurant/bar and snack bar (all season). Small playground. Fishing. Riding arranged (collected from site). Torches helpful. English is spoken. Off site: Shops, bars and restaurants in Pechón , plus a disco/bar 1 km. Golf 28 km.

Open: 1 June - 30 September.

Directions

On A8 from Santander, take km. 272 exit for Unquera (N621) at end of motorway section. Take first exit Ca380 signed Pechón and site. From Oviedo/Gijón on A8/N634 at km. 272 take N621 slip-road for Unquera (do not join motorway), then as above. GPS: N43:23.491 W04:30.635

Charges guide

Per person	€ 4,50
pitch incl. electricity	€ 10,60 - € 13,40

All plus 7% VAT.

ES8971 Camping Caravaning Playa de Oyambre

San Vicente de la Barquera, Finca Peña Guerra, E-39547 San Vicente de la Barquera (Cantabria)

Tel: **942 711 461**. Email: **camping@oyambre.com**

This exceptionally well managed site is ideally positioned to use as a base to visit the spectacular Picos de Europa or one of the many sandy beaches along this northern coast. Despite its name, it is in fact a kilometre from the beach on foot, further if you go by car. The 100 touring pitches all have 10A electricity (long leads needed in places). The fairly flat central area is allocated to tents while caravans are mainly sited on wide terraces (access to some could be a little tight for larger units) and there is some shade. There may be some traffic noise on the lower terraces.

Facilities

Good, clean sanitary facilities are in one, well kept block. Showers are spacious but have a frustrating mixture of push-button hot and ordinary cold controls. Facilities for babies and disabled visitors. Washing machines. Motorcaravan services. Well stocked supermarket (15/6-15/9). Restaurant. Bar and takeaway. Swimming pools with lifeguard (1/6-15/9). Playground. Off site: Bus service at site entrance. Fishing and superb beach 1 km. Golf 2 km. Riding 5 km. San Vicente de la Barquera 5 km.

Open: Easter/1 April - 30 September.

Directions

From A8 (Santander - Oviedo) take exit at km. 258 (Caviedes) and join N634. Turn towards San Vicente. Site is signed at junction to Comillas, at km. 265 on the E70, 5 km. east of San Vicente. The entrance is quite steep. Another 'Camping La Playa' at Oyambre within 500 m. (on the beach) is not recommended.

Charges 2007

Per person	€ 4,15
pitch incl. electricity	€ 11,50

All plus VAT.

ES8973 Camping Santillana

Ctra de Comilias s/n, E-39330 Santillana del Mar (Cantabria)

Tel: **942 818 250**. Email: **complejosantillana@cantabria.com**

This is an attractive site on a hill above the charming mediaeval village of Santillana del Mar and five to ten kilometres from some of Costa Verde's good beaches. There are 400 pitches, all with access to electricity (5A), some mainly for tents informally arranged on a slope, with others for caravans and motorcaravans on the lower part of the site. Where the pitches are numbered but unmarked some overcrowding may occur in high season and those alongside the road will experience some noise as this is a busy route. There are also 64 chalets and mobile homes for hire.

Facilities

Toilet blocks are well placed (only one open in low season), fully equipped and with facilities for disabled campers. Washing machines. Supermarket and souvenir shop (1/6-30/9). Bar/restaurant and self-service café (all year). Swimming pool (1/5-30/9). Play areas. Minigolf. Tennis. Bicycle hire. Entertainment in high season. Off site: Riding 300 m. Fishing 5 km.

Open: All year.

Directions

Santillana is 30 km. west of Santander. From A8 (Santander - Oviedo) take km. 234 exit west of Torrelavega and follow Ca133 north to Santillana. Turn left at T-junction (busy) towards Comillas and site is 300 m. GPS: N43:25.572 W04:06.789

Charges 2006

Per person	€ 4,80 - € 5,46
pitch	€ 6,00 - € 9.13

No credit cards. Camping Cheques accepted.

ES9000 Camping Playa Joyel

Playa de Ris, E-39180 Noja (Cantabria)

Tel: **942 630 081**. Email: **playajoyel@telefonica.net**

This very attractive holiday and touring site is some 40 kilometres from Santander and 80 kilometres from Bilbao. It is a busy, high quality, comprehensively equipped site by a superb beach providing 1,000 well shaded, marked and numbered pitches with 3A electricity available. These include 80 large pitches of 100 sq.m. Some 250 pitches are occupied by tour operators or seasonal units. This well managed site has a lot to offer for family holidays with much going on in high season when it gets crowded.The swimming pool complex with lifeguard is free to campers and the superb beaches are cleaned daily 15/6-20/9. One of the beach exits leads to the main beach, or if you turn left out of the other you will find a safe, placid estuary with water at rising tide. An unusual feature is the natural park within the site boundary which has a great selection of animals to see. It overlooks a protected area of marsh where European birds spend the winter. There are security patrols at night.

Facilities

Six excellent, spacious and fully equipped toilet blocks include baby baths. Large laundry. Motorcaravan services. Gas supplies. Freezer service. Supermarket (all season). General shop. Kiosk. Restaurant and takeaway (1/7-31/8). Bar and snacks (all season). Swimming pools, bathing caps compulsory (20/5-15/9). Entertainment organised with a soundproof pub/disco (July-Aug). Gym park. Tennis. Playground. Riding. Fishing. Natural animal park. Hairdresser (July/Aug). Medical centre. Torches necessary in some areas. Dogs and other animals are not accepted. Off site: Bicycle hire and large sports complex with multiple facilities including an indoor pool 1 km. Sailing and boat launching 10 km. Riding and golf 20 km.

Open: Easter - 30 September.

Directions

From A8 (Bilbao - Santander) take km. 185 exit and N634 towards Beranga. Almost immediately turn right on Ca147 to Noja. In 10 km. turn left at multiple campsite signs and go through town. At beach roundabout turn left and continue to site at end of road. GPS: N43:29.369 W03:32.220

Charges 2007

Per person	€ 3,70 - € 5,50
child (3-9 yrs)	€ 2,50 - € 4,00
pitch	€ 12,00 - € 21,00
electricity	€ 3,00 - € 4,00

All plus 7% VAT. No credit cards.

Camping Cheques accepted.

ES8985 Camping Valderredible

Ctra Polientes - Ruerrero s/n, Valderredible, E-39220 Polientes (Cantabria)

Tel: **942 776 138**. Email: **valderrecamp@mundivia.es**

This is a pleasant site owned and designed by the Gutierrez brothers, José and Jesús, who are very keen to welcome you. The site is about 110 km. south of Santander and could provide a peaceful break on the way south – you might just decide to stay! All the facilities on the site are modern and kept spotlessly clean. There are 80 flat pitches for tourers (60 with 6A electricity) and an area for tents. Trees have been planted, although there is little shade at the moment. The pools enjoy river and mountain views, as does the patio to the bar/snack bar.

Facilities

The good central sanitary block is fully equipped and comfortable. Two washing machines (free) and a dryer. No facilities for disabled campers. Small well stocked shop. Bar selling tapas and more formal restaurant, good service and reasonably priced. Swimming pool and children's pool (1/7-15/9; caps required). Play area (supervision required). Off site: Canoeing and fishing in river Ebro 200 m. (March - June). Riding and bicycle hire 15 km. Bars and restaurant in village 800 m.

Open: 1 April - 4 November.

Directions

Polientes is west of the N623 Burgos - Santander road. Near km. 61, north of village of Quintanilla Escalada, turn west on Bu643/Ca275 towards Polientes. Site is signed along the 21 km. of road and is just past village of Ruijas. GPS: N42:48.358 W03:55.651

Charges guide

Per person	€ 3,30 - € 3,50
child (3-10 yrs)	€ 3,00 - € 3,10
pitch	€ 6,80 - € 7,20
electricity	€ 2,50
Plus 7% VAT.	

ES8995 Camping Los Molinos

Ctra La Ria s/n, E-39180 Noja (Cantabria)

Tel: **942 630 426**. Email: **losmolinos@ceoecant.es**

Camping Los Molinos is close to the village of Noja, a seaside resort that gets very busy in high season. It is on the coast of Cantabria, a ten minute walk from the Playa del Ris beach which has fine sand and clear water. The site is divided into two main areas, both with a large number of permanent units, some of which look a little run down. There are 180 average sized touring pitches for caravans or motorcaravans on level ground, but with little shade; all have 3A electricity. A large separate area without electricity is used for tents.

Facilities

Four fully equipped toilet blocks, two recently refurbished, are kept clean. Facilities for disabled campers. Washing machines. Supermarkets and butcher (1/6-30/9). Restaurant (July/Aug). Bars and café bar serving tapas and pizzas (1/6-30/9). Swimming pool and children's pool with lifeguard (24/6-4/9). Play area. Tennis. Medical room. ATM. Torch useful. Off site: Beach and fishing 300 m. Indoor pool and bicycle hire 500 m. Golf 9 holes 1 km, 18 holes 20 km. Boat launching 7 km. Riding 10 km. Free bus hourly to the beach and town in high season.

Open: 1 June - 30 September.

Directions

From A8 (Bilbao - Santander) take km. 185 exit, join N634 towards Beranga and almost immediately turn right on Ca147 to Noja. In 10 km. turn left and go down through town. At beach roundabout turn left and then left again just before Camping Playa Joyel at large sign for site. GPS: N43:29.155 W03:32.281

Charges 2007

Per person	€ 4,50 - € 6,00
child	€ 3,00 - € 4,50
pitch	€ 8,50 - € 12,00
electricity	€ 3,00
No credit cards.	

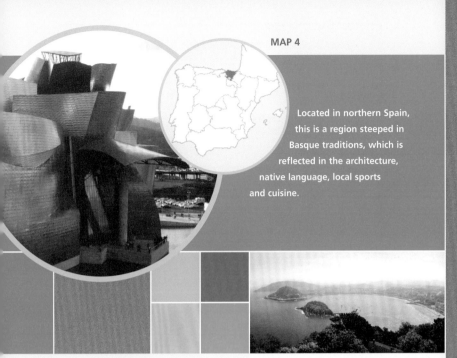

MAP 4

Located in northern Spain, this is a region steeped in Basque traditions, which is reflected in the architecture, native language, local sports and cuisine.

Pais Vasco-Euskadi

THERE ARE THREE PROVINCES: ALAVA, GIPUZKOA AND BIZKAIA

THE REGIONAL CAPITAL IS VITORIA

The province of Gipuzkoa adjoins France in the east. Its capital, San Sebastian, is a bustling, picturesque seaside town with a strong Basque identity. Overlooking La Concha Bay and enclosed by rolling low hills, this popular resort boasts four good beaches, including the celebrated La Concha Beach. As cider production is one of oldest traditions in Basque country there are also plenty of sidrerías (cider houses) to visit. Heading along the rocky fringe of Costa Vasca towards Bilbao in Bizkaia are more excellent beaches and pretty fishing villages including Orio, Zarautz and Getaria. The biggest attraction in Bilbao is the famous Guggenheim Museum. Opened in 1997 this spectacular building is completely covered with titanium sheets and houses a collection of modern and contemporary art from around the world. The city also boasts a beautiful old quarter with a Gothic cathedral, the Plaza Nueva and a museum. Further inland in Alava is Vitoria, the region's capital. Its medieval streets intermingle with Renaissance Palaces and fine churches and are lined with lively bars and tavernas. In the summer the city plays host to a jazz festival. Elsewhere in the province are several nature reserves.

Places of interest

Encartanciones: one of the world's largest cave chambers Torca del Carlista, wildlife sanctuary

Hondarribia: fishing port, beaches, charming walled old town

Laguardia: old walled town with cobbled streets, historic buildings, in wine-growing district of Rioja Alavesa

Oñati: Baroque architecture, old university

Tolosa: impressive old town square, carnival in February

Zarautz: seaside town, famous for production of *txakoli*

Zumaia: beaches, good coastal walks, July fiesta with Basque sports, dancing and bull racing

Cuisine of the region

Basque cuisine is considered to be the finest in Spain. Tapas or *pintxos* is readily available in bars, served with the local white wine *txakoli*. Fish is popular, especially *bacalao* (cod) and seafood is often used to make casseroles and sauces. Lots of milk based desserts. Founded in the 19th century, the tradition of dining clubs or *txokos* are unique to the Basque country

Alubias pochas: white haricot bean stew

Chipirones en su tinta: squid cooked in its ink

Goxua: sponge cake with whipped cream and caramel

Intxaursalsa: milk pudding with cinnamon and walnuts

Marmitaco: fish and potato stew

Pantxineta: custard slice

ES9035 Camping Portuondo

Ctra Gernika - Bermeo, E-48360 Mundaka (Bizkaia)

Tel: **946 877 701**. Email: **recepcion@campingportuondo.com**

From some of the 98 pitches on this well kept site there are stunning views over the ocean and estuary. Among the lovely gardens, the pitches are mainly for tents and smaller vans, but there are six large pitches at the lower levels for caravans and motorhomes. However, it must be stressed that access is difficult as the road is very steep and there is no turning space. In high season (July/August) it is best to ring to book your space. English is spoken and the friendly owner Imanol and his staff are keen to help you.

Facilities

Two fully equipped toilet blocks can be heated and include mostly British WCs and a smart baby room. Washing machines and dryers. Shop . Bar and two restaurants, all open to public (16/1-14/12). Takeaway (15/6-15/9). Swimming pools (15/6-15/9). Barbecue area. Torches may be helpful. Off site: Fishing 100 m. Beaches 500 m bracing walk. Surfing on Mundaka beach 500 m. Boat launching 1 km. Shops, bars and restaurants 2 km. Riding 8 km. Bicycle hire 10 km. Golf 40 km. Buses to Bilbao and Gernika (every 30 mins) 300 m.

Open: All year.

Directions

Mundaka is 35 km. northeast of Bilbao. From A8 (San Sebastián - Bilbao) take exit 18 and follow signs for Gernika on Bi635. Continue on Bi2235 towards Bermeo. Site is on right approaching Mundaka but because of oblique, steep (18%) access, continue nearly 2 km. and use slip road to turn in filling station on left. GPS: N43:23.951 W02:41.766

Charges 2006

Per person	€ 4,75 - € 5,20
child (under 10 yrs)	€ 3,95 - € 4,55
pitch	€ 10,00 - € 10,45
incl. electricity	€ 13,40 - € 13,85

All plus 7% VAT. Less 5-10% for longer stays.

ES9045 Camping Angosto

Ctra Villanañe - Angosto no. 2, E-01425 Villanañe (Araba)

Tel: 945 353 271. Email: info@camping-angosto.com

This is a smart eco-friendly site with excellent facilities surrounded by wooded hills near the Valderejo National Park. Opened in 1999, the facilities are improving every year remaining smart and clean. A keen young team run things here and the site is geared towards families. In high season it is bustling and very Spanish! The 80 touring pitches are flat and of average size, 56 having electricity. There is a large area for tents. Young trees have been planted around the site and are beginning to provide a little shade. The attractive new, heated pool has a sliding roof for inclement weather.

Facilities

Fully equipped and well maintained toilet block with facilities for disabled campers. Washing machine. Good shop (1/3-30/9). Stylish bar with takeaway and separate restaurant. Small fenced play area close to entrance and grass toddler play area. Activities for children (high season). Mountain bike hire. Fishing. Ice machine. Off site: Many outdoor activities arranged locally. Riding 30 km. Sailing 40 km. Golf 45 km. Sea 60 km.

Open: 15 February - 30 November

Directions

Villanañe is 25 km. northwest of Miranda de Ebro. From Miranda de Ebro, take A1 towards Burgos, leave at exit 5 and take A2122 to Puentelarrá and on to Espejo. From N1 Burgos - Vitoria road, turn north on A2625 (west of Ameyugo) to Sta Gadea and Espejo. Site is just after village, clearly signed. GPS: N42:50.548 W03:04.119

Charges 2006

Per person	€ 3,70
pitch	€ 3,45 - € 4,20

All plus 7% VAT.

ES9039 Gran Camping Zarautz

Monte Talai-Mendi, Ctra N634 San Sebastian - Bilbao, E-20800 Zarautz (Gipuzkoa)

Tel: 943 831 238. Email: info@grancampingzarautz.com

This friendly site sits alongside vines high in the hills to the east of the Basque town of Zarautz and has commanding views of the excellent beaches and the island of Getaria. A quarter of the 400 pitches are seasonal which brings Spanish life and colour to the site at weekends and in high season. The pitches are of average size, shaded by mature trees and are reasonably level; 200 have 5A electricity. We recommend a call to reserve (if you are lucky!) one of the perimeter pitches which enjoy magnificent views over the bay.

Facilities

Three well-equipped toilet blocks, one heated in winter. The central one is more modern and has facilities for disabled campers and a third block serves an outlying area. Washing machines. Bar/snack-bar with TV plus terrace. Play area. Restaurant with menú del dia and á la carte meals. Well stocked shop (all facilities open all year). Off site: Beach and fishing 1 km. Golf (9 holes) 2 km. Bicycle hire 3 km. Shops, restaurants, bars, indoor pool plus bus/train services in Zarautz 2 km.

Open: All year.

Directions

Zarautz is 20 km. west of San Sebastián. From the A8 (San Sebastián - Bilbao) take exit 11 for Zarautz and turn east on N634 towards Orio. Entrance road to site is on left in 200 m. If using the N634 coast road, site is signed near km. 17 marker. GPS: N43:17.410 W02:08.780

Charges 2007

Per person	€ 4,70
pitch incl. car	€ 9,90

VAT included. Camping Cheques accepted.

ES9030 Camping Igueldo

Paseo Padre Orkolaga no. 69, Barrio de Igueldo, E-20008 San Sebastian (Gipuzkoa)

Tel: 943 214 502. Email: info@campingigueldo.com

A five kilometre drive from the city takes you to this terraced campsite, high above San Sebastian, between the mountains and the sea. It offers mostly level, shaded, small (max. 70 sq.m.) grass pitches with electricity and drainage. The restaurant and bar are open all year and a sun terrace looks toward the mountains. An excellent bus service to and from San Sebastian runs every 30 minutes (all year). There are 17 attractive chalets to rent at the entrance to the site. With few sporting facilities, this site is for those wishing to mix quiet surroundings with city life. English is spoken in reception.

Facilities

Three traditional toilet blocks are clean and light. Facilities for disabled people and babies (accessed by key). Motorcaravan service point. Shop for basics (20/6-15/9). Bar/restaurant (all year, Wed-Sun in early/late season, every day in summer). Play area. Off site: The town is within walking distance with shops, restaurants and bars. Bicycle hire and fishing 5 km. Beach 5 km. Golf 9 km.

Open: All year.

Directions

From A8 exit 8 for San Sebastian West (oeste). At Playa de Ondarreta, follow beach road. At T-junction turn left. Keep right on Pase O De Igueldo. Continue for 5 km. to site. GPS: N43:18.276 W02:02.763

Charges 2006

Per unit incl. 2 persons	€ 14,30 - € 27,00
electricity	€ 3,50

All plus 7% VAT. Special winter prices available.

MAP 4

This small region located in the north eastern part of the country is the most outstanding wine-growing area in Spain. Its production, Rioja wine, figures among the finest wines in the world.

THIS IS A ONE PROVINCE REGION

THE CAPITAL IS LOGROÑO.

The capital of the region Logroño did not gain importance till the 11th century, when the rise in popularity of the Pilgrims' Route to Santiago de Compostela attracted people. Indeed the 12th century Codex Calixtinus, the first guide to the route, mentions the city. And throughout the region, every town along the way has a church dedicated to the saint. Pilgrimages aside, La Rioja is best known for its wine. At the centre of the region's wine production is Haro, a stately town northwest of Logroño, and obviously a good place to stock up on a bottle or two! For those interested in the wine processes the Museum of Wine is worth a visit; admission includes cheese and wine tasting. During the last week of June the town comes alive with festivities. With free outdoor concerts, costumed characters on giant stilts, wine tastings and bargain buys, the climax of these fiestas is the Battle of the Wine, where thousands of people happily gather to be drenched in wine.

Places of interest

Calahorra: main town in Lower Rioja, Cathedral Museum.

Ezcaray: in the Sierra de la Demanda mountains, the surrounding area is made up of streams, forests and peaks over 2,000 metres high.

Nájera: monastery of Santa María la Real, built in 1032, History and Archaeological Museum.

San Millán de la Cogolla: traditional town, Monasteries of Suso and Yuso where the first texts written in Spanish are preserved.

Santo Domingo de la Calzada: last great staging post of the Pilgrim's Route in La Rioja, Cathedral of San Salvador.

Cuisines of the region

Asparagus, beans, peppers, garlic, artichokes and other vegetables and pulses are the basic ingredients of a long list of dishes such as vegetable stew, potatoes a la riojana, lamb cutlets with vine shoots or stuffed peppers. Traditional desserts include pears in wine, almond pastries from Arnedo or marzipan from Soto.

Camerano Cheese: cheese made from goat's milk, typical of La Rioja, usually eaten as a dessert with honey.

Fardelejo: pastry cake filled with marzipan.

Riojan-style potatoes: prepared with chorizo, peppers, garlic and lamp chops (optional).

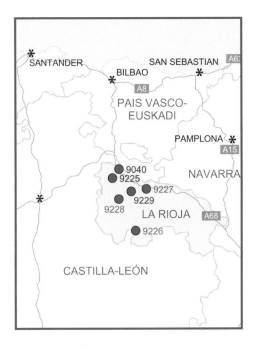

ES9040 Camping de Haro

Avenida Miranda 1, E-26200 Haro (La Rioja)
Tel: **941 312 737**. Email: **campingdeharo@fer.es**

This quiet riverside site is on the outskirts of Haro, the commercial centre for the renowned Rioja wines. It is a family run site with excellent pools. Staff in the modern reception are helpful and you may well get a cheery welcome from Carlos, the owner's son, who speaks excellent English. All of the 230 pitches are on level ground and of reasonable size. About 50% are occupied on a seasonal basis. Many of the touring pitches have some shade, a few have a great deal. Electricity connections are provided, although long leads may be required on some pitches.

Facilities

Two toilet blocks, one heated in winter, the other with facilities for disabled campers. Laundry. Bar/snack bar with small counter selling basic provisions and adjacent swimming pool (16/6-18/9). Play area and animation for children in season. Fishing. Torch useful. Off site: Large municpal pool complex nearby. Shops, bars, restaurants within walking distance. Bicycle hire 1 km. Riding 3 km. Boat launching 6 km. Golf 20 km.

Open: All year excl. 10 December - 10 January.

Directions

Haro is between Miranda de Ebro and Logroño. From A68 (Bilbao - Logroño) take exit 9 to Haro. Keep to LR-111 (Vitoria) bearing left, crossing lights and over river where site is signed to left. From N124 (Vitoria - Logroño) leave at exit north of Haro onto LR-111 towards town and turn right before bridge (site signed). Avoid other turnings into town centre! GPS: N42:34.691 W02:51.257

Charges 2006

Per person	€ 3,40 - € 4,01
child (3-10 yrs)	€ 2,70 - € 3,17
pitch	€ 5,56 - € 6,90
electricity (3/6A)	€ 3,25

Camping Cheques accepted.

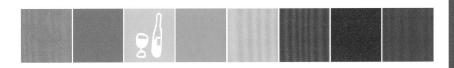

ES9225 Camping De La Rioja

Ctra. de Haro - Sto. Domingo de la Calzada, E-26240 Castanares de Rioja (La Rioja)

Tel: **941 300174**. Email: **info@campingdelarioja.com**

This site is situated just beyond the town of Castanares de Rioja. This is a busy site during the peak season with many sporting activities taking place. In low season it becomes rather more quiet with limited facilities available. There are 30 level, grass touring pitches, out of a total of 250, and these are separated by hedges and trees allowing privacy. Each has their own water, drainage and electricity connection. To the rear of the site is the Oja River which is ideal for fishing and there are views of the Obarenes mountains in the distance. Some noise from the main road is possible.

Facilities

The central sanitary facilities are old and traditional in style but clean. Open style washbasins and controllable showers. Laundry and dishwashing facilities. Shop, bar, restaurant, takeaway (on request) all open 20/6-20/9. Outdoor swimming pool (20/6-20/9 supervised). Multisport court. Football. Volleyball. Tennis. River fishing. Riding. Children's cycle circuit. Play area. No individual barbecues. Off site: Town centre 1.5 km. The Guggenheim Museum in Bilbao. City of San Sebastian with beaches and aquarium.

Open: 1 January - 9 December.

Directions

Head west on N120. Turn right onto LR111 signed Castanares de Rioja. Continue through town towards Haro. Site is on left, 800 m. after leaving town speed restriction.

Charges 2006

Per person	€ 5,20
child	€ 4,50
pitch	€ 11,40
electricity	€ 3,15

ES9226 Camping Los Cameros

Ctra de la Virgen de Lomos de Orios, km. 3, E-26125 Villoslada de Cameros (La Rioja)

Tel: **941 747021**. Email: **info@camping-loscameros.com**

Situated 3 km. from the small town of Villoslada de Cameros, this site is in a quiet location, in a valley surrounded by tree-covered mountains. The area provides the opportunity for plenty of hill walking and a footpath from the site takes you into the town. Of the 150 pitches, 40 are available for touring. They are open with some shade and have 5A electricity. This is a simple site with limited facilities available but it is well kept and has character; ideal for relaxation.

Facilities

One heated sanitary block provides WCs, washbasins with cold water only (one with hot water) and cubicled showers. No facilities for disabled visitors. Cold water only for washing machine and dishwashing. No shop but bread and gas available. Bar with games. Restaurant with comprehensive menu and takeaway to order. Playing field and play area. Picnic area. Off site: Town 3 km. with shops, bars and restaurants and swimming pool.

Open: All year.

Directions

From Logrono (AP68) turn left onto N111 heading south towards Soria and Madrid. At sign for Villoslada de Cameros turn right, pass the centre and turn left by camping sign (LR448). Site on left in 3 km. Road bumpy and uneven, drive with care and watch for animals on road.

Charges 2006

Per person	€ 4,25
child (under 10 yrs)	€ 3,60
pitch incl. electricity	€ 7,93 - € 12,88

ES9227 Camping Navarrete

Ctra de Entrena km. 1, E-26370 Navarrete (La Rioja)

Tel: **941 440169**. Email: **campingnavarette@fer.es**

Camping Navarrete is a spotlessly clean site in which the owners take great pride. Ideal as a base for exploring the surrounding countryside and sampling wonderful wines as it is located in the heart of La Rioja. Many of the 180 pitches are taken up by static caravans but a designated grassy area has been set aside for 40 unmarked, spacious touring pitches with 5A electricity connections. Some have shade and there are good views of the Rioja valley. Facilities on site are limited until the height of the season but the area is surrounded by many villages and places of artistic and historical importance. Possible traffic noise from main road.

Facilities

One modern central sanitary block is clean. No facilities for disabled visitors. Laundry facilities. Shop (15/6-15/9). Bar and takeaway (both limited opening in low season). Restaurant. Motorcaravan services. Outdoor swimming and paddling pools (15/6-15/9). Tennis. Bicycle hire. Unfenced play area. No barbecues on pitches. Off site: Large town of Logrono 10 km.

Open: All year.

Directions

From Logroño proceed west along AP68. Exit at junction 11 signed Navarrete. At town centre turn left onto LR137 signed Entrena. Site on right in 800 m.

Charges 2006

Per person	€ 3,95 - € 4,55
child (under 10 yrs)	€ 3,65 - € 4,15
pitch incl. electricity	€ 7,40 - € 12,25

ES9228 Camping Berceo

Ctra de Nájera - Sto. Domingo, E-26227 Berceo (La Rioja)

Tel: **941 373227**

Camping Berceo would ideally suit those looking for a quiet break at a site with limited facilities. It sits low in the San Millan valley in the heart of the Sierra de la Demanda and a steep walk of about 20 minutes will take you into the village. Here you will find several bars and restaurants, but little English is spoken. The 30 touring pitches are varied in size and separated by hedges. Some have shade and there are views of the green valley and mountains. Apart from the swimming pool which is open in peak season, there are few activities provided.

Facilities

One main toilet block providing sufficient facilities, but none for disabled visitors. Laundry and dishwashing areas. Shop for basic supplies. Bar/restaurant. Takeaway on request. TV in bar and games area. Swimming and paddling pools. Play area. Off site: Berceo village 20 minute uphill walk. San Millan monasteries.

Open: All year.

Directions

From A68 head west until N120 exit. Turn left onto N120 signed Najera. Turn left onto LR113 (Bobadilla). Within 5 km. turn right onto 205 (Cárdenas) until Berceo village. In village centre follow site arrow down steep hill. Site on left within 500 m.

Charges 2006

Per person	€ 4,20
child	€ 3,60
pitch	€ 4,20 - € 8,50
electricity	€ 3,00

ES9229 Camping El Ruedo

Pso. San Julián 24, E-26300 Najera (La Rioja)

Tel: **941 360102**

Camping El Ruedo is situated 500 m. from the town of Najera and the river Rio Najerilla runs close by. There are numerous walks possible and seating provided along the riverbank. This is a small site with a total of 20 touring pitches on level ground, unmarked and with no separation. You can pitch at your own discretion. The traditional style sanitary block is kept clean and tidy with ample provision for the small amount of visitors. Extremely quiet and with very basic facilities, this site would suit those looking for peace and tranquillity. The site is not suitable for large units. No English is spoken.

Facilities

One immaculate toilet block with washbasins and showers. No facilities for disabled visitors. Washing machines (rather old). No shop, but provisions in town. Swings. No site lighting so torches useful. Off site: Town 500 m. (10 minutes walk).

Open: 1 April - 10 September.

Directions

From Logrono head west on AP68 until sign for N120 Najera. Turn left onto LR113 signed Najera. At traffic lights turn sharp left immediately before cobbled bridge. Site on left within 500 m. Poorly signed after A12.

Charges 2006

Per person	€ 4,20
child (under 10 yrs)	€ 4,00
pitch	€ 4,00 - € 8,00
electricity	€ 3,00

MAP 5

The region of Navarra lie the north of Spain, sepa from France by the Pyre With mountain retreats, beautiful valleys and an ar of attractive towns and histor buildings, it is also popular for thos wishing to follow the Pilgrim's Rou to Santiago de Compostela.

THERE IS ONLY ONE PROVINCE ALSO KNOWN AS NAVARRA

THE CAPITAL IS PAMPLONA

Founded by the Roman general Pompey in 75 BC, the region's capital Pamplona is perhaps best known for the Fiestas de San Fernmín (July), when the encierro takes place – a tradition which involves people running through the streets in front of bulls. The city also boasts its fair share of sights including the old town, with its ancient churches and elegant buildings. Outside the city is the Sierra de Aralar, with well-marked paths of all grades. A wander through here will take you past waterfalls and caves and in Excelsis you'll come across Navarra's oldest church, the Sanctuario de San Miguel, a popular pilgrimage destination. In the south, the historic medieval town of Olite is home to an outstanding 15th century castle, with turrets galore, and a Romanesque and Gothic church. To the west is the Urbasa and Andía Nature Reserve. Further north and in the east, the villages and valleys of the Pyrenees provide some of the most beautiful landscapes in the province and offer the perfect place to relax. Of particular note are the Valle de Baztán and the Valle de Salazar. For the more active, the Valle de Roncal is a good place to explore the mountains as is the Pirenaico National Park.

Places of interest

Andía Nature Reserve: forests, ponds, wildlife including the golden eagle, wild boar and wildcat.

Camino de Santiago: ancient Pilgrim's route. There are variants but the most popular point of entry into Spain was the pass of Roncesvalles, in the Pyrenees. It then continues south through Navarra via Sangüesa, Puente La Reina and Estella, then west through the provinces of La Rioja and Castilla-León till it reaches Santiago in the Galicia province.

Orreaga-Roncesvalles: a town established as a sanctuary and hospital in 1132 and first staging post for pilgrims, museum with exhibition on Pilgrim's Route.

Sangüesa: small town, 14th century churches, medieval hospital.

Ujué: medieval defensive village, Romanesqe church.

Cuisine of the region

Typical products found in abundance in this area include asparagus grown on the river banks, small red peppers and artichokes from Tudela, pork from Estella, cherries from Ciriza, cheese made in the Roncal Valley and *chorizo* from Pamplona.

Ajoarriero: cod cooked with garlic, potato, 'choricero' peppers and tomatoes.

Canutillos de Sumbilla: sweet pastry made with aniseed, filled with lemon flavouring.

Chorizo: shaped like a candle, stuffed in thick tripe with pork and beef, seasoned with salt, paprika, garlic and sugars.

Cordero al chilindrón: lamb stew.

Cuajada: made from sheep's milk and natural curd, sweetened by honey or sugar.

Pacharán: traditional aniseed liquor.

ES9042 Camping Etxarri

Paraje Dambolintxulo s/n, E-31820 Etxarri-Aranatz (Navarra)

Tel: **948 460 537**. Email: info@campingetxarri.com

Situated in the Valle de la Burunda the site is a peaceful oasis with superb views of the 1,300 m. high San-Donato Mountains. The approach to the constantly improving site is via a road lined by huge 300 year old oak trees, which are a feature of the site. Reception is a purpose built chalet with a touring reference library (mostly in Spanish). There are 100 average sized pitches on flat ground, 50 for tourers, with 6A electricity to all and water to 25. The site is well placed for fascinating walks in unspoilt countryside and is close to three recognised nature walks. Animation is organised in August for children. The site gets very crowded during the Fiestas de San Fermín (bull-running) in Pamplona early in July. It is essential to make a reservation if you wish to stay. A visit to Pamplona is recommended. Parking is difficult – try to the west of the bullring, then wander down to Plaza de Toros (renamed Plaza Hemingway), to savour the atmosphere. It is common to use dual-naming of places and roads (one in the Spanish language, the other in Basque and it can be confusing) – ask for advice if in doubt.

Facilities

The single toilet block has good facilities including baby bath. Laundry. Gas supplies. Essential supplies kept in high season. Bar (1/4-30/9). Restaurant and takeaway (1/6-15/9). Large swimming pool with children's pool (15/6-15/9) also open to the public and can get crowded. Bicycle hire. Minigolf. Play area. Off site: Bus and trains nearby. Bars, restaurants and shops 2 km. Golf, fishing, riding all 20 km. Pamplona 40 km.

Open: 1 April - 1 October.

Directions

Etxarri-Aranatz is 40 km. northwest of Pamplona. From A8 (San Sebastian - Bilbao) take A15 towards Pamplona, then 20 km. northwest of Pamplona, take A10 west towards Vitoria/Gasteix. At km. 19 take NA120 to and through town following site signs. Turn left after crossing railway to site at end of road.

Charges 2006

Per person	€ 2,90 - € 3,95
child	€ 2,70 - € 3,65
pitch	€ 2,90 - € 4,95
electricity	€ 3,80

ES9049 Camping Baztan

Ctra. Francia . s/n., E-31714 Erratzu (Navarra)

Tel: **948 453 133**. Email: **campingbaztan@campingbaztan.com**

Driving through the small town of Erratzu extreme caution is required due to the narrowness of the streets and is not advised for large units. This site's rural setting and the mountain views make this a retreat for those who enjoy camping in quiet surroundings. It consists of a main building housing reception, a shop, bar and a small restaurant and above, 14 tidy apartments. There are also ten timber cottages for rent. Tarmac roads lead to the grass touring pitches which are shady and of a good size, with both water and electricity (10A). Most are level. In early and late season the campsite is open, but a telephone call is necessary to gain access. You may be the only occupants. The one toilet block is open and cleaned but facilities are minimal.

Facilities

The single sanitary block is clean and has facilities for disabled visitors. Covered dishwashing and laundry. Shop, bar and restaurant (weekends only outside 1/6-20/9). Swimming pool (1/6-20/9, 12.00 – 20.00 only). In April, May and 20 Sept – 1 Nov. the site is only open at weekends. If you wish to stay on weekdays, entry can be obtained by dialling a number displayed at reception (sanitary block will be open). Off site: Excursions arranged to activity centre (horse riding, kayaking, rafting) 15 km. away. Buses run to Pamplona and San Sebastian (3 per day, all year). Village (5 mins walk) offers a small supermarket, bars and restaurant. River fishing 50 m. Golf (in France) 20 km. Bicycle hire 15 km.

Open: 1 June - 20 September
(fully open, other times see above).

Directions

From Hendaye head south on the N121A. Turn east on N121B. Continue north to the junction with NA2600. Turn right to Erratzu. Proceed through village, bear left at sign 'Francia NA2600' and site is on the right.

Charges 2006

Per person	€ 4,00 - € 5,50
child (2-10 yrs)	€ 2,50 - € 3,50
pitch incl. electricity	€ 7,50 - € 15,00

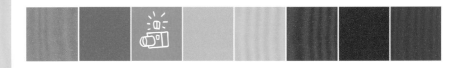

ES9048 Camping Urrobi

Ctra Pamplona - Valcarlos, km. 42. N 135, E-31694 Espinal (Navarra)

Tel: **948 760 200**. Email: **info@campingurrobi.com**

This large site is in a beautiful location with mountain views. At the entrance is a lively bar, a reasonably priced restaurant and a well stocked shop. The site is popular with Spanish families and there are many mobile homes, so it can be busy at holiday times and weekends. However, there is plenty of room on the 150 unmarked grass pitches. All have electricity points (6A) and there are plenty of water taps. Water activities of all types are catered for with both a swimming pool and an area of the river sectioned off for safe bathing and paddling. With many walks and bicycle tracks, there is plenty of scope for discovering this delightful area. This is a suitable site for families.

Facilities

Clean sanitary blocks include facilities for disabled visitors (key from reception). Laundry facilities. Motorcaravan service point. Shop, bar and restaurant (all season). Swimming pool. Games room with TV (Spanish). Internet facility. Minigolf. Tennis court. Playing field. Play area. Off site: Village 1 km. with shops, restaurant and bars. Forest of Irati 15 mins. Bicycle hire 15 km. Golf and riding 40 km. Beach 70 km. One bus per day to and from Pamplona.

Open: 1 April - 31 October.

Directions

From Pamplona take N135 northeast for 42 km. After village of Auritzberri turn right onto NA172. Site is on the left. GPS: N42:58.389 W01:21.109

Charges 2006

Per person	€ 4,20
child (2-12 yrs)	€ 3,40
pitch	€ 7,60 - € 9,05
electricity	€ 4,20

ES9043 Camping Caravanning Errota el Molino

E-31150 Mendigorria (Navarra)

Tel: **948 340 604**. Email: **info@campingelmolino.com**

This is an extensive site set by an attractive weir near the town of Mendigorria, alongside the river Arga. It takes its name from an old disused watermill (molino) close by. The site is split into separate permanent and touring sections. The touring area is a new development with good-sized flat pitches with electricity and water for tourers, and a separate area for tents. Many trees have been planted around the site but there is still only minimal shade. The chirpy owner Anna Beriain will give you a warm welcome. Reception is housed in the lower part of a long building along with the bar/snack bar which has a cool shaded terrace, a separate restaurant and a supermarket. The upper floor of this building is dormitory accommodation for backpackers. The site has a sophisticated dock and boat launching facility and an ambitious watersport competition programme in season with a safety boat present at all times. There are pedaloes and canoes for hire. The site is very busy during the festival of San Fermín (bull running) in July in Pamplona (28 km). Tours of the local bodegas (groups of ten) to sample the fantastic Navarra wines can be organised by reception.

Facilities

The well equipped toilet block is very clean and well maintained, with cold water to washbasins. Facilities for disabled campers. Washing machine. Large restaurant, pleasant bar. Supermarket (Easter - Sept). Superb new swimming pools for adults and children. Bicycle hire. Riverside bar. Weekly animation programme (July/Aug) and many sporting activities. Squash courts. Internet access. Pleasant river walk. Torches useful. Off site: Bus to Pamplona 500 m. Riding 15 km. Golf 35 km.

Open: All year.

Directions

Mendigorria is 30 km. southwest of Pamplona. From A15 San Sebastian - Zaragoza motorway, leave Pamplona bypass on A12 towards Logroño. Leave at km. 23 on NA601 to hill-top town of Mendigorria. At crossroads turn right towards Larraga and down hill to site. GPS: N42:37.497 W01:50.533

Charges 2006

Per person	€ 4,30
child	€ 3,50
pitch incl. car and electricity	€ 11,90

Plus 7% VAT. Discounts outside high season. Camping Cheques accepted.

MAP 5

In the north eastern par
Spain, Aragón borders F
with the Pyreenes lying
between them. It is a regi
rich in folklore, with rural,
mountainside villages renowned
their Romanesque architecture, bea
valleys and awe-inspiring peaks.

ARAGÓN IS MADE UP OF THREE PROVINCES:
HUESCA, ZARAGOZA AND TERUEL

THE CAPITAL OF THE REGION IS ZARAGOZA

The region can be separated into three different areas: the central area consisting of the Ebro basin, a vast flat lowland, the northern Pyrenees, and the area made up of the Iberian mountain range in the northwest and southeast of the region. The northern-most province of Huesca is located in the foothills of the Pyrenees Mountains, a beautiful area with plenty of picturesque towns and villages to visit. It is also good walking country with numerous trails offering anything from short day-walks in the valleys to long-distance treks in the mountains. Skiing is popular too. Bordering Huesca, the province of Zaragoza is home to the region's capital, also of the same name. Zaragoza is a lively town with plenty of bars and restaurants, plus numerous museums and architectural treasures. Outside the capital you'll find more villages, countryside, and vineyards where the best of the region's wine is produced; the mapped out Ruta del Vino will take you through the area. The third province of Teruel is largely comprised of the Iberian mountain range, with attractive towns, medieval sights and more dramatic scenery to admire.

Places of interest

Aljafería Palace: spectacular Moorish monument.

Basílica de Nuestra Señora del Pilar: Baroque temple from the 17th and 18th centuries.

Benasque: attractive alpine town, gateway to Pyrenees.

Casa-Museo de Goya: art museum, including engravings by Goya.

Jaca: home of the country's oldest Romanesque cathedral.

Monasterio de San Juan de la Peña: 17th century Baroque monastery and 10th century Old monastery in Romanesque style.

Parque Nacional de Ordesa y Monte Perdido: alpine national park.

Cuisine of the region

Specialities include lamb, locally-produced ham and sausages; fruit is also used a lot in desserts.

Chilindrones: sauces of tomato and pepper.

Frutas de Aragón: sugar-candied fruits covered in chocolate.

Pollo al chilindrón: chicken (or lamb) stew with onions, tomatoes and red peppers.

Salmorrejos: cold soups.

Suspiros de amante: dessert with cheese and egg.

Ternasco: roast lamb.

Tortas de alma: made with pumpkin, honey and sugar.

Trenza de Almudévar: with nuts and raisins soaked in liqueur.

ES9058 Camping Baliera

Ctra N260, km. 355.5, E-22486 Bonansa (Huesca)

Tel: **974 554 016**. Email: **info@baliera.com**

With its wonderful location in a quiet river valley with views of the surrounding mountains all around, Camping Baliera is an excellent site for enjoying this beautiful area. Combining camping with timber chalets and apartments, the site has 200 well kept grass touring pitches (80-120 sq.m) all with electricity (5/10A). The pitches are mostly located close to the attractive, stone built reception building which also houses a comfortable bar and shop. The approach to this site is by narrow and winding mountain roads and it is 5 km. from the nearest village. However, for all but the largest units, the trip is well worth making. An outdoor swimming pool is open in high season. At this time an entertainment team organises excursions in the local area and activities such as cinema, handicrafts and sports. With two National Parks within 10 km. the site is ideally positioned for activities such as walking, cycling, fishing and winter skiing.

Facilities

Two toilet blocks, one part of the apartment block near the entrance, the other in the reception building (this closed in low season). Heated, they are good with well equipped showers, vanity style washbasins. Laundry room and drying room. Motorcaravan services. Shop (1/7-31/8) and bar (all season). Swimming pool (15/7-15/9). Fitness equipment. Play area. Entertainment in high season. Off site: National parks and outdoor activities. Nearest village 5 km.

Open: All year exc. November.

Directions

On N230, 34 km. south of Vielha, turn on N260 for 2-3 km, then onto A1605 signed Bonsana for 100 m. to site on left. Reception is 200 m. through the site. Approach roads are narrow and winding, but navigable. GPS: N42:26.211 E00:41.539

Charges 2007

Per person	€ 3,96 - € 4,95
child (2-10 yrs)	€ 3,72 - € 4,65
pitch with electricity	€ 11,60 - € 13,50
dog	€ 1,84 - € 2,30

VAT included.
Camping Cheques accepted.

ES9060 Camping Peña Montañesa

Ctra Ainsa - Francia, km. 2, E-22360 Labuerda (Huesca)
Tel: **974 500 032**. Email: **info@penamontanesa.com**

A large site situated quite high up in the Pyrenees near the Ordesa National Park, Peña Montanesa is easily accessible from Ainsa or from France via the Bielsa Tunnel (steep sections on the French side). The site is essentially divided into three sections opening progressively throughout the season and all have shade. The 288 pitches on fairly level grass are of about 75 sq.m. and 10A electricity is available on virtually all. Grouped near the entrance are the facilities that make the site so attractive, including a fair sized outdoor pool and a glass-covered indoor pool with jacuzzi and sauna.

Facilities

A newer toilet block, heated when necessary, has free hot showers but cold water to open plan washbasins. Facilities for disabled visitors. Small baby room. An older block in the original area has similar provision. Washing machine. Bar. Restaurant. Takeaway. Supermarket. Outdoor pool (1/3-1/10). Indoor pool (all year). Playground. Bicycle hire. Riding. Rafting. Only gas barbecues are permitted. Off site: Fishing 100m. Skiing in season. Canoeing near.

Open: All year.

Directions

Site is 2 km. from Ainsa, on the road from Ainsa to France. GPS: N42:26.112 E00:08.171

Charges 2006

Per person	€ 4,40 - € 5,75
child (1-9 yrs)	€ 3,44 - € 4,50
pitch	€ 12,00 - € 16,50
electricity	€ 4,75

All plus 7% VAT.

ES9062 Camping Boltaña

Ctra N-260, km 442, E-22340 Boltaña (Huesca)
Tel: **974 502 347**. Email: **info@campingboltana.com**

Nestled in the Rio Ara valley, surrounded by the Pyrennees mountains and below a tiny but enchanting, historic, hill top village, is the very pretty, thoughtfully planned Camping Boltana. Generously sized, grassy pitches have good shade from a variety of trees and a stream meanders through the campsite. The landscaping includes ten charming rocky water gardens (though these can dry up in summer months) and a covered pergola doubles as an eating and play area. A stone building houses the site's reception, social room and supermarket. Opposite is a terrace for enjoying tapas, listening to music, casual eating, animation and games.

Facilities

Two modern sanitary blocks include facilities for disabled visitors and laundry facilities. Casual restaurant and bar and a more formal restaurant (April-Oct). Supermarket. Swimming pools (15/5-30/9). Playground. Barbecues. Animation for children (high season). Pentanque. Guided tours, plus hiking, canyoning, rafting, climbing, mountain biking and caving. Torches useful in some parts. Off site: Local bus service.

Open: All year.

Directions

South of the Park Nacional de Ordesa, site is about 50 km. from Jaca near Ainsa. From Ainsa travel northwest on N260 toward Boltaña (near 443 km. marker) and 1 km. from Boltaña turn south toward Margudged. Site is well signed and is 1 km. along this road. GPS: N42:25.811 E00:04.729

Charges 2006

Per person	€ 5,00
child (1-10 yrs)	€ 4,00
pitch incl. car	€ 10,00 - € 10,60

Camping Cheques accepted.

ES9064 Camping Gavin

Ctra N260, km 503, E-22639 Gavin (Huesca)
Tel: **974 485090**. Email: **info@campinggavin.com**

Camping Gavin is set on a terraced, wooded hillside and you will find a friendly welcome. The site offers 150 pitches of 80 sq m. in size and with electricity available to all (6/10A). In some areas the terracing means that some pitches are quite small. The main site buildings are built of natural stone. There are also 11 superb, balconied apartments for 4 to 6 persons. At about 900 m. the site is surrounded by towering peaks at the portal of the Tena Valley. One can enjoy the natural beauty of the Pyrenees and venture near or far along the great Pyrenean footpaths.

Facilities

Excellent shower and toilet facilities in three main buildings with subtle, tasteful décor include facilities for babies and disabled people. Laundry facilities. Bar and snacks. Supermarket. Swimming pool. Tennis. Playground. Barbecues are not permitted at some times of the year. Off site: Rafting, windsurfing, riding, fishing, walking and climbing. Bicycle hire 2 km.

Open: All year.

Directions

Site is off the N260, 2 km. from Biescas at km 503. GPS: N42:37.164 W00:18.245

Charges 2006

Per person	€ 3,80 - € 5,25
pitch	€ 7,70 - € 10,50
electricity	€ 4,40 - € 5,10

Camping Cheques accepted.

ES9070 Centro de Vacaciones Pirineos

Ctra N240, km. 300, E-22791 Santa Cilia de Jaca (Huesca)

Tel: **974 377 351**. Email: **pirineos@pirinet.com**

This pretty site which is open most of the year, is directly on the pilgrimage route to Santiago. The area has a mild climate, being near the River Aragon, not too high and it is convenient for touring the Pyrenees. This is a friendly site which is useful for transit stops and off-season camping on the large, mostly level wooded area which can accommodate 250 units (no marked pitches), with electric points throughout. The trees provide good shade and the attractive swimming pool is being rebuilt and updated. There is some road noise along the south side of the site.

Facilities

One heated sanitary block is open all year, providing a quite satisfactory supply. A second, more modern block is open April - Sept. only. Launderette. Restaurant. Bar. Supermarket (15/6-15/9, otherwise essentials kept in bar). Swimming pools (15/6-15/9). Two tennis courts. Playground. Games room. Petanque. Bicycle hire. Gas supplies. Torches required in some areas. Off site: Fishing and bathing in river 200 m.

Open: All year excl. 3 November - 3 December.

Directions

Site is 15 km. west of Jaca on N240 at the km. 300 point (65 km. northwest of Huesca). GPS: N42:33.040 W00:45.660

Charges 2006

Per person	€ 4,30
child (2-9 yrs)	€ 4,00
pitch	€ 7,60 - € 8,30
electricity (6A)	€ 5,35

All plus 7% VAT. 20% discount in low season.

ES9125 Camping Lago Barasona

Ctra N-123a, km. 25, E-22435 La Puebla de Castro (Huesca)

Tel: **974 545 148**. Email: **info@lagobarasona.com**

This site, alongside its associated ten room hotel, is beautifully positioned on terraces across a road from the shores of the Lago de Barasona (a large reservoir), with views of hills and the distant Pyrenees. The very friendly, English speaking owner is keen to please and has applied very high standards throughout the site. The grassy, fairly level pitches are generally around 100 sq.m. with 35 high quality pitches of 110 sq m for larger units. All have electricity (6/10A), many are well shaded and some have great views of the lake and/or hills. Waterskiing and other watersports are available in July and August.

Facilities

Two toilet blocks in modern buildings have high standards and hot water throughout including cabins (3 for ladies, 1 for men). Bar/snack bar and two excellent restaurants (open all season). Shop (15/5-15/9). Swimming pools (15/5-15/9). Tennis. Mountain bike hire. Canoe, windsurfing motor boat and pedalo hire. Mini-club (high season). Lake swimming, fishing, canoeing, etc. Walking (maps provided). Money exchange. Mini-disco. Off site: Riding 4 km.

Open: All year.

Directions

Site is on the west bank of the lake, close to km. 25 on the N123A, 6 km. south of Graus (about 80 km. north of Lleida/Lerida). Travelling from the south, the site is on the left from a newly built roundabout and slip road. GPS: N42:08.498 E00:18.915

Charges 2007

Per person	€ 3,90 - € 5,50
child (2-10 yrs)	€ 3,20 - € 4,65
pitch	€ 4,30 - € 10,40
electricity	€ 4,30 - € 5,40

Plus 7% VAT.
Camping Cheques accepted.

ES9095 Camping Ciudad de Albarracin

Junto al Polideportivo, E-44100 Albarracin (Teruel)

Tel: **978 710 197**

Albarracin, in southern Aragon is set in the 'Reserva Nacional de los Montes Universales' and is a much frequented, fascinating town with a Moorish castle. The old city walls towering above date from its days when it attempted to become a separate country within Spain. This neat and clean family site is set on three levels on a hillside behind the town, with a walk of 1 km. to the centre. It is very modern and has high quality facilities including a superb building for barbecuing (all materials provided). There are 140 pitches (70 for touring units), all with electricity and separated by trees.

Facilities

The two spotless, modern sanitary buildings provide British style WCs, quite large showers and hot water throughout. Baby bath. Washing machines. Bar/restaurant (all season). Essentials from bar. Special room for barbecues with fire and wood provided. Play area. Fronton. Torches required in some areas.
Off site: Municipal swimming pool 100 m. (high season). Town shops, bars and restaurants 500 m.

Open: 1 March - 31 October.

Directions

From Teruel north on the N330 for about 8 km. then west onto A1512 for 30 km. Well signed in town.

Charges 2007

Per person	€ 3,15
child (under 14)	€ 2,40
tent	€ 3,15
electricity	€ 2,65
Plus 7% VAT.	

ES9105 Camping Lago Park

Ctra Alhama de Aragon-Nuevalos, E-50210 Nuevalos (Zaragoza)

Tel: **976 849 038**

Lago Park is situated in an attractive area which receives many visitors for the Monasterio de Piedra just 3 km. distant and it enjoys pleasant views of the surrounding mountains. This site is suitable for transit stops or if you wish to visit the monasterio as it is the only one hereabouts and appears to make the most of that fact. It is not recommended for extended stays. Set on a steep hillside, the 300 pitches (250 for tourers) are on terraces. Only the lower rows are suitable for large caravans. These pitches are numbered and marked by trees, most having electricity (10A).

Facilities

The single sanitary block has Turkish and British style WCs. washbasins with hot water and controllable hot showers (no dividers). Restaurant/bar (June-Sept). Shop (all season). Swimming pool (late June-Sept). Play area. Gas supplies. Torches needed in some areas. Off site: Fishing 300 m. Riding 2 km.

Open: 1 April - 30 September.

Directions

From Zaragoza (120 km.) take fast A2/N11/E90 road and turn onto C202 road beyond Calatayud to Nuévalos (25 km). From Madrid, exit A2 at Alhama de Aragón (13 km). Follow signs for Monasterio de Piedra from all directions.

Charges 2007

Per person	€ 5,60
child (3-10 yrs)	€ 5,50
pitch incl. car	€ 5,80 - € 9,90
electricity	€ 4,70

Check real time availability and at-the-gate prices...

www.**alanrogers**.com

Menorca, steeped in history and blanketed by mystery, is an enchanting island of roughly 270 square miles in area.

The C721 highway provides the back-bone to the island, connecting modest market towns to Mahon (the main town) in the east and Ciutadella in the west.

Mahon's classic Georgian style buildings, complete with sash windows, will endear them to the British traveller. Its impressive harbour was captured by the British in 1708 during the Spanish War of Succession. In complete contrast, Ciutadella has a more Gothic feel to it. A labyrinth of tiny streets entwine the 'little city', most of which can only be accessed on foot. Monte Toro stands proudly at the centre of the island surveying all. To the south a greener lush terrain exists with long, luxurious beaches, while to the north a giant rockery erupts riddled with caves and prehistoric finds.

ES8000 Camping Son Bou

Ctra de San Jaime km 3.5, Apdo. de Correus 85, Alayor, E-07730 Menorca (Menorca)
Tel: **971 372 605**. Email: **info@campingsonbou.com**

Camping Son Bou was opened in 1996 and has been purpose built in local style providing a large irregular shaped pool with marvellous view across to Monte Toro and overlooked by a pine shaded, terraced bar and restaurant. The 313 large pitches are arranged in circles radiating out from the main facilities and clearly edged with stones. Natural pine tree shade covers most but the outer ring. Drinking water and refuse points are well placed. Electricity (6A) is available on nearly all pitches. The ground is hard and devoid of grass except where sprinklers operate. The beautiful island of Menorca cries out to be explored. It is peaceful and tranquil, with its characteristic dry stone walls, its low white buildings with terracotta tiled roof, its beautiful coastline, ancient monuments and pretty villages with their cycle of fiestas of religious origin with the noble horse as the central element. The site gets very busy with Spanish people from the mainland in high season. Earlier in the year it is quieter and greener. If you do not fancy the ferry crossings the site has some neat wooden chalets and ready erected tents. The site is more than happy to arrange the overnight ferry crossing from Barcelona or Valencia (discounts available).

Facilities

Well designed toilet block of good quality, open plan in places. Some washbasins in cabins (cold water). Baby room. Facilities for disabled visitorst. Serviced wash available. Shop (from 1/5). Bar. Restaurant. Outdoor pool (from 1/5). Tennis. Play area. Bicycle hire. English spoken. Open air cinema most evenings. Occasional barbecue with guitarist. Comprehensive activity programme. Off site: Riding 3 km. Village 0.75 km. with sandy beach.

Open: 7 April - 25 September.

Directions

From Mahon (Mao) follow main road to Ciutadella. Go past Alaior (bypassed) and watch for restaurant on left and sign for San Jaime/Son Bou. Continue for 3.5 km.and site on right.

Charges 2006

Per person	€ 5,40 - € 6,60
child (3-13 yrs)	€ 4,00 - € 4,85
tent for one person	€ 3,05 - € 3,70
tent for 2 persons	€ 6,00 - € 7,25
car	€ 3,65 - € 4,45
All plus 7% VAT.	

Portugal is a relatively small country occupying the southwest corner of the Iberian peninsula, bordered by Spain in the north and east, with the Atlantic coast in the south and west. In spite of its size, the country offers a tremendous variety in both its way of life and traditions.

Most visitors looking for a beach type holiday head for the busy Algarve, with its long stretches of sheltered sandy beaches, and warm, clear Atlantic waters, great for bathing and watersports. With its monuments and fertile rolling hills, central Portugal adjoins the beautiful Tagus river that winds its way through the capital city of Lisbon, on its way to the Altantic Ocean.

Lisbon city itself has deep rooted cultural traditions, coming alive at night with buzzing cafes, restaurants and discos. Moving south east of Lisbon the land becomes rather impoverished, consisting of stretches of vast undulating plains, dominated by cork plantations. Most people head for the walled town of Evora, an area steeped in two thousand years of history. The Portuguese consider the Minho area in the north to be the most beautiful part of their country, with its wooded mountain and wild coastline, a rural and conservative region with picturesque towns.

Population: 10 million

Capital: Lisbon

Climate: The country enjoys a maritime climate with hot summers and mild winters with comparatively low rainfall in the south, heavy rain in the north

Language: Portuguese, but English is widely spoken in cities, towns and larger resorts. French can be useful

Currency: The Euro (€)

Telephone: The country code is 00 351

Banks: Mon-Fri 08.30-11.45 and 13.00-14.45. Some large city banks operate a currency exchange 18.30-23.00

Shops: Mon-Fri 0900-1300 and 1500-1900. Sat 0900-1300.

Public Holidays: New Year; Carnival (Shrove Tues); Good Fri; Liberty Day 25 Apr; Labour Day; Corpus Christi; National Day 10 June; Saints Days; Assumption 15 Aug; Republic Day 5 Oct; All Saints 1 Nov; Immaculate Conception 8 Dec; Christmas 24-26 Dec

Tourist Office:
ICEP Portuguese Trade & Tourism Office,
Second Floor, 22/25a Sackville Street, London W1S 3LY

Tel: 09063 640 610   E-mail: iceplondt@aol.com
Fax: 020 7494 1868   Internet: www.portugalinsite.com

MAP 7

Algarve

The Algarve, Portugal's southernmost province, is a true sunseekers paradise, offering all year round sunshine and over 150 miles of beautiful sandy beaches.

THE ALGARVE HAS ONE DISTRICT: FARO

The coast of the Algarve offers mile after mile of golden beaches and small sandy coves with interesting rock formations, interspersed with busy fishing ports. The capital, Faro, boasts excellent beaches, while the thriving fishing port and market centre of Lagos is one of the most popular destinations in the Algarve. Although the earthquake of 1755 caused great damage to Lagos, the streets and squares of the town have retained much of their charm. Within walking distance are some superb beaches, including Praia de Dona Ana, which is considered to be the most picturesque of all, and the smaller coves of Praia do Pinhão and Praia Camilo. Further inland and to the north, the hills mark the edge of a greener and more fertile region, brilliantly coloured by fig-trees, orange-groves and almond-trees that come into blossom in the winter. Here you will also find a series of typical villages that have successfully preserved their ancestral traditions. The walled town of Silves has a Moorish fortress, 13th century cathedral and archaeology musuem. Nearby, the narrow streets of the old spa town of Monchique wind up a steep hillside, revealing magnificent views.

Places of interest

Albufeira: popular resort, daily market, good nightlife.

Cape São Vicente: south westernmost point of Europe.

Faro: monuments, churches, museums, Gothic cathedral, good shopping centre.

Sagres: 17th century fortress.

Tavira: picturesque town, 17th and 18th century architecture.

Vilamoura: good sporting facilities including golf courses.

Cuisine of the region

Fresh fish and seafood are popular; the local speciality is *Ameijoas na Cataplana* (clams steamed in a copper pan). One of the most traditional dishes is *caldeiradas* (stew made with all kinds of different fish) and *sardinha assada* (grilled sardines). Given the abundance of trees in the region, figs and almonds are used a lot in desserts including *bolinhos de amêndoa* (small cakes made from marzipan and almond paste), which are moulded into the shape of fruits and vegetables in all kinds of different sizes.

PO8230 Camping Olhão

Pinheiros de Marim, P-8700 Olhão (Faro)

Tel: **289 70 03 00**. Email: **parque.campismo@sbsi.pt**

This site, with around 800 pitches, is open all year. It has many mature trees providing good shade. The pitches are marked, numbered and in rows divided by shrubs, although levelling will be necessary and the trees make access tricky on some. There is electricity for 102 pitches (6A) and a separate area for tents. Permanent and long stay units take 20% of the pitches, the touring pitches filling up quickly in July and August, so arrive early. There is some noise nuisance from an adjacent railway. The site has a relaxed, casual atmosphere. Amenities include very pleasant swimming pools and tennis courts, a reasonable restaurant/bar and a café/bar with TV and games room. All are very popular with the local Portuguese who pay to use the facilities. The large, sandy beaches in this area are on offshore islands reached by ferry and are, as a result, relatively quiet; some are reserved for naturists. This site can get very busy in peak periods and maintenance can be variable. There was a large, low season British contingent when we visited, enjoying the low prices.

Facilities

Eleven sanitary blocks are adequate, clean when seen, and are specifically sited to be a maximum of 50 m. from any pitch. One block has facilities for disabled visitors. Laundry. Excellent supermarket. Kiosk. Restaurant/bar (all year). Café and general room with cable TV. Playgrounds. Swimming pools (April - Sept) and tennis courts (fees for both). Bicycle hire. Internet at reception. Off site: Bus service to the ferry at Olhao 50 m. from site. Indoor pool 2 km. Riding 1 km. Fishing 2 km. Golf 20 km.

Open: All year.

Directions

Just over 1 km. east of Olhão, on EN125, take turn to Pinheiros de Marim. Site is back off the road on the left. Look for very large, white, triangular entry arch as the site name is different on the outside wall. GPS: N37:02 W07:49

Charges 2006

Per person	€ 2,20 - € 4,00
child (5-12 yrs)	€ 1,20 - € 2,20
pitch	€ 3,45 - € 10,80
electricity	€ 1,50

Less for longer winter stays.

PO8210 Parque de Campismo Albufeira

EN 125 Ferreiras-Albufeira, P-8200-555 Albufeira (Faro)

Tel: 289 58 76 29. Email: campingalbufeira@mail.telepac.pt

The spacious entrance to this site will accommodate the largest of units (watch for severe speed bumps at the barrier). One of the better sites on the Algarve, it has pitches on fairly flat ground with some terracing, trees and shrubs giving reasonable shade in most parts. There are some marked and numbered pitches of 50-80 sq.m. Winter stays are encouraged with many facilities remaining open including a pool. An attractively designed complex of traditional Portuguese style buildings on the hill, with an unusually shaped pool and two more for children, forms the central area of the site. It has large terraces for sunbathing and pleasant views and is surrounded by a variety of flowers, shrubs and well watered lawns, complete with a fountain. The 'à la carte' restaurant, impressive with its international cuisine, and the very pleasant self-service one both have views across the three pools. A pizzeria, bars and a soundproofed disco are great for younger campers.

Facilities

The toilet blocks include hot showers. Launderette. Very large supermarket. Tabac (English papers). Waiter and self-service restaurants. Pizzeria. Bars. Satellite TV. Soundproof disco. Swimming pools. Tennis. Playground. Internet access. First aid post. Car wash. ATM. Car hire. Off site: Site bus service from gate to Albufeira every 45 minutes (2 km). Theme parks nearby. Beaches.

Open: All year.

Directions

From N125 coast road or N264 (from Lisbon) at new junctions follow N395 to Albufeira. Site is about 2 km. on the left. GPS: N37:06 W08:15

Charges 2006

Per person	€ 5,20
child (4-10 yrs)	€ 2,60
pitch	€ 5,60 - € 11,95
electricity (10A)	€ 2,85

PO8200 Orbitur Camping Valverde

Estrada da Praia da Luz, Valverde, P-8600-148 Lagos (Faro)

Tel: 282 78 92 11. Email: info@orbitur.pt

A little over a kilometre from the village of Praia da Luz and its beach and about 7 km. from Lagos, this large, well run site is certainly worth considering for your holiday stay in the Algarve. It has 600 numbered pitches, of varying size, which are enclosed by hedges. All are on flat ground or broad terraces with good shade in most parts from established trees and shrubs. The site has a swimming pool with a long curling slide and a paddling pool (under 10s free, adults charged). This is an excellent site with well maintained facilities and good security. It attracts a good number of long-term winter visitors and is one of the better Orbitur sites.

Facilities

Six large, clean, toilet blocks have some washbasins and sinks with cold water only, and hot showers. Units for disabled people. Laundry. Motorcaravan services. Supermarket (all year), shops, restaurant and bar complex with both self-service and waiter service in season (closed November). Takeaway. Coffee shop. Swimming pool (April - Sept) with slide and paddling pool (June - Sept). Playground. Tennis. Satellite TV in bar. Disco. Pub. Excursions. Off site: Bus service from site gate. Beach and fishing 1.5 km. Bicycle hire 3 km. Golf 10 km.

Open: All year.

Directions

From Lagos on N125 road, after 7 km. turn south to Praia da Luz. At the town follow Orbitur camping signs. The beach road is narrow and cobbled and is very challenging in a large unit. GPS: N37:05 W08:43

Charges 2007

Per person	€ 2,90 - € 5,40
child (5-10 yrs)	€ 1,45 - € 2,70
caravan and car	€ 6,70 - € 13,10
electricity	€ 2,40
Off season discounts (up to 70%).	

PO8220 Orbitur Camping Quarteira

Estrada da Fonte Santa, Avenida Sá Cameiro, P-8125-618 Quarteira (Faro)

Tel: **289 30 28 26**. Email: **info@orbitur.pt**

This is a large, busy attractive site on undulating ground with some terracing, taking 795 units. On the outskirts of the popular Algarve resort of Quarteira, it is 600 m. from a sandy beach which stretches for a kilometre to the town centre. Many of the unmarked pitches have shade from tall trees and there are a few small individual pitches of 50 sq.m. with electricity and water which can be reserved. There are 680 electrical connections. Like others along this coast, the site encourages long winter stays. There is a large restaurant and supermarket which have a separate entrance for local trade. The swimming pools are excellent, featuring pools for adults (with a large flume) and children (with fountains), incurring an extra charge.

Facilities

Five toilet blocks provide British and Turkish style toilets, washbasins with cold water, hot showers plus facilities for disabled visitors. Washing machines. Motorcaravan services. Gas supplies. Supermarket. Self-service restaurant (closed Nov). Separate takeaway (from late May). Swimming pools (April - Sept). General room with bar and satellite TV. Tennis. Open air disco (high season). Off site: Bus from gate to Faro. Fishing 1 km. Bicycle hire (summer) 1 km. Golf 4 km.

Open: All year.

Directions

Turn off N125 for village of Almancil. In the village take road south to Quarteira. Site is on the left 1 km. after large, official town welcome sign. GPS: N37:04 W08:05

Charges 2007

Per person	€ 2,90 - € 5,40
child (5-10 yrs)	€ 1,45 - € 2,70
caravan and car	€ 6,70 - € 13,10
electricity	€ 2,40
Off season discounts (up to 70%).	

PO8440 Parque de Campismo Quintos dos Carriços

Praia da Salema, Vila do Bispo, P-8650-196 Budens (Faro)

Tel: **282 69 52 01**. Email: **quintacarrico@oninet.pt**

This is an attractive and peaceful, valley site with a dedicated naturist area. A traditional tiled Portuguese style entrance leads you down a steep incline into this excellent and well maintained site which has a village atmosphere. With continuing improvements, the site has been developed over the years by the Dutch owner. It is spread over two valleys (which are real sun-traps), with the 300 partially terraced pitches marked and divided by trees and shrubs (oleanders and roses). A small stream (dry when seen) meanders through the site. The most remote part, 250 m. from the main site, is dedicated to naturists. Although the site is lit, torches may be required in more remote areas. A very popular site for summer and winter sun-worshippers, within easy driving distance of resorts. The many fine beaches in the region provide ample opportunities for diving, swimming and fishing.

Facilities

Four modern, spacious sanitary blocks, well tiled with quality fittings, are spotlessly clean. Washbasins with cold water, hot showers on payment. Washing machine. Excellent facility for disabled people. Gas supplies. Mini-market (all year). Restaurant (1/3-15/10). Bar (daily in season, once a week only 15/10-1/3). TV (cable). WiFi internet. Games room. Bicycle, scooter, moped and m/cycle hire. Off site: Fishing, golf and beach 1 km. Riding 8 km. Bus service to town (not beach) from site.

Open: All year.

Directions

Turn off RN125 (Lagos-Sagres) road at junction to Figuere and Salema (17 km. from Lagos); site is signed. GPS: N37:04 W08:49

Charges 2007

Per person	€ 4,60
child	€ 2,30
car and caravan	€ 11,10
motorcaravan	€ 6,90 - € 8,30
Discounts for long winter stays.	

PO8202 Camping Turiscampo

Estrada Nacional, 125, Espiche, P-8600 Lagos (Faro)

Tel: **282 789 265**. Email: **info@turiscampo.com**

This site is being thoughtfully refurbished and updated to include most of the existing infrastructure since it was purchased by the friendly Coll family, who are known to us from their previous Spanish site. Work was still in progress when we visited but the site does show great promise and will become a quality site. The site provides 250 pitches for tourers mainly in rows of terraces, all with electricity and some with shade. They vary in size (70-120 sq.m). The upper areas of the site are being developed and are mostly destined for bungalows (which are generally separate from the touring areas). A new, elevated Californian style pool plus a children's pool have been constructed and the supporting structure is a clever water cascade and surround. There is a large sun lounger area on astroturf. One side of the pool area is open to the road. The restaurant/bar has been tastefully refurbished and Giovanni and staff are delighted to use their excellent English to provide good fare at most reasonable prices (bargain menu of the day for € 6.50). The restaurant has two patios one of which is used for live entertainment and discos in season and the other for dining out. The sea is 2 km. and the city of Lagos 4 km. with all the attractions of the Algarve within easy reach. When complete this will be a very good site for families and for 'Snowbirds' to 'over-winter'.

Facilities

The two existing toilet blocks have been refurbished and a new block added containing modern facilities for disabled campers. Hot water throughout. Facilities for children. Washing machines. Shop (all year). Gas supplies. Restaurant/bar (all year). Swimming pool (March - Oct). Bicycle hire. Internet. Cable TV. Entertainment in high season on the bar terrace. Playground on sand. Adult art workshops, aqua gymnastics and mini-club (5-12 yrs) in season. Bungalows to rent. Petanque. Sports field with basketball, volleyball etc. Off site: Bus to Lagos and other towns from Praia da Luz village 1.5 km. Fishing and beach 2 km. Golf 4 km. Riding 10 km. Sailing 5 km. Boat launching 5 km.

Open: All year.

Directions

Take the N125 from Lagos to Sagres. The impressive entrance is about 3 km. on the right.
GPS: N37:06 W08:43

Charges 2007

Per person	€ 2,90 - € 5,40
child (3-10 yrs)	€ 1,60 - € 2,80
pitch	€ 4,75 - € 12,00
electricity (6/10A)	€ 2,85 - € 3,60
Camping Cheques accepted.	

PO8410 Parque de Campismo de Armacão de Pera

P-8365 Armacão de Pera (Faro)

Tel: **282 31 22 96**. Email: **camping_arm_pera@hotmail.com**

A modern site with a wide attractive entrance and a large external parking area, the 1,200 pitches are in zones on level grassy sand. They are marked by trees that provide some shade, and are easily accessed from tarmac and gravel roads. Electricity is available for most pitches. The facilities are good. The self service restaurant, bar and well stocked supermarket should cater for most needs, and you can relax around the swimming pools. The disco near the entrance and café complex is soundproofed which should ensure a peaceful night for non-revellers. The site is within easy reach of Albufeira and Portimao. It is 40 km. from Faro and makes an excellent base for stays in this region and for winter sun-seekers.

Facilities

Three modern sanitary blocks provide British and Turkish style WCs and showers with hot water on payment. Facilities for disabled campers. A reader reports that maintenance can be variable. Laundry. Supermarket. Self-service restaurant (all year). Three bars (one all year). Swimming and paddling pools (May - Sept; charged per day; no lifeguard). Games and TV rooms. Tennis. Well maintained play area. ATM. Off site: Bus to town from gate. Fishing, bicycle hire and watersports nearby.

Open: All year.

Directions

Site is west of Albufeira. Turn off N125/IC4 road in Alcantarilha, taking the EN269-1 towards the coast. Site is on left before Armação de Pêra. There are sites with similar names in the area, so be sure to find the right one. GPS: N37:06 W08:21

Charges 2006

Per person	€ 2,50 - € 5,50
child (4-10 yrs)	€ 1,60 - € 3,20
pitch	€ 4,00 - € 7,50
electricity (6A)	€ 2,50 - € 4,00

Min. stay 3 nights 1 June - 31 Aug.

PO8430 Orbitur Camping Sagres

Cerro das Moitas, P-8650-998 Sagres (Faro)

Tel: **282 62 43 71**. Email: **info@orbitur.pt**

Camping de Sagres is a pleasant site at the western tip of the Algarve, not very far from the lighthouse in the relatively unspoilt southwest corner of Portugal. With 960 pitches for tents and 120 for tourers, the sandy pitches, some terraced, are located amongst pine trees that give good shade. There are some hardstandings for motorhomes and electricity throughout. The fairly bland restaurant, bar and café/grill provide a range of reasonably priced meals. This is a reasonable site for those seeking winter sun, or as a base for exploring this 'Land's End' region of Portugal. It is away from the hustle and bustle of the more crowded resorts. The beaches and the town of Sagres (the departure point of the Portuguese navigators) with its fort, are a short drive.

Facilities

Three spacious toilet blocks are showing some signs of wear but provide hot and cold showers and washbasins with cold water. Washing machines. Motorcaravan services. Supermarket (all year). Restaurant/bar and café/grill (all Easter and June-Oct). TV room. Satellite TV in restaurant. Bicycle hire. Barbecue area. Playground. Fishing. Medical post. Car wash. Off site: Buses from village 1 km. Beach and fishing 2 km. Boat launching 8 km. Golf 12 km.

Open: All year.

Directions

From Sagres, turn off the N268 road west onto the EN268. After about 2 km. the site is signed off to the right. GPS: N37:01 W08:56

Charges 2007

Per person	€ 2,40 - € 4,40
child (5-10 yrs)	€ 1,20 - € 2,20
caravan and car	€ 5,40 - € 10,60
electricity (6A)	€ 2,40

Off season discounts (up to 70%).

MAP 7

Alentejo

With huge, sparsely populated plains dominated by vast cork plantations, which provide nearly half of the world's cork, Alentejo's main attractions include the historic city of Évora and the coastal resorts with their fine, sandy beaches.

ALENTEJO IS MADE UP OF FOUR DISTRICTS: BEJA, ÉVORA, SETÚBAL AND PORTALEGRE

One of the most impressive cities in Portugal, Évora lies on a gently sloping hill rising out of the huge Alentejo plain. A city steeped in history, it was occupied by the Romans and Moors for centuries. With its narrow streets, of Moorish origin, and white-washed houses, it also boasts one of the best-preserved Roman temples in the country plus various palaces and monuments, the majority dating from the 14th-16th centuries. One of the more extraordinary sights can be found in the Capela dos Ossos in the church of São Francisco – adorning the walls and pillars of this chamber are the bones of more than 5000 monks. On the Alentejo coast is the small peaceful town of Santiago do Cacém, which has two of the best beaches in Portugal. The nearby archaelogical site at Miróbriga includes ruins of a hippodrome, several houses (some of which have mural paintings) and a clearly defined acropolis. Further south along the coast is Porto Côvo and the larger, popular resort of Vila Nova de Milfontes, which has a little castle and ancient port.

Places of interest

Arraiolos: ancient town, 17th century castle, famous for its carpets.

Beja: provincial town founded by Julius Caesar, 13th century castle.

Borba: pretty town, noted for its marble and wine.

Elvas: ancient fortress town, 15th century aqueduct.

Estremoz: market town, medieval castle.

Odemira: quiet, characterful country town.

Reguengos de Monsaraz: charming, unspoiled village with whitewashed houses.

Vila Viçosa: attractive hillside town, 16th century convent.

Cuisine of the region

Alentejo was traditionally an important wheat-growing region (it is frequently referred to as the 'granary of Portugal'). Local specialities include *sopa de cação* (skate soup), made from fish and bread, and *ensopado de borrego* (lamb-stew). Cheeses of the region include *queijo de Serpa* and *queijos de Niza*, made from goats milk. The *queijos de Évora*, made from ewe's milk, is smaller in size with a strong, spicy flavour. *Arroz Doce* (rice pudding topped with cinnamon) is the traditional dessert for festivals and parties and is to be found all over the country.

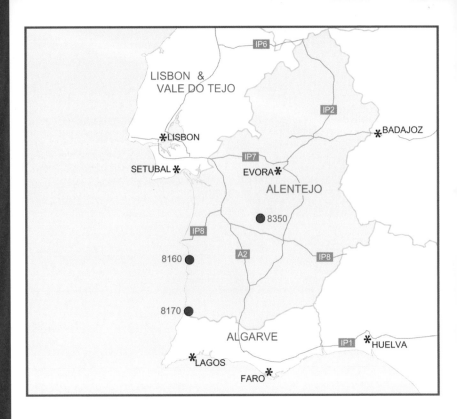

PO8170 Parque de Campismo São Miguel

São Miguel, Odeceixe, P-7630-592 Odemira (Beja)

Tel: **282 947145**. Email: **camping.sao.miguel@mail.telepac.pt**

Nestled in green hills near two pretty white villages, 4 km. from the beautiful Praia Odeceixe (beach) is the attractive camping park São Miguel. Unusually the site works on a maximum number of 700 campers, you find your own place (there are no defined pitches) under the tall trees, there are ample electrical points, and the land slopes away gently. Wooden chalet style accommodation to rent is in a separate area, but some mobile homes share the two traditional older style but clean sanitary blocks. The main building with its traditional Portuguese architecture is built around two sides of a large grassy square. It houses reception, restaurant, bars and supermarket. There are 'Lisbon Arcade' style verandas to sit under and enjoy a drink, coffee or meal while enjoying the view across the square to the pool, tennis courts and camping which is hidden under a canopy of trees. An outdoor cinema operates in summer showing films for children and adults. The self service restaurant and bars are excellent and there is a pizzeria by the pool with its own terrace (summer only). For those who want to self cater the supermarket has a bakery, as well as a wide range of goods including cooked chicken, fresh fruit and vegetables.

Facilities

Two older style toilet blocks with British style WCs and free hot showers. Washing machines. Toilets and basins for disabled campers but no shower. Shop (June -Sept). Self-service restaurant (March-Oct). Bar, snacks and pizzeria (June-Sept). Satellite TV. Playground. Tennis (charged). Swimming pool (charged). Dogs are not accepted. Torches useful. Off site: Bus service from gate. Historic village of Odeceixe 2 km. Beach, fishing and sailing 4 km. Riding 20 km. Site is inside the Alentejo nature park.

Open: All year.

Directions

Between Odemira and Lagos on the N120 just before the village of Odeceixe on the main road well signed. GPS: N37:26 W08:45

Charges 2006

Per person	€ 3,50 - € 5,50
child (5-10 yrs)	€ 2,00 - € 3,00
pitch	€ 7,00 - € 12,50
electricity	€ 2,75
Plus 7% VAT.	

PO8160 Parque de Campismo Porto Covo

Estrada Municipal 55u, P-7520-436 Porto Covo (Setubal)

Tel: **269 90 51 36**

This is a site in a popular, small seaside resort where a fairly large proportion of the pitches are occupied by Portuguese units. However, it has a reasonable sense of space as you pass the security barrier to reception which is part of an uncluttered and attractively designed 'village square' area with some well established apartments for rent. The pitches are somewhat small but are hedged, reasonably level, all have electricity (5A), and are shaded. The beaches are a short walk and feature steep cliffs and pleasant sandy shores. If you do not want to venture out to the beach then the site has a swimming pool located behind the restaurant and with areas for sunbathing. Dedicated barbecue areas are close to the pools. A mini market stocks the essentials and some souvenirs. A jolly bar and restaurant with terrace cleverly operates across the boundary of the site and it offers a varied Portuguese menu (popular with the locals) at very reasonable prices. A second smaller restaurant operates in the site in low season.

Facilities

The toilet blocks are clean with the usual amenities including hot showers. Motorcaravan services. Restaurant (10/6-30/9). Bar with satellite TV. Mini-market in season. Recreation room with games and a TV. Play area. Swimming pools (10/6-30/9). Tennis. Barbecue areas. Boat trips and fishing trips organised. Off site: The village is a short walk with shops, bars and restaurants. Bus service to Lisbon 300 m. from site. Fishing 500 m. Riding 20 km. Golf 25 km.

Open: All year.

Directions

From E120-1 Cercal - Sines road (the road changes from the E120 at Tanganheira). Turn left (southwest) to Porto Covo and follow site signs. Do not be surprised to be led through a new housing estate - look for large white water tower with site logo.

Charges 2006

Per person	€ 3,20
child	€ 1,60
pitch	€ 8,00 - € 11,10
electricty	€ 2,95

All plus 7% VAT. Reductions in low season.

PO8350 Camping Markádia

Barragem de Odivelas, Apartado 17, P-7920-999 Alvito (Beja)

Tel: **284 76 31 41**

A tranquil, lakeside site in an unspoilt setting, this will appeal most to those nature lovers who want to 'get away from it all' and to those who enjoy country pursuits such as walking, fishing or riding. There are 130 casual unmarked pitches on undulating grass and sand with ample electricity hook-ups (16A). The site is lit but a torch is required. The friendly Dutch owner has carefully planned the site so each pitch has its own oak tree to provide shade. The open countryside and lake provide excellent views and a very pleasant environment, albeit somewhat remote. The lake is in fact a 1,000 hectare reservoir, and more than 120 species of birds can be found in the area. The stellar views in the very low ambient lighting are wonderful at night. The bar/restaurant with a terrace is open daily in season but weekends only during the winter. One can swim in the reservoir and rowing boats, pedaloes and windsurfers are available for hire. You may bring your own boat, although power boats are not allowed on environmental grounds.

Facilities

Four modern, clean and well equipped toilet blocks are built in traditional Portuguese style with hot water throughout. Washing machines. Motorcaravan services. Bar and restaurant (1/4-30/9). Shop (all year, bread to order). Lounge. Playground. Fishing. Boat hire. Tennis. Riding. Medical post. Car wash. Dogs are not accepted in July/August. Facilities and amenities may be reduced outside the main season. Off site: Swimming and boating in the lake.

Open: All year.

Directions

From A2 between Setabul and the Algarve take exit 10 on IP8 signed Ferreira and Beja. Take road to Torrao and 13 km. later, 1 km. north of Odivelas, turn right towards Barragem and site is 3 km. after crossing head of reservoir following small signs (one small section of poor road).
GPS: N38:11.22 W08:06.22

Charges 2006

Per person	€ 4,80
child (5-10 yrs)	€ 2,40
pitch	€ 4,80 - € 9,60
electricity	€ 2,40

Discounts of 10-20% outside June - Aug, and for longer stays. No credit cards.

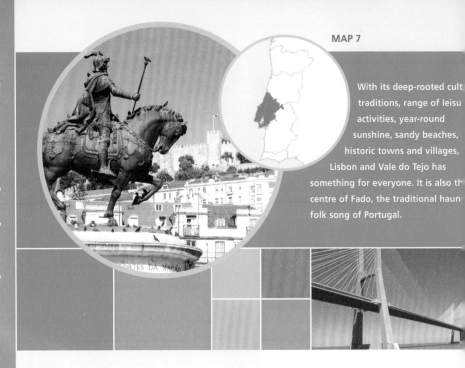

MAP 7

With its deep-rooted cult
traditions, range of leisu
activities, year-round
sunshine, sandy beaches,
historic towns and villages,
Lisbon and Vale do Tejo has
something for everyone. It is also th
centre of Fado, the traditional haun
folk song of Portugal.

THIS REGION IS DIVIDED INTO FOUR DISTRICTS:
LEIRIA, LISBON, SANTARÉM AND SETÚBAL

(PART OF SETÚBAL ALSO FEATURES IN THE
ALENTEJO REGION)

Standing on the banks of the river Tagus, Lisbon has been the capital of Portugal since 1255. Places of interest in the city include the medieval quarters of Alfama and Mouraria, with their cobbled streets and alleys, colourful buildings, markets and castles, and Belém, with its tower and the 16th century Jerónimos monastery. Lisbon also boasts an assortment of museums. Not far from the capital lies the romantic town of Sintra, which has an array of cottages, manor houses and palaces. Its mountains also form part of the Sintra-Cascais Natural Park. Along the Atlantic coast, high sweeping cliffs lead down to white sandy beaches, backed by lagoons. Europe's westernmost point, Cabo da Roca, is found here as are plenty of coastal towns and villages including Peniche, Nazaré and Óbidos, a small medieval walled town with cobbled streets, tiny whitewashed houses and balconies brimming with flowers. Further inland, at Alcobaça, Tomar and Batalha, are ancient monasteries, with castles in Leiria, Tomar and Santarém. Recreational pursuits include water sports, fishing and golf. In summer there are open air music festivals.

Places of interest

Estoril: casino, golf course and racing track.

Fátima: one of the most important centres of pilgrimage in the Catholic world.

Leiria: medieval royal castle, 16th century cathedral, Romanesque church.

Mafra: 18th century Palace-Convent, the largest Portuguese religious monument.

Santarém: castle, archaeology museum, Gothic convent and churches.

Sesimbra: picturesque small fishing town, medieval castle, the Lagoa de Albufeira is a favourite spot for windsurfers.

Setúbal: natural reserve, beaches, golf courses.

Tomar: 12th century Templars' Castle, Gothic and Renaissance churches, 15th century synagogue.

Cuisine of the region

Fish soups, stews and seafood are popular, including *sardinha assada* (grilled sardines) and *Bifes de Espardarte* (swordfish steaks). Sintra is famed for its cheesecakes, which according to ancient documents were already being made in the 12th century, and were part of the rent payments. Wine-producing regions include Azeitão, Bucelas, Carcavelos and Colares.

Caldeiradas: fish stews.

Queijadas: cheese tarts.

Pastéis de Belém: custard tarts.

Travesseiros: puff pastries stuffed with a sweet eggy mixture.

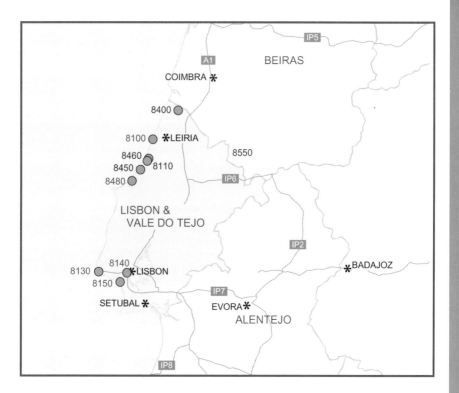

PO8150 Orbitur Camping Costa da Caparica

Avenida Alfonso de Albuquerque, Quinta de St Antonio, P-2825-450 Costa da Caparica (Setubal)

Tel: **212 90 13 66**. Email: **info@orbitur.pt**

This is very much a site for 600 permanent caravans but it has relatively easy access to Lisbon (just under 20 km.) via the motorway, by bus or even by bus and ferry if you wish. It is situated near a small resort, favoured by the Portuguese themselves, which has all the usual amenities plus a good sandy beach (200 m. from the site) and promenade walks. There is a small area for touring units which includes some larger pitches for motorcaravans. We see this very much as a site to visit Lisbon rather than for prolonged stays. Some activities and shows are organised in season in an outdoor disco and entertainment area.

Facilities

The three toilet blocks have mostly British style toilets, washbasins with cold water and some hot showers - they come under pressure when the site is full. Facilities for disabled visitors. Washing machine. Motorcaravan services. Supermarket. Large bar/restaurant (not Nov). TV room (satellite). Playground. Gas supplies. Off site: Bus service from site gate. Fishing 1 km. Riding 4 km. Golf 5 km.

Open: All year.

Directions

Cross the Tagus bridge (toll) on A2 motorway going south from Lisbon, immediately take the turning for Caparica and Trafaria. At 7 km. marker on IC20 turn right (no sign) - the site is at the second roundabout. GPS: N38:39.22 W09:14.33

Charges 2007

Per person	€ 2,70 - € 4,80
child (5-10 yrs)	€ 1,35 - € 2,40
caravan and car	€ 6,70 - € 12,50
electricity	€ 2,40 - € 3,00
Off season discounts (up to 70%).	

PO8130 Orbitur Camping Guincho

E.N. 247, Lugar da Areia - Guincho, P-2750-053 Cascais (Lisbon)

Tel: **214 87 04 50**. Email: **info@orbitur.pt**

Although this is a popular site for permanent Portuguese units with 1,295 pitches, it is nevertheless quite attractively laid out among low pine trees and with the A5 autostrada connection to Lisbon (30 km), it provides a useful alternative to sites nearer the city. This is viewed as an alternative for visiting Lisbon, not a holiday site. There is a choice of pitches (small – mainly about 50 sq.m.) mostly with electricity, although siting amongst the trees may be tricky, particularly when the site is full. Located behind sand dunes and a wide, sandy beach, the site offers a wide range of facilities. These include a fairly plain bar/restaurant, supermarket (all year), general lounge with pool tables, electronic games, TV room and a good laundry.

Facilities

Three sanitary blocks, one refurbished, are in the older style but are clean and tidy. Washbasins with cold water but hot showers. Facilities for disabled visitors. Washing machines and dryers. Motorcaravan services. Gas. Supermarket. Restaurant, bar and terrace (all year). General room with TV. Tennis. Playground. Entertainment in summer. Chalets to rent. Off site: Bus service from gate. Excursions. Riding 500 m. Beach 800 m. Fishing 1 km. Golf 3 km.

Open: All year.

Directions

Approach from either direction on N247. Turn inland 6.5 km. west of Cascais at camp sign. Travelling direct from Lisbon, the site is well signed as you leave the A5 autopista. GPS: N38:43.27 W09:28.00

Charges 2007

Per person	€ 2,70 - € 4,80
child (5-10 yrs)	€ 1,35 - € 2,40
caravan and car	€ 6,70 - € 12,50
electricity	€ 2,40 - € 3,00

Off season discounts (up to 70%).

PO8140 Lisboa Camping-Parque Municipal de Monsanto

Estrada da Circunvalacao, P-1400-061 Lisboa (Lisbon)

Tel: **217 623 100**

This very large site is professionally operated by many uniformed staff, providing a quality service at a good price. The wide entrance with its ponds, fountains and the trees, lawns and flowering shrubs leading up to the swimming pool, is a most attractive feature. On sloping ground, the site's many terraces are well shaded by trees and shrubs. The 400 good pitches include 170 serviced pitches on concrete hardstandings. There is a huge separate area for tents, and 70 chalet style bungalows are for hire. Central Lisbon is 8 km. with two bus routes giving a regular service from the gate. A decent beach is 10 km. Athough a city site, it is big enough to generate a park atmosphere and when we visited we spotted many red squirrels and an abundance of birds. This is a most pleasant site for visiting Lisbon or just relaxing using the impressive facilities.

Facilities

Eight solar-powered toilet blocks contain quality facilities, including those for disabled people. Launderette. Motorcaravan service point. Shops, bar and restaurants (all year). Two swimming pools (with lifeguard; May - Sept). Tennis. Minigolf. Sports field. Playgrounds. Roman theatre. Entertainment in high season. General and TV (cable) rooms. Internet café. Organised excursions. Off site: Excellent bus service from site gate. Lisbon city. Beaches 10 km. Bicycle hire 2 km. Golf 5 km. Riding 16 km.

Open: All year.

Directions

From Lisbon take A5 motorway towards Estoril and site is signed from junction 4 onto the 1C17 (huge site signs at first exit to Buraca). Site is immediately on the right. Enter to the right of the fountain on the tiled road. GPS: N38:43.48 W09:12.38

Charges 2006

Per person	€ 4,20 - € 5,60
child (6-12 yrs)	€ 2,10 - € 2,80
pitch incl. electricity	€ 6,75 - € 10,30

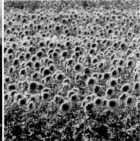

PO8100 Orbitur Camping São Pedro de Moel

Rua Volta do Sete, P-2430 São Pedro de Moel (Leiria)

Tel: **244 59 91 68**. Email: **info@orbitur.pt**

This quiet and very attractive site is situated under tall pines, on the edge of the rather select small resort of São Pedro de Moel. This is a shady site which can be crowded in July and August. The 525 pitches are in blocks and are unmarked (cars may be parked separately) with 404 electrical connections. A few pitches are used for permanent units. Although there are areas of soft sand, there should be no problem in finding a firm place. The large restaurant and bar are modern as is the superb swimming pool, paddling pool and flume (there is a lifeguard). The attractive, sandy beach is about 500 m. walk downhill from the site (you can take the car, although parking may be difficult in the town) and is sheltered from the wind by low cliffs.

Facilities

Four clean toilet blocks have mainly British style toilets (some with bidets), some washbasins with hot water. Hot showers are mostly in one block. Laundry. Motorcaravan services. Gas supplies. Supermarket (all year). Large restaurant and bar with terrace (closed in November). Swimming pools (31/3-30/9). Satellite TV. Games room. Playground. Tennis. Off site: Bus service 100 m. Beach 500 m. Fishing 1 km.

Open: All year.

Directions

Site is 9 km. west of Marinha Grande, on the right as you enter São Pedro de Moel.
GPS: N39:45.45 W09:01.60

Charges 2007

Per person	€ 2,70 - € 4,80
child (5-10 yrs)	€ 1,30 - € 2,40
caravan and car	€ 6,70 - € 12,50
electricity	€ 2,40 - € 3,00

Off season discounts (up to 70%).

PO8110 Orbitur Camping Valado

Rua dos Combatentes do Ultramar, 2, Valado, P-2450-148 Nazaré (Leiria)

Tel: **262 56 11 11**. Email: **info@orbitur.pt**

This popular site is close to the old, traditional fishing port of Nazaré which has now become something of a holiday resort and popular with coach parties. The large sandy beach in the town (about 2 km. steeply downhill from the site) is sheltered by headlands and provides good swimming. The campsite is on undulating ground under tall pine trees, has 503 pitches and, although some smallish individual pitches with electricity and water can be reserved, the bulk of the site is not marked out and units are close together during July/August. About 375 electrical connections are available. The functional restaurant and bar are contained in one white-walled block and are open 18.00 - 21.00 only. Essential supplies are available from reception.

Facilities

The three toilet blocks have British and Turkish style WCs, washbasins (some cold water) and 17 hot showers, all very clean when inspected. Laundry. Motorcaravan services. Gas supplies. Supermarket (all season). Bar, snack bar and restaurant with terrace (Easter and June-Oct). TV/general room. Playground. Tennis. Off site: Bus service 20 m. Fishing and bicycle hire 2 km.

Open: 1 February - 30 November.

Directions

Site is on the Nazaré - Alcobaca N8-5 road, 2 km. east of Nazaré.

Charges 2007

Per person	€ 2,20 - € 4,00
child (5-10 yrs)	€ 1,10 - € 2,00
caravan and car	€ 4,65 - € 9,90
electricity	€ 2,40

Off season discounts (up to 70%).

Check real time availability and at-the-gate prices...

www.**alanrogers**.com

PO8400 Campismo O Tamanco

Casas Brancas II, P-3100-231 Louriçal (Leiria)

Tel: **236 95 25 51**. Email: **campismo.o.tamanco@mail.telepac.pt**

O Tamanco is a peaceful countryside site, with a homely, almost farmstead atmosphere. You will have chickens and ducks wandering around and there is a Burro here. The young Dutch owners, Irene and Hans, are sure to give you a warm welcome at this delightful little site. The 100 good sized pitches are separated by cordons of all manner of fruit trees, ornamental trees and flowering shrubs, on level grassy ground. There is electricity (6/16A) to 72 pitches and 5 pitches are suitable for large motorhomes. The site is lit and there is nearly always space available. The swimming pool is very pleasant, as is the small bar and a restaurant (with vegetarian menu options). Courses in printing and sculpture are arranged at certain times of the year. There may also be entertainment for the children during the day. The site is extremely popular with the Dutch, mature couples and winter campers. One can fish or swim in a nearby lake and the resort beaches are a short drive. There is some road noise on pitches at the front of the site.

Facilities

The single toilet block provides very clean and generously sized facilities including washbasins in cabins, with easy access for disabled visitors. As facilities are limited they may be busy in peak periods. Hot water throughout. Washing machine. Bar/restaurant. Roofed patio with fireplace. TV room/lounge (satellite). Internet access. Swimming pool. Off site: Bus service 1 km. Lake 2 km. Beach 11 km. Market in nearby Lourical every Sunday.

Open: 1 February - 31 October.

Directions

From N109/IC1 (Leira - Figuera de Foz) road, 25 km. south of Figuera in Matos de Carriço, turn on to N342 road (signed Louriçal 6 km). Site is 1.5 km. on the left. GPS: N39:59.50 W08:47.31

Charges 2006

Per person	€ 3,30
child (up to 5 yrs)	€ 1,75
pitch	€ 4,90 - € 6,00
electricity (6A)	€ 2,45 - € 3,35

Winter discounts up to 40%. No credit cards.

PO8450 Parque de Campismo Colina do Sol

Serra Dos Mangues, P-2465 São Martinho do Porto (Leiria)

Tel: **262 98 97 64**. Email: **parque.colima.sol@dix.pt**

Colina do Sol is a well appointed site with its own swimming pool and near the beach. Only 2 km. from the small town of São Martinho do Porto, it has around 350 pitches marked by fruit and ornamental trees on grassy terraces. Electricity (6A) is available. The attractive entrance with its beds of bright flowers, is wide enough for even the largest of outfits, and the surfaced roads are very pleasant for manoeuvring. There is a warm welcome and good English is spoken. The beach is at the rear of the site, with access via a gate which is locked at night. We are told that swimming in the sea requires great care when there are large waves – there is no lifeguard. The site has a well stocked supermarket, a restaurant and a bar with a delightful paved terrace beside the large clean swimming and paddling pools. This is a convenient base for exploring the Costa de Prata and for excursions to old town of Leiria, with its crenulated walls towering high above the rock faces, and to the famous shrine of Fátima. Market in São Martinho do Porto is on Sunday.

Facilities

Two large, clean and modern toilet blocks provide British style WCs (some with bidets), washbasins - some with hot water. Dishwashing and laundry sinks are outside but covered. Motorcaravan services. Supermarket. Bar and restaurant (1/7-31/8). Satellite TV. Swimming pool (1/7-10/9). Off site: Bus from the gate to nearby towns. Shop, restaurant and bar within 200 m. Beach (no lifeguard).

Open: All year excl. 25 December.

Directions

Turn from EN 242 (Caldas-Nazaré) road northeast of San Martinho do Porto. Site is clearly signed. GPS: N39:31.37 W09:07.38

Charges 2006

Per person	€ 3,65 - € 4,30
child (4-10 yrs)	€ 1,79 - € 2,10
pitch	€ 6,92 - € 9,85
electricity	€ 2,60

Less in low seasons.

PO8460 Camping Caravaning Vale Paraiso

E.N. 242, P-2450-138 Nazaré (Leiria)

Tel: 262 56 18 00. Email: info@valeparaiso.com

A pleasant, well managed site, Vale Paraiso improves every year, with the latest additions being new reception buildings and pool areas. The owners are keen to welcome British visitors and English is spoken. The site is by the main N242 road in eight hectares of undulating pine woods. There are over 600 shady pitches, many on sandy ground only suitable for tents. For other units there are around 250 individual pitches of varying size on harder ground with electricity available. A large range of sporting and leisure activities includes an excellent outdoor pool and paddling pool with sunbathing areas. The adventure playground is very safe with new equipment. There is a pleasant bar, and innovative takeaway selling roasts and a lower level restaurant/bar. Several long beaches of white sand are within 2-15 km. allowing windsurfing, sailing or surfing. Animation for children and evening entertainment is organised in season. Nazaré is an old fishing village with narrow streets, a harbour and marina and many outdoor bars and cafés, with a lift to Sitio. There is much of historical interest in the area although the mild Atlantic climate is also conducive to just relaxing.

Facilities

Spotless sanitary facilities have hot water throughout. Nearly all WCs are British style. Modern facilities for disabled people. Baby baths. Washing machine and dryers. Motorcaravan services. Supermarket (1/5-30/9). Restaurant (March - Sept). Café/bar with satellite TV (all year). Brilliant takeaway. Tabac. Swimming and paddling pools (March - Sept; free for under 11s). Petanque. Leisure games. Amusement hall. Bicycle hire. Safety deposit. Gas supplies. E-mail and fax facilities. Apartments to rent. Off site: Bus service from gate. Fishing 1.5 km. Boat launching 2.5 km. Riding 5 km. Golf 35 km.

Open: All year excl. 10-26 December.

Directions

Site is 2 km. north of Nazaré on the EN242 Marinha Grande road.

Charges 2007

Per person	€ 3,10 - € 4,20
child (3-10 yrs)	€ 1,50 - € 2,00
electricity (4-10A)	€ 2,50

Credit cards accepted for amounts over € 150. Camping Cheques accepted.

vale paraíso camping

Apartments Bungalows Chalets

Reservations on-line - www.valeparaiso.com
Estrada Nacional 242
2450-138 Nazaré-PORTUGAL
Tel. 351 262 561 800   Fax. 351 262 561 900
info@valeparaiso.com

NATURE • SEA • CULTURE

PO8480 Orbitur Camping Foz do Arelho

Rua Maldonado Freitas, P-2500-516 Foz do Arelho (Leiria)

Tel: **262 97 86 83**. Email: **info@orbitur.pt**

This is a large and roomy ex-municipal site and improvements are still taking place. It is 2 km. from the beach and has a new central complex with a most impressive swimming pool and separated children's pool with lifeguard. Pitches are generally sandy with some hardstandings. They vary in size and are unmarked on two main levels with wide tarmac roads. There is some shade and all touring pitches have electricity (5/15A). The large two storey, brick-faced building contains all the site's leisure facilities but has no ramped access and there are no sanitary facilities anywhere on site for disabled campers. This building is somewhat sterile and the furniture is bland but there are pleasant views over the pool from the restaurant and terrace. This is a pleasant site with sound facilities but probably not recommended if you have special needs. Some permanent Portuguese units are occupied in high season and weekends at other times.

Facilities

Four identical modern sanitary buildings (solar heating) with seatless British and Turkish style WCs and free showers. Washing machine in one. No facilities for disabled campers. No chemical disposal point. Supermarket (all year). Bar/snacks and restaurant. (closed November). Children's club. Games room. Small new amphitheatre. Playground – supervision needed. Bus service. Doctor's room. Torches useful. Off site: Bus 500 m. Seaside town 2 km. Fishing 2 km.

Open: All year.

Directions

Site is north of Lisbon and west of Caldos la Rainha. From the A8 take N360 to Foz de Arelho. Site is well signed. GPS: N39:25.84 W09:12.05

Charges 2007

Per person	€ 2,60 - € 4,60
child (5-10 yrs)	€ 1,30 - € 2,30
caravan and car	€ 5,80 - € 11,20
electricity	€ 2,40

PO8550 Camping Quinta da Cerejeira

P-2240-33 Ferreira do Zêzere (Santarem)

Tel: **249 361756**. Email: **info@cerejeira.com**

This is a delightful, small, family owned new venture run by Gert and Teunie Verheij assisted by their children. It is a converted farm (quinta) and has been coaxed into a very special campsite. The pitches are on flat grass or on long terraces under fruit and olive trees. There are 18 pitches with electricity (6A) from a central server. There is some shade and the site is full of rustic charm and craft works. It is very peaceful with views of the surrounding green hills from the charming vine-covered patio above a small swimming pool. You will notice the working well, no longer powered by a donkey but you can see where he used to circle to pump water. The charmimg restaurant offers an extremely reasonable menu of the day. This site packs a punch in that it has several rooms set aside for art and craft activities and quality workshops are offered in a range of subjects including pottery, painting and Portuguese cooking. Live entertainment is arranged in season. Visits are arranged to local vineyards and we recommend a picnic at the nearby lake which also offers all manner of watersports. A visit to Tomar to explore the temple and legends of Knights Templar is fun. If you like a small peaceful, friendly site this is for you.

Facilities

The single rustic sanitary building has seatless British style WCs with hot showers. It could be busy at peak periods. Washing machine. No facilities for disabled campers. No shop but just ask and the baker calls daily. Bar with snacks and restaurant. Children's club room. Separate games and rest room with satellite TV. Artistic workshops. Internet terminals. One swing for children. Torches useful. Off site: Bus service from town 1 km. Town has shops, bars and restaurants. Fishing 5 km. Watersports 5 km. Riding 11 km.

Open: All year excl. December & January (but see above).

Directions

From Lisbon take A1/A23 to Torres Novas then IC3 to Tomar and N238 to Ferreira do Zezere. Take road N348 to Vila de Rei and the site is 1 km. from Ferreira do Zezere to the eastern side of town (do not go into the town). GPS: N39:42.2 W08:16.69

Charges 2006

Per person	€ 2,70 - € 3,00
child (under 10 yrs)	€ 1,50 - € 1,35
pitch incl. car	€ 4,25 - € 5,75
electricity	€ 2,25

Check real time availability and at-the-gate prices...

www.alanrogers.com

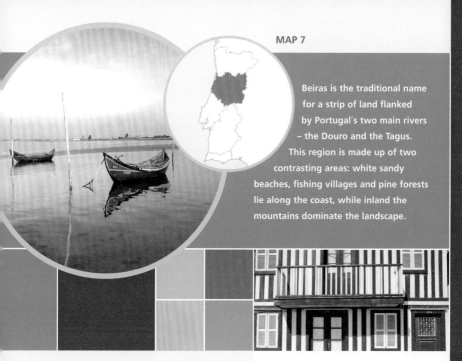

MAP 7

Beiras is the traditional name for a strip of land flanked by Portugal's two main rivers – the Douro and the Tagus. This region is made up of two contrasting areas: white sandy beaches, fishing villages and pine forests lie along the coast, while inland the mountains dominate the landscape.

BEIRAS HAS FIVE DISTRICTS: AVEIRO, COIMBRA, CASTELO BRANCO, GUARDA AND VISEU

One of Europe's oldest university towns, Coimbra was Portugal's capital from 1143 to 1255. The university, founded in 1290, has kept its academic traditions, as seen in the black-capped students, in the soulful tones of the fado de Coimbra (a traditional song sung to the sound of guitars by the students) and in the Queima das Fitas (Burning of the Ribbons), a boisterous celebration of graduating students. Coimbra also boasts a Romanesque cathedral and south of the town lies Conímbriga, with the most important Roman remains in Portugal. Surrounded by the original walls, the archaeological site features an early Christian burial ground, a set of hot springs and a museum. Further north lies Aveiro. Famous for its lagoon, the town is crisscrossed by canals where colourfully painted moliceiro boats sail. To the east lies the Serra de Estrela, the highest mountain range in the country. It is home to the textile town of Covilha, attractive villages including Gouveia, Manteigas and Seia, plus the mountain resort of Guarda. Along the coast, the pretty seaside resorts of São Martinho do Porto, Nazaré and Figueira da Foz offer fine sandy beaches, good seafood restaurants and water sports facilities.

Places of interest

Belmonte: hilltop town, castle, Romanesque-Gothic church.

Bussaco: national park founded by monks in the 6th century.

Castelo Branco: 13th century castle, medieval quarter, 16th-18th century churches.

Curia and *Luso*: spa towns.

Monsanto: historic village, 12th-century castle, 18th-century manor-houses.

Viseu: remains of Gothic walls, cathedral.

Cuisine of the region

Roast pork, lamb stew, seafood and fresh fish are popular, including *truta* (trout) from the mountains of Serra da Estrela. The famous ewe's milk cheese Queijo da Serra, is also a produced in the mountains, and can be bought at Cheese Fairs held in villages and towns throughout the region during February and March. Regional desserts include hard and sweet biscuits, pancakes and sponge cake (*ovos-moles, pão-de-ló*).

Chanfana: lamb stewed in red wine.

Leitão assado da Bairrada: roast pork.

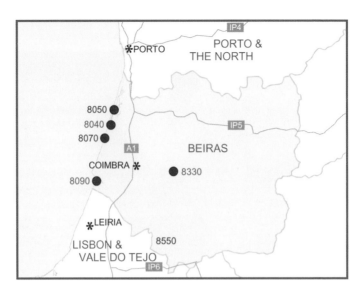

PO8040 Parque de Campismo da Vagueira

Gafanha da Vagueira, Gafanha da Boa Hora, P-3840-254 Vagos (Aveiro)

Tel: **234 797526**

This is a large site set 1.5 km. from the beach and 500 m. from the 'Ria da Gosta Nova' river. It is shaded under tall pine trees and has comprehensive facilities and reasonable prices. The 800 pitches are unmarked, on sand and pine needles with a large number of permanent Portuguese units which are here in high season and weekends at other times. Groups are taken in high season. All touring pitches have electricity (6A). In sympathy with the surroundings, the modern buildings have clean lines and include a restaurant and bar with a disco area outside where music is played at weekends.

Facilities

Seven modern sanitary buildings with British and Turkish style WCs and free showers. Facilities for disabled campers (unlocked). Washing machines. Bar/snacks and separate (June-Sept). Large supermarket. Children's club. Outdoor disco. Games room. Playground. Tennis (charge). Satellite TV. Internet room. Torches useful. Off site: Seaside town has shops bars and restaurants. River fishing 500 m. Watersports at beach 1.5 km. Golf 1 km. Riding 1 km. Bus 500 m.

Open: All year.

Directions

Site is south of Aveiro. Take N109 south from Aveiro towards Mira. At Vagos take the N333 right turn towards Vagueira. Site is well signed at this turn and is just off the roundabout you arrive at on the beach road. GPS: N40:33.475 W08:44.71

Charges 2006

Per person	€ 1,83 - € 3,65
child	€ 0,95 - € 1,85
pitch and car	€ 3,25 - € 8,50
electricity	€ 2,00

PO8050 Orbitur Camping São Jacinto

E.N. 327, km 20, São Jacinto, P-3800-909 Aveiro (Aveiro)

Tel: **234 83 82 84**. Email: **info@orbitur.pt**

This small site is in the São Jacinto nature reserve, on a peninsula between the Atlantic and the Barrinha, with views to the mountains beyond. The area is a weekend resort for locals and can be crowded in high season – it may therefore be difficult to find space in July/Aug, particularly for larger units. This is not a large site, taking 169 units on unmarked pitches, but in most places trees provide natural limits and shade. Swimming and fishing are both possible in the adjacent Ria, or the sea, 20 minutes walk from a guarded back gate.

Facilities

Two toilet blocks, very clean when inspected, contain the usual facilities. Dishwashing and laundry sinks. Washing machine and ironing board in a separate part of the toilet block. Motorcaravan services. Shop (all season). Restaurant, bar and snack bar (Easter and June-Oct). Playground. Five bungalows to rent. Off site: Bus service 20 m. Fishing 200 m. Bicycle hire 10 km.

Open: 1 February - 31 October.

Directions

Turn off N109 at Estarreja to N109-5 to cross bridge over Ria da Gosta Nova and on to Torreira and São Jacinto. From Porto go south N1/09, turn for Ovar on the N327 which leads to São Jacinto.

Charges 2007

Per person	€ 2,20 - € 4,00
child (5-10 yrs)	€ 1,10 - € 2,00
pitch incl. electricity	€ 7,05 - € 12,30
Off season discounts (up to 70%).	

PO8070 Orbitur Camping Mira

Estrada Florestal no. 1 - km 2, Dunas de Mira, P-3070-792 Praia de Mira (Coimbra)

Tel: **231 47 12 34**. Email: **info@orbitur.pt**

A small, peaceful seaside site set in pinewoods, Orbitur Camping Mira is situated to the south of Aveiro and Vagos, in a quieter and less crowded area. It fronts onto a lake at the head of the Ria de Mira, which eventually runs into the Aveiro Ria. A back gate leads directly to the sea and a wide quiet beach 300 m. away. A road runs alongside the site boundary where the restaurant complex is situated resulting in some road noise. The site has around 225 pitches on sand, which are not marked but with trees creating natural divisions. Electricity and water points are plentiful.

Facilities

The modern toilet blocks are clean, with 14 free hot showers and washing machines. Facilities for disabled visitors. Motorcaravan services. Gas supplies. Shop (all season). Restaurant, bar and snack bar (Easter and June-Oct). TV room. Play area. Bicycle hire. Bungalows (7) to rent. Off site: Bus service 150 m. (summer only). Fishing 500 m. Indoor pool, lake swimming and riding 7 km.

Open: 1 January - 30 November.

Directions

Take the IP5 (A25) southwest to Aveiro then the A17 south to Figuera da Foz. Then take the N109 north to Mira and follow signs west to Praia de Mira.

Charges 2007

Per person	€ 2,40 - € 4,40
child (5-10 yrs)	€ 1,20 - € 2,20
caravan and car	€ 5,40 - € 10,60
electricity	€ 2,40 - € 3,00

Off season discounts (up to 70%).

PO8090 Orbitur Camping Gala

E.N. 109 - km 4 - Gala, P-3080-458 Figueira da Foz (Coimbra)

Tel: **233 43 14 92**. Email: **info@orbitur.pt**

This site of around 450 pitches is on sandy terrain under a canopy of pine trees and well cared for. Some pitches near the road are rather noisy. One can drive or walk the 300 m. from the back of the site to a private beach; you should swim with caution when it is windy – the warden will advise. The site fills in July/August and units may be very close together, but there should be plenty of room at other times. Besides the beach, Coimbra and the nearby Roman remains are worth visiting.

Facilities

The three toilet blocks have British and Turkish style toilets, individual basins (some with hot water) and free hot showers. Laundry. Motorcaravan services. Gas supplies. Supermarket and restaurant/bar with terrace (all open all year). Lounge. Playground. Tennis. TV. Doctor visits in season. Car wash area. Open-air pool (June-Sept). Off site: Beach 300 m. Fishing 1 km. Bicycle hire and riding 3 km.

Open: All year.

Directions

Site is 4 km. south of Figueira da Foz beyond the two rivers; turn off N109 1 km. from bridge on southern edge of Gala, look for Orbitur sign on roundabout it is then 600 m. to site.
GPS: N40°07.11 W08°51.41

Charges 2007

Per person	€ 2,60 - € 4,60
child (5-10 yrs)	€ 1,30 - € 2,30
caravan and car	€ 5,80 - € 11,20
electricity	€ 2,40

Off season discounts (up to 70%).

PO8330 Camping Municipal Arganil

E.N. 17 - km5, Sarzedo, P-3300 Arganil (Coimbra)

Tel: **235 20 57 06**

This peaceful, inland site is attractively located in the hamlet of Sarzedo, some 2 km. from the town of Arganil. A spacious and well planned site, it is of a high quality for a municipal and prices are very reasonable! Delightfully situated among pine trees above the River Alva where one can swim, fish or canoe. The 150 pitches, most with electricity (15A), are of a reasonable size, mainly on flat sandy grass terraces and most shaded by tall trees. The site is kept beautifully clean and neat and access roads are tarmac. An excellent, small restaurant has an unusual attached bar with terrace.

Facilities

Sanitary facilities are clean and well maintained, with Turkish and British style WCs, controllable hot showers, washbasins in semi-private partitioned cabins and a hairdressing area. Ramped entrances make it suitable for disabled visitors. Washing machines. Bar, restaurant and snacks (all year). Shop (July - Sept). TV room. Tennis. Off site: Bus service 50 m. River beach and fishing 100 m. Watersports 200 m. Swimming pool in nearby Arganil. Golf 25 km.

Open: All year.

Directions

From EN17/N2 Coimbra - Sarzedo at 324.4 km. marker exit to Sarzedo (site signed). Ignore first site sign to Avelar as there is a better access 500 m. further up the road on the right, also signed.

Charges 2006

Per person	€ 1,60 - € 1,80
child (5-10 yrs)	€ 1,10 - € 1,30
pitch	€ 3,10 - € 7,00
electricity	€ 2,00 - € 2,40

Plus 7% VAT.

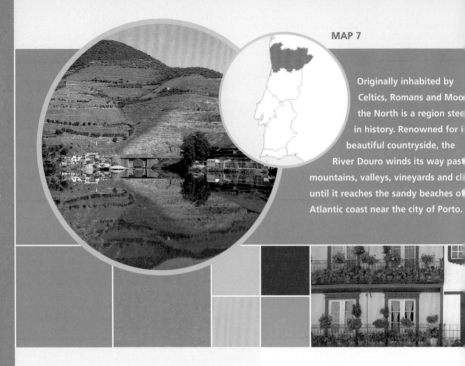

MAP 7

Originally inhabited by Celtics, Romans and Moo the North is a region stee in history. Renowned for i beautiful countryside, the River Douro winds its way past mountains, valleys, vineyards and cl until it reaches the sandy beaches of Atlantic coast near the city of Porto.

THE REGION IS COMPRISED OF FIVE DISTRICTS: BRAGA, BRAGANÇA, PORTO, VIANA DO CASTELO AND VILA REAL

Situated in the north western corner of Portugal, the Costa Verde boasts lush green pine forests and unspoilt sandy beaches, dotted with picturesque seaside villages, including Caminha and Vila Nova de Cerveira. It is also renowned for its wine, being the home of Port and Vinho Verdo. Located on the banks for the River Douro, the attractive city of Porto is the centre of the Port wine trade – free tastings are offered at the wine cellars in Vila Nova de Gaia – and terraced vineyards can be found across the Douro Valley. The region is also a perfect place for walking, mountain trekking, canoeing or simply relaxing in the spa towns of Carvalhelhos, Chaves and Pedras Salgadas. Vidago has a magnificent park with swimming pools and a golf course, while the mountains of Peneda, Soajo and Gerês form the Peneda Geres National Park, an area covering 170,000 acres, with an abundance of wildlife. Vila Nova de Foz is the centre for visits to the Côa Archaeological Park, which houses one of the world's largest collections of outdoor Palaeolithic rock art, dating back 22,000 years.

Places of interest

Barcelos: medieval walled town with dungeon, ceramics museum, archaeology museum.

Bragança: medieval castle and walls, 16th century cathedral, railway museum with 19th century locomotives and carriages.

Chaves: Roman bridge, 14th century castle with Archaeology and Epigraphy Museum.

Guimarães: medieval castle and walls, palace.

Lamego: medieval castle, 12th century fortress.

Ponte de Lima: beautiful small town, Roman bridge, medieval towers, manor houses.

Viana do Castelo: town famous for its handicrafts and colourful regional costumes.

Vila do Conde: ancient medieval shipyard, famous for its manufactured lace.

Cuisine of the region

Typical dishes include *bacalhau* (dried and salted cod), *rabanadas*, *papos-de-anjo* and *barrigas-de-freiras* (sweetmeats). Porto has its own tripe dish *Tripas à moda do Porto*.

The Minho region is renowned for its *Vinhos Verdes*, whose vines are grown on trellises (being suspended high in the air on special frames). In the Douro region, the vines are grown on terraces, giving the impression of huge natural staircases leading down to the banks of the river. Both red and white wines are produced here including the famous *Vinho do Porto* (Port Wine).

Caldo verde: thick soup made with green cabbage, potatoes and spicy sausage.

Feijoada à transmontana: bean stew.

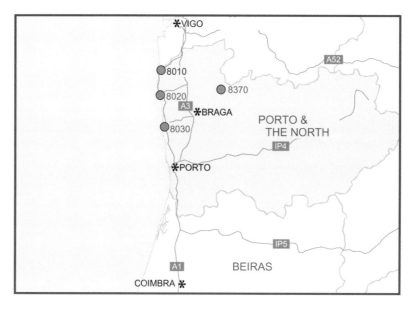

PO8010 Orbitur Camping Caminha

EN13 - km. 90, Mata do Camarido, P-4910-180 Caminha (Viana do Costelo)

Tel: **258 92 12 95**. Email: **info@orbitur.pt**

In northern Portugal close to the Spanish border, this pleasant site is just 200 metres from the beach. It has an attractive and peaceful setting in woods alongside the river estuary that marks the border with Spain and on the edge of the little town of Caminha. The site is shaded by tall pines with other small trees planted to mark large sandy pitches. The main site road is surfaced but elsewhere take care not to get trapped in soft sand. Pitching and parking can be haphazard.

Facilities	Directions
The clean, well maintained toilet block has British style toilets, washbasins (cold water) and hot showers, plus beach showers, extra dishwashing and laundry sinks (cold water). Laundry. Motorcaravan services. Small restaurant/bar with snacks (all Easter and 1/6-15/9), supermarket (all year). Bicycle hire. Off site: Beach 200 m. Bus service 800 m. Fishing 200 m.	From the north, turn off the main coast road (N13-E50) just after camping sign at end of embankment alongside estuary, about 1.5 km. south of ferry. From the south on N13 turn left at Hotel Faz de Minho at start of estuary. Follow for 1 km. to site.

Open: All year.

Charges 2007

Per person	€ 2,40 - € 4,40
pitch incl. electricity	€ 7,80 - € 14,10

Off season discounts (up to 70%).

PO8020 Orbitur Camping Viana do Castelo

Rua Diogo Alvares, Cabadelo, P-4900-161 Darque (Viana do Costelo)

Tel: **258 32 21 67**. Email: **info@orbitur.pt**

This site in northern Portugal is worth considering as it has the advantage of direct access, through a gate in the fence (locked at night) to a large and excellent soft sand beach (400 m.) which is popular for windsurfing. There are 225 pitches on undulating sand, most with good shade from pine trees and with electricity in all areas (long leads may be needed). Some flat good sized pitches are reserved for caravans and motorcaravans. As usual with Orbitur sites, most pitches are not marked and it could be crowded in July/August. A pleasant restaurant terrace overlooks the pool.

Facilities	Directions
Toilet facilities are in two blocks, both with washbasins with cold water and hot showers. Facilities for disabled campers. Laundry. Motorcaravan services. Gas supplies. Supermarket (all year). Small restaurant with terrace and bar (all Easter and 1/6-30/9). Open-air pool (June-Sept.). Reading room with TV, video and fireplace. Playground. Tennis. Medical post. Off site: Fishing 100 m. Beach 50 m.	On N13 coast road driving north to south drive through Viana do Castelo and over estuary bridge. Turn right off N13 towards Cabedelo and the sea. Site is the third camp signed.

Open: All year.

Charges 2007

Per person	€ 2,60 - € 4,60
child (5-10 yrs)	€ 1,30 - € 2,30
pitch incl. electricity	€ 8,20 - € 13,60

Off season discounts (up to 70%).

PO8030 Orbitur Camping Rio Alto

E.N. 13 - km 13 - Rio Alto-Est, Estela, P-4570-275 Póvoa de Varzim (Porto)

Tel: **252 61 56 99**. Email: **info@orbitur.pt**

This site makes an excellent base for visiting Porto which is some 35 km. south of Estela. It has around 700 pitches on sandy terrain and is next to what is virtually a private beach. There are some hardstandings for caravans and motorcaravans and electrical connections to most pitches (long leads may be required). The area for tents is furthest from the beach and windswept, stunted pines give some shade. There are arrangements for car parking away from camping areas in peak season. There is a quality restaurant, snack bar and a large swimming pool plus across the road from reception. An 18 hole golf course is adjacent and huge nets along one side of the site protect campers from any stray balls. The beach is accessed via a novel double tunnel in two lengths of 40 metres under the dunes (open 09.00-19.00). The beach shelves steeply at some tidal stages (lifeguard 15/6-15/9).

Facilities

Four well equipped toilet blocks have hot water. Washing machines and ironing facilities. Facilities for disabled campers. Gas supplies. Restaurant, bar, snack bar and mini-market (all year). Swimming pool (1/6-30/9). Tennis. Playground. Games room. Surfing. TV. Medical post. Car wash. Evening entertainment twice weekly in season. Off site: Fishing 800 m. Golf 1 km. Bicycle hire 13 km. Riding 19 km.

Open: All year.

Directions

From A28 take exit 7 for Estela to EN13 coast road. Turn north for 1 km. and at hotel turn left towards the sea, 12 km. north of Póvoa de Varzim. Travel 2.6 km. along the narrow cobbled road. Look to the right for an Orbitur sign (well back from the road) and take for 0.8 km. to site (speed bumps).

Charges 2007

Per person	€ 2,70 - € 4,80
child (5-10 yrs)	€ 1,35 - € 2,40
caravan and car	€ 6,70 - € 12,50
electricity (5/15A)	€ 2,40 - € 3,00
Off season discounts (up to 70%).	

PO8370 Parque de Campismo de Cerdeira

P-4840 Campo do Gerês (Braga)

Tel: **253 35 1005**. Email: **info@parquecerdeira.com**

Located in the National Park of Peneda Gerês, amidst spectacular mountain scenery, this excellent site offers modern facilities in a truly natural area. The National Park is home to all manner of flora, fauna and wildlife, including the roebuck, wolf and wild boar. The well fenced, professional and peaceful site has some 600 good sized, unmarked, mostly level, grassy pitches in a shady woodland setting. Electricity is available for most pitches, though some long leads may be required. A very large timber complex, tastefully designed with the use of noble materials, granite and wood, provides a superb restaurant with a comprehensive menu. A pool with a separated section for toddlers is a welcome, cooling relief in the height of summer. There are unlimited opportunities in the immediate area for fishing, riding, canoeing, mountain biking and climbing, so take advantage of this quality mountain hospitality.

Facilities

Four very clean sanitary blocks provide mixed style WCs, controllable showers and hot water. Dishwashing and laundry sinks under cover. Laundry. Gas supplies. Mini-market. Restaurant/bar (15/4- 30/9, plus weekends and holidays). Playground. Bicycle hire. TV room (satellite). Medical post. Good tennis courts. Minigolf. Car wash. Barbecue area. Torches useful. English spoken. Attractive bungalows to rent. Dogs are not accepted in July/August. Off site: Fishing and riding 800 m. Off site: Fishing and riding 800 m.

Open: All year.

Directions

From north, N103 (Braga-Chaves), turn left at N205 (7.5 km north of Braga). Follow N205 to Caldelas Terras de Bouro and Covide where site is clearly marked to Campo do Geres. An eastern approach from the N103 is for the adventurous but will be rewarded by magnificent views over mountains and lakes. GPS: N41:45.811 W08:11.33

Charges 2007

Per person	€ 3,20 - € 4,50
child (5-11 yrs)	€ 2,00 - € 3,00
pitch	€ 4,30 - € 7,50
electricity (6/10A)	€ 2,50 - € 3,50

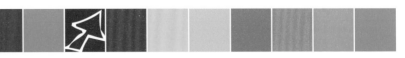

Travelling

When taking your car (and caravan, tent or trailer tent) or motorcaravan to the continent you do need to plan in advance and to find out as much as possible about driving in the countries you plan to visit. Whilst European harmonisation has eliminated many of the differences between one country and another, it is well worth reading the short notes we provide in the introduction to each country in this guide in addition to this more general summary.

Of course, the main difference from driving in the UK is that in mainland Europe you will need to drive on the right. Without taking extra time and care, especially at busy junctions and conversely when roads are empty, it is easy to forget to drive on the right. Remember that traffic approaching from the right usually has priority unless otherwise indicated by road markings and signs. Harmonisation also means that most (but not all) common road signs are the same in all countries.

Your vehicle

Book your vehicle in for a good service well before your intended departure date. This will lessen the chance of an expensive breakdown. Make sure your brakes are working efficiently and that your tyres have plenty of tread (3 mm. is recommended, particularly if you are undertaking a long journey).

Also make sure that your caravan or trailer is roadworthy and that its tyres are in good order and correctly inflated. Plan your packing and be careful not to overload your vehicle, caravan or trailer – this is unsafe and may well invalidate your insurance cover (it must not be more fully loaded than the kerb weight of the insured vehicle).

Check all the following:

☐ GB sticker. If you do not display a sticker, you may risk an on-the-spot fine as this identifier is compulsory in all countries. Euro-plates are an acceptable alternative within the EU (but not outside). Remember to attach another sticker (or Euro-plate) to caravans or trailers. Only GB stickers (not England, Scotland, Wales or N. Ireland) stickers are valid in the EU.

☐ Headlights. As you will be driving on the right you must adjust your headlights so that the dipped beam does not dazzle oncoming drivers. Converter kits are readily available for most vehicle, although if your car is fitted with high intensity headlights, you should check with your motor dealer. Check that any planned extra loading does not affect the beam height.

☐ Seatbelts. Rules for the fitting and wearing of seatbelts throughout Europe are similar to those in the UK, but it is worth checking before you go. Rules for carrying children in the front of vehicles vary from country to country. It is best to plan not to do this if possible.

☐ Door/Wing mirrors. To help with driving on the right, if your vehicle is not fitted with a mirror on the left hand side, we recommend you have one fitted.

☐ Fuel. Leaded and Lead Replacement petrol is increasingly difficult to find in Northern Europe.

Travelling continued

Compulsory additional equipment

The driving laws of the countries of Europe still vary in what you are required to carry in your vehicle, although the consequences of not carrying a required piece of equipment are almost always an on-the-spot fine.

To meet these requirements we suggest that you carry the following:

- ☐ Fire extinguisher
- ☐ Basic tool kit
- ☐ First aid kit
- ☐ Spare bulbs
- ☐ Two warning triangles – two are required in some countries at all times, and are compulsory in most countries when towing.
- ☐ High visibility vest – now compulsory in Spain, Italy and Austria (and likely to become compulsory throughout the EU) in case you need to walk on a motorway.

Insurance and Motoring Documents

Vehicle insurance

Contact your insurer well before you depart to check that your car insurance policy covers driving outside the UK. Most do, but many policies only provide minimum cover (so if you have an accident your insurance may only cover the cost of damage to the other person's property, with no cover for fire and theft).

To maintain the same level of cover abroad as you enjoy at home you need to tell your vehicle insurer. Some will automatically cover you abroad with no extra cost and no extra paperwork. Some will say you need a Green Card (which is neither green nor on card) but won't charge for it. Some will charge extra for the Green Card. Ideally you should contact your vehicle insurer 3-4 weeks before you set off, and confirm your conversation with them in writing.

Breakdown insurance

Arrange breakdown cover for your trip in good time so that if your vehicle breaks down or is involved in an accident it (and your caravan or trailer) can be repaired or returned to this country. This cover can usually be arranged as part of your travel insurance policy (see below).

Documents you must take with you

You may be asked to show your documents at any time so make sure that they are in order, up-to-date and easily accessible while you travel. These are what you need to take:

- ☐ Passports (you may also need a visa in some countries if you hold either a UK passport not issued in the UK or a passport that was issued outside the EU).
- ☐ Motor Insurance Certificate, including Green Card (or Continental Cover clause)
- ☐ DVLC Vehicle Registration Document plus, if not your own vehicle, the owner's written authority to drive.
- ☐ A full valid Driving Licence (not provisional). The new photo style licence is now mandatory in most European countries).

insure **4** campers.com

Taking your own caravan, motorhome or tent abroad?

European Camping Holiday Insurance

Our specially tailored travel insurance policies provide exactly the right cover for a self-drive camping holiday in Europe at the lowest possible price. Our policies have been adapted to cover the often-unique risks associated with a camping holiday in Europe. For example, policies include cover for valuables stored in your vehicle overnight on a campsite* (loss from unattended vehicles is often excluded from general travel insurance policies).

Specialist insurance for campers and caravanners can include*:

- **Payment towards additional accommodation costs following loss of own tent**
- **Specific tent and camping equipment cover**
- **Reimbursement of caravan insurance excess.**
- **Theft of valuables from an unattended vehicle whilst parked on a campsite.**
- **Increased car hire limits when towing a caravan or trailer (Plus policies)**

* see policy wording for details

Single Trip Policies

Our **Personal Insurance** provides access to the services of Inter Group Assistance Services (IGAS) and Global Excel, two of the UK's largest assistance companies. Experienced multi-lingual personnel provide a caring, efficient service 24 hours a day. They are backed by a medical team who include in-house doctors and nurses headed by specialist medical consultants.

- **24 hour travel advice line and medical assistance**
- **Authorisation of medical costs and payment guarantees**
- **Air ambulance repatriation/evacuation**
- **Repatriation due to serious illness of relatives at home**
- **Medical escorts and regular liaison with overseas doctors providing treatment**

Our **European Vehicle Assistance** cover is provided by Green Flag who, with over 25 years' experience, provide assistance to over 3 million people each year. With a Europe-wide network of over 7,500 garages and agents, you know you're in very safe hands.

Both IGAS and Green Flag are very used to looking after the needs of campsite-based holidaymakers and are very familiar with the location of most European campsites, with contacts at garages, doctors and hospitals nearby.

Green Flag
motoring assistance

Combined Personal and Vehicle Assistance Insurance

PREMIER COUPLES PACKAGE
£57* 18 days cover for motorhome + 2 adults

PREMIER FAMILY PACKAGE
£89* 18 days cover for car + caravan + 2 adults + dependent children under 16

* Based on vehicles under 5 years old

SAVE WITH ANNUAL POLICIES

If you are likely to take more than one overseas holiday in the next 12 months then our Annual multi-trip policies could save you a great deal of money. European self-drive personal cover for a couple starts at just **£69** and the whole family can be covered for just **£89**.

One call and you're covered **0870 405 4059**

Travelling continued

Personal Holiday insurance

Even though you are just travelling within Europe you must take out travel insurance. Few EU countries pay the full cost of medical treatment even under reciprocal health service arrangements. The first part of a holiday insurance policy covers people. It will include the cost of doctor, ambulance and hospital treatment if needed. If needed the better companies will even pay for English language speaking doctors and nurses and will bring a sick or injured holidaymaker home by air ambulance.

The second part of a good policy covers things. If someone breaks into your motorhome and steals your passports and money, one phone call to the insurance company will have everything sorted out. If you manage to drive over your camera, it should be covered. NB – most policies have a maximum payment limit per item, do check that any valuables are adequately covered.

An important part of the insurance, often ignored, is cancellation (and curtailment) cover. Few things are as heartbreaking as having to cancel a holiday because a member of the family falls ill. Cancellation insurance can't take away the disappointment, but it makes sure you don't suffer financially as well. For this reason you should arrange your holiday insurance at least eight weeks before you set off.

Whichever insurance you choose we would advise reading very carefully the policies sold by the High Street travel trade. Whilst they may be good, they may not cover the specific needs of campers, caravanners and motorcaravanners.

Telephone 0870 405 4059 for a quote for our European Camping Holiday Insurance with cover arranged through Green Flag Motoring Assistance and Inter Group Assistance Services, one of the UK's largest assistance companies. Alternatively visit our website at www.insure4campers.com.

European Health Insurance Card (EHIC)

Important Changes since E111: Since September 2005 new European Health Insurance Cards have replaced the E111 forms .

Make sure you apply for your EHIC before travelling in Europe. Eligible travellers from the UK are entitled to receive free or reduced-cost medical care in many European countries on production of an EHIC. This free card is available by completing a form in the booklet 'Health Advice for Travellers' from local Post Offices. One should be completed for each family member. Alternatively visit www.dh.gov.uk/travellers and apply on-line. Please allow time to send your application off and have the EHIC returned to you.

The EHIC is valid in all European Community countries plus Iceland, Liechtenstein, Switzerland and Norway. If you or any of your dependants are suddenly taken ill or have an accident during a visit to any of these countries, free or reduced-cost emergency treatment is available - in most cases on production of a valid EHIC. Only state-provided emergency treatment is covered, and you will receive treatment on the same terms as nationals of the country you are visiting. Private treatment is generally not covered, and state-provided treatment may not cover all of the things that you would expect to receive free of charge from the NHS.

Remember an EHIC does not cover you for all the medical costs that you can incur or for repatriation - it is not an alternative to travel insurance. You will still need appropriate insurance to ensure you are fully covered for all eventualities.

Open All Year

The following campsites are understood to accept caravanners and campers all year round. It is always wise to phone the site to check as the facilities available, for example, may be reduced.

SPAIN

Cataluña-Catalunya

ES8008	Joncar Mar
ES8130	Calonge
ES8228	Blanes
ES8235	Bon Repos
ES8240	Bona Vista Kim
ES8390	Vilanova Park
ES8395	Arc de Bara
ES8482	Pineda de Salou
ES8483	Tamarit
ES8502	Montblanc Park
ES8506	Serra de Prades
ES8508	Poboleda
ES8535	Cala d`Oques
ES8536	Ametlla
ES8555	Eucaliptus
ES9121	Vall d'Ager
ES9123	El Solsones
ES9140	Pedraforca

Comunidad Valenciana

ES8558	Vinaros
ES8559	Azahar
ES8560	Playa Tropicana
ES8570	Torre La Sal 2
ES8580	Bonterra
ES8590	Monmar
ES8612	Euro Camping
ES8615	Kiko
ES8620	L`Alqueria
ES8625	Kiko Rural
ES8645	Mariola
ES8675	Vall de Laguar
ES8681	Villasol
ES8683	Benisol
ES8685	El Raco
ES8687	Cap Blanch
ES8689	Playa del Torres
ES8690	Costa Blanca
ES8742	La Marina
ES8743	Marjal
ES8754	Javea
ES8755	Moraira

Murcia

ES8745	La Fuente
ES8748	Los Madriles
ES8752	El Portus
ES8753	La Manga

Andalucia

ES8749	Sopalmo
ES8751	Cuevas Mar
ES8762	Los Escullos
ES8763	Cabo de Gata
ES8765	La Garrofa
ES8782	Laguna Playa
ES8783	Almanat
ES8790	La Laguna

ES8800	Marbella Playa
ES8802	Cabopino
ES8803	La Buganvilla
ES8809	El Sur
ES8850	Paloma
ES8855	Tarifa
ES8865	Playa Las Dunas
ES8871	Giralda
ES9078	Los Villares
ES9080	El Brillante
ES9081	Villsom
ES9082	Sevilla
ES9085	Carlos III
ES9089	Despenaperros
ES9270	Suspiro-Moro
ES9275	Los Avellanos
ES9285	Las Lomas
ES9290	El Balcon
ES9292	Puerta de La Alpujarra
ES9295	Don Cactus
ES9296	Castillo de Banos

Extremadura

ES9027	Monfrague
ES9086	Cáceres
ES9087	Merida

Castilla La-Mancha

ES9090	El Greco
ES9096	El Mirador
ES9097	Los Batanes

Madrid

ES9200	El Escorial
ES9210	Pico-Miel

Castilla y León

ES9021	Fuentes Blancas
ES9022	El Folgoso
ES9025	Regio
ES9250	Costajan
ES9253	Picon del Conde
ES9257	Frias

Galicia

ES9024	As Cancelas

Asturias

ES8940	Los Cantiles
ES8965	Picos-Europa

Cantabria

ES8964	Molino
ES8973	Santillana

Pais Vasco-Euskadi

ES9030	Igueldo
ES9035	Portuondo
ES9039	Gran Zarautz

La Rioja

ES9226	Los Cameros
ES9227	Navarrete
ES9228	Berceo

Navarra

ES9043	Errota el Molino

Aragón

ES9060	Peña Montañesa
ES9062	Boltana
ES9064	Gavín
ES9125	Lago Barasona

PORTUGAL

Algarve

PO8200	Valverde
PO8202	Turiscampo
PO8210	Albufeira
PO8220	Quarteira
PO8230	Olhao
PO8410	Armacao-Pera
PO8430	Sagres
PO8440	Quintos

Alentejo

PO8160	Porto Covo
PO8170	São Miguel
PO8350	Markádia

Lisbon & Vale do Tejo

PO8100	S Pedro-Moel
PO8130	Guincho
PO8140	Monsanto
PO8150	Caparica
PO8480	Foz do Arelho

Beiras & Centre

PO8040	Vagueira
PO8090	Gala
PO8330	Arganil

Porto & North

PO8010	Caminha
PO8020	Viana-Castelo
PO8030	Rio Alto
PO8370	Cerdeira

Dogs

For the benefit of those who want to take their dogs with them or for people who do not like dogs at the sites they visit, we list here the sites that have indicated to us that they do not accept dogs. If you are, however, planning to take your dog we do advise you to contact them first to check – there may be limits on numbers, breeds, etc. or times of the year when they are excluded.

Never – these sites do not accept dogs at any time:

SPAIN

Cataluña-Catalunya

ES8090	Cypsela
ES8101	Playa Brava
ES8103	El Maset
ES8420	Stel (Roda)
ES8481	Cambrils
ES8530	Playa Montroig
ES8537	Templo del Sol
ES8540	Torre del Sol

ES9123	El Solsones
ES9143	Pirineus

Comunidad Valenciana

ES8560	Playa Tropicana
ES8681	Villasol

Murcia

ES8748	Los Madriles

Extremadura

ES9086	Cáceres

Castilla y León

ES9251	Rio Lobos

Cantabria

ES9000	Playa Joyel

PORTUGAL

Alentejo

PO8170	São Miguel

Maybe – accepted at any time but with certain restrictions:

SPAIN

Cataluña-Catalunya

ES8080	Delfin Verde
ES8160	Cala Gogo
ES8232	Bella Terra
ES8533	Els Prat

Comunidad Valenciana

ES8559	Azahar
ES8580	Bonterra

Andalucia

ES8803	La Buganvilla
ES9295	Don Cactus

PORTUGAL

Alentejo

PO8350	Markádia

Porto & North

PO8370	Cerdeira

Fishing

We are pleased to include details of sites which provide facilities for fishing on site. However, it is always best to contact sites directly to check that they provide for your individual requirements.

SPAIN

Cataluña-Catalunya

ES8010	Castell Mar
ES8015	La Laguna
ES8030	Nautic Almata
ES8031	Gaviota
ES8032	Riu
ES8035	Amfora
ES8040	Las Dunas
ES8050	Aquarius
ES8060	Ballena Alegre 2
ES8064	Bassegoda
ES8074	Paradis
ES8080	Delfin Verde
ES8101	Playa Brava
ES8140	Treumal
ES8160	Cala Gogo
ES8200	Cala Llevadó
ES8228	Blanes
ES8232	Bella Terra
ES8235	Bon Repos
ES8238	Caballo de Mar
ES8420	Stel (Roda)
ES8483	Tamarit
ES8486	Torre de la Mora
ES8520	Marius
ES8530	Playa Montroig
ES8533	Els Prat
ES8535	Cala d'Oques
ES8536	Ametlla
ES8537	Templo del Sol

ES8540	Torre del Sol
ES9142	Solana del Segre
ES9143	Pirineus

Comunidad Valenciana

ES8560	Playa Tropicana
ES8570	Torre La Sal 2
ES8612	Euro Camping (Oliva)
ES8615	Kiko
ES8689	Playa del Torres
ES8743	Marjal

Murcia

ES8752	El Portus
ES8753	La Manga

Andalucia

ES8765	La Garrofa
ES8782	Laguna Playa
ES8783	Almanat
ES8855	Tarifa
ES9295	Don Cactus
ES9296	Castillo de Banos

Castilla La-Mancha

ES9090	El Greco
ES9098	Rio Mundo

Castilla y León

ES9257	Frias

Asturias

ES8945	Lagos-Somiedo
ES8950	Costa Verde

ES8960	La Paz
ES8965	Picos-Europa

Cantabria

ES8962	La Isla
ES8964	Molino
ES8970	Arenas-Pechon
ES9000	Playa Joyel

Pais Vasco-Euskadi

ES9035	Portuondo
ES9045	Angosto

La Rioja

ES9040	Haro

Navarra

ES9043	Errota el Molino
ES9048	Urrobi

Aragón

ES9058	Baliera
ES9060	Peña Montañesa

PORTUGAL

Alentejo

PO8350	Markádia

Porto & North

PO8030	Rio Alto

Bicycle Hire

We understand that the following sites have bicycles to hire on site or can arrange for bicycles to be delivered. However, we would recommend that you contact them directly to check as the situation can change.

SPAIN

Cataluña-Catalunya

ES8030	Nautic Almata
ES8031	Gaviota
ES8032	Riu
ES8033	Las Palmeras
ES8035	Amfora
ES8040	Las Dunas
ES8050	Aquarius
ES8060	Ballena Alegre 2
ES8064	Bassegoda
ES8072	Les Medes
ES8074	Paradis
ES8080	Delfin Verde
ES8090	Cypsela
ES8100	Inter-Pals
ES8160	Cala Gogo
ES8180	Sant Pol
ES8210	Tucan
ES8340	Rupit
ES8390	Vilanova Park
ES8392	El Garrofer
ES8410	Playa Bara
ES8420	Stel (Roda)
ES8482	Pineda de Salou
ES8502	Montblanc Park
ES8506	Serra de Prades
ES8530	Playa Montroig
ES8533	Els Prat
ES8536	Ametlla
ES8537	Templo del Sol
ES8540	Torre del Sol
ES8555	Eucaliptus
ES9123	El Solsones
ES9140	Pedraforca
ES9144	Stel

Comunidad Valenciana

ES8559	Azahar
ES8560	Playa Tropicana
ES8580	Bonterra
ES8615	Kiko
ES8625	Kiko Rural
ES8743	Marjal

Murcia

ES8745	La Fuente
ES8748	Los Madriles

Andalucia

ES8762	Los Escullos
ES8763	Cabo de Gata
ES9290	El Balcon
ES9295	Don Cactus

Extremadura

ES9027	Monfrague
ES9087	Merida

Castilla La-Mancha

ES9098	Rio Mundo

Castilla y León

ES9023	Santiago
ES9250	Costajan

Galicia

ES9024	As Cancelas

Cantabria

ES8962	La Isla
ES8973	Santillana

Pais Vasco-Euskadi

ES9045	Angosto

Navarra

ES9042	Etxarri
ES9043	Errota el Molino

Aragón

ES9060	Peña Montañesa
ES9064	Gavín
ES9125	Lago Barasona

Balears

ES8000	Son Bou

PORTUGAL

Algarve

PO8202	Turiscampo
PO8210	Albufeira
PO8230	Olhao
PO8430	Sagres
PO8440	Quintos

Alentejo

PO8160	Porto Covo

Lisbon & Vale do Tejo

PO8460	Vale Paraiso
PO8480	Foz do Arelho
PO8550	Quinta Da Cerejeira

Beiras & Centre

PO8040	Vagueira

Porto & North

PO8010	Caminha
PO8370	Cerdeira

Horse Riding

We understand that the following sites have horse riding stables on site. Where facilities are within easy reach and we have been given details, we have included this information in the individual site reports. However, we recommend that you contact the site to check that they meet your requirements.

SPAIN

Cataluña-Catalunya
ES8015   La Laguna
ES8030   Nautic Almata
ES8506   Serra de Prades

Andalucia
ES9290   El Balcon

Extremadura
ES9027   Monfrague

Asturias
ES8945   Lagos-Somiedo

Cantabria
ES8962   La Isla
ES8970   Arenas-Pechon

Aragon
ES9060   Peña Montañesa

PORTUGAL

Alentejo
PO8350   Markádia

Boat Launching

We understand that the following sites have boat slipways on site. Where facilities are within easy reach and we have been given details, we have included this information in the individual site reports. However, we recommend that you contact the site to check that they meet your requirements.

SPAIN

Cataluña-Catalunya
ES8030   Nautic Almata
ES8032   Riu
ES8101   Playa Brava
ES8530   Playa Montroig
ES8533   Els Prat
ES8540   Torre del Sol

Comunidad Valenciana
ES8612   Euro Camping (Oliva)
ES8615   Kiko
ES8689   Playa del Torres

Murcia
ES8752   El Portus

Andalucia
ES8765   La Garrofa
ES8782   Laguna Playa
ES8855   Tarifa

Cantabria
ES8970   Arenas-Pechon

Navarra
ES9043   Errota el Molino

Aragón
ES9125   Lago Barasona

PORTUGAL

Alentejo
PO8350   Markádia

Reports by Readers

We always welcome reports from readers concerning sites which they have visited. Generally reports provide us with invaluable feedback on sites already included in the Guide or, in the case of those not featured in our Guide, they provide information which we can follow up with a view to adding them in future editions. However, if you have a complaint about a site, this should be addressed to the campsite owner, preferably in person before you leave.

Please make your comments either on this form or on plain paper. It would be appreciated if you would indicate the approximate dates when you visited the site and, in the case of potential new sites, provide the correct name and address and, if possible, include a campsite brochure. Send your reports to:

Alan Rogers Guides, Spelmonden Old Oast, Goudhurst, Kent TN17 1HE

Name of Site and Ref. No. (or address for new recommendations)

Dates of visit:

Comments:

Reader's Name and Address:

Name and reference number of the campsite (or address for new recommendations):

_____

_____

Dates of visit: _____

Comments:

Reader's Name and Address: _____

_____

_____

_____

How can I pack more into my holiday in

Spain?

We know a way

Take our Plymouth to Santander service, and pack your car with all the things you need to enjoy your holiday to the full.

Enjoy superb on-board facilities on the shortest direct ferry crossing from the UK to Spain. And all for less than you'd expect.

brittanyferries.com
0870 908 9516

Great magazines for touring, holidays and inspirational ideas!

For buying information, top tips and technical help, **Caravan, Motor Caravan Magazine** and **Park Home & Holiday Caravan** are all you need — every month!

Subscribe today and save 30%

☎ 0845 676 7778

Lines are open seven days a week, 9am – 9pm. Closing date 31 December 2007
Quote code Caravan XCV 38E or Motor Caravan XMV 39A or
Park Home & Holiday Caravan XPH 35H when calling

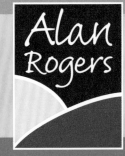

Sample any of the magazines below for just £1 each for your first three issues

3 issues for £1 each
then £7.99 every 3 months, saving 14%

The UK's favourite and best-selling motorcaravan magazine for 40 years

3 issues for £1 each
then £6.00 every 3 months, saving 35%

The UK's leading magazine for motorhome buyers

3 issues for £1 each
then £7.00 every 3 months, saving 21%

Dedicated to the wonderful world of caravanning, motorcaravanning and camping

3 issues for £1 each
then £7.00 every 3 months, saving 22%

Britain's best guide to buying new and used caravans

3 issues for £1 each
then £5.50 every 3 months, saving 41%

The UK's only magazine for backpackers and family campers

CALL OUR HOTLINE TODAY ON 01778 391180

quoting ref: ALANROGERS07. Please have your bank details ready when calling
Offers are open to UK residents and close on 31st December 2007

Offers can be used by existing subscribers to renew/extend an existing subscription
Your subscription(s) will start with the next available issue.

Ref: ALANROGERS07

CANTABRIA PAIS VASCO-EUSKADI
ASTURIAS
FRANCE
GALICIA
NAVARRA
ANDORRA
LA RIOJA
CASTILLA Y LEON
CATALUNYA
NORTH
ARAGON
BEIRAS
MADRID
LISBON AND VALE DO TEJO
EXTREMADURA CASTILLA-LA-MANCHA
COMUNIDAD VALENCIANA
ALENTEJO
MURCIA
ANDALUCIA
ALGARVE

Widely regarded as the 'Bible' by site owners and readers alike, there is no better guide when it comes to forming an independent view of a campsite's quality. When you need to be confident in your choice of campsite, you need the Alan Rogers Guide.

✓ Sites only included on merit

✓ Sites cannot pay to be included

✓ Independently inspected, rigorously assessed

✓ Impartial reviews

✓ 40 years of expertise

INSPECTED CAMPSITES & SELECTED

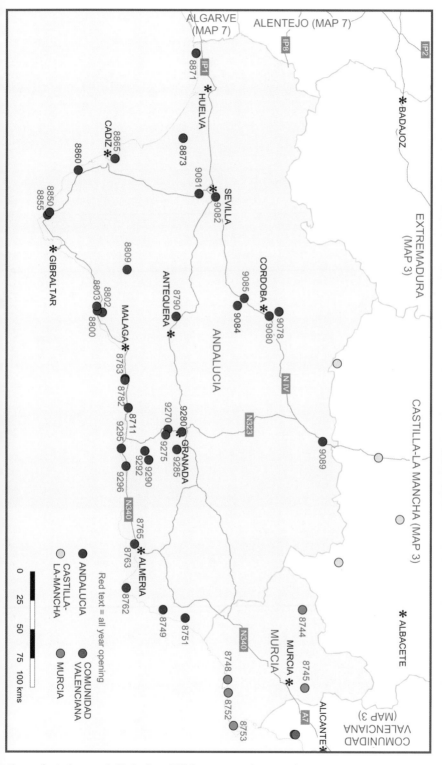

ALGARVE
(MAP 7)

ALENTEJO (MAP 7)

EXTREMADURA
(MAP 3)

CASTILLA-LA MANCHA (MAP 3)

ANDALUCIA

MURCIA

COMUNIDAD
VALENCIANA
(MAP 3)

* BADAJOZ

* ALBACETE

IP2

IP8

IP1

8871

* HUELVA

8873

9081

* SEVILLA
9082

8865 * CADIZ

8860

8850
8855

* GIBRALTAR

8809

8803 8802
8800

ANTEQUERA
8790
*

MALAGA
*

8783

8782

8711

9270

9280
* GRANADA
9275
9285
9292
9290
9296

8765

8763

* ALMERIA

8762

8749

8751

9085

CORDOBA
* 9080
9084

9078

N IV

N323

9089

8744

MURCIA
* 8745

8748

8752

8753

A7

* ALICANTE

N340

N340

Red text = all year opening

ANDALUCIA

CASTILLA-
LA-MANCHA

COMUNIDAD
VALENCIANA

MURCIA

0   25   50   75   100 kms

Please refer to the numerical index (page 202) for exact campsite page references.

195

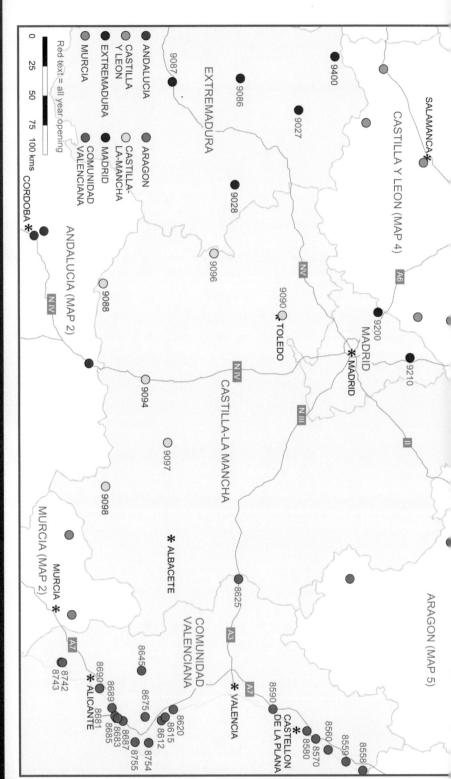

Red text = all year opening

●	ANDALUCIA
○	CASTILLA Y LEON
●	EXTREMADURA
●	MURCIA
●	ARAGON
○	CASTILLA-LA-MANCHA
●	MADRID
●	COMUNIDAD VALENCIANA

0   25   50   75   100 kms

CASTILLA Y LEON (MAP 4)

SALAMANCA ✳

EXTREMADURA

9400

9086

9027

9028

9087

9096

9090 ✳ TOLEDO

9088

9094

9097

9098

CORDOBA ✳

ANDALUCIA (MAP 2)

N IV

MADRID

MADRID ✳

9200

9210

CASTILLA-LA MANCHA

N V

N III

III

A6

ARAGON (MAP 5)

✳ ALBACETE

MURCIA (MAP 2)

MURCIA (MAP 2) ✳

8625

COMUNIDAD VALENCIANA

A3

A7

✳ VALENCIA

8445

8675

8620

8615

8612

8687

8685

8683

8689

8690

8691

8742

8743

✳ ALICANTE

8754

8755

A7

8590

CASTELLON DE LA PLANA ✳

8560

8570

8580

8559

8558

Please refer to the numerical index (page 202) for exact campsite page references.

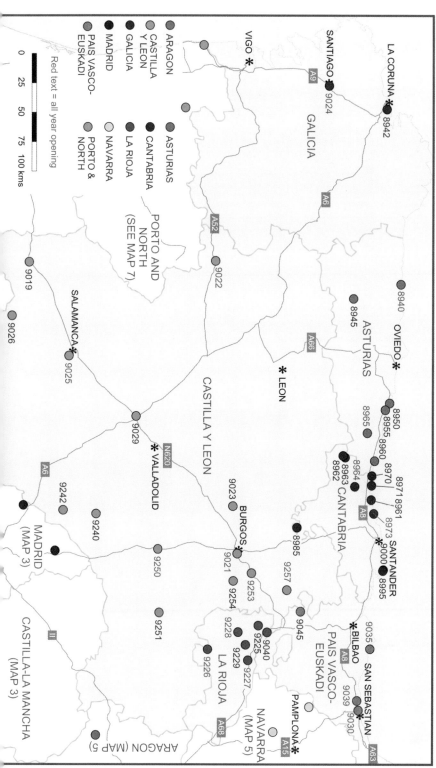

Red text = all year opening

⬤ ARAGON	⬤ PORTO & NORTH
⬤ CASTILLA Y LEON	⬤ NAVARRA
⬤ GALICIA	⬤ LA RIOJA
⬤ MADRID	⬤ CANTABRIA
⬤ PAIS VASCO-EUSKADI	⬤ ASTURIAS

0 25 50 75 100 kms

GALICIA

VIGO ✱

SANTIAGO 9024

LA CORUNA ✱ 8942

A9

A6

A52

PORTO AND NORTH
(SEE MAP 7)

9022

9019

9026

SALAMANCA ✱ 9025

9029

A6

N620

✱ VALLADOLID

CASTILLA Y LEON

✱ LEON

ASTURIAS

OVIEDO ✱

8940

8945

A66

8950
8955 8960
8965
8964 8970
8963 8961
8962
8971
8973
9000 ✱ SANTANDER
8985
8995

CANTABRIA

A8

9023

BURGOS ✱

9021 ✱

9253
9254
9257

9228 9229
9225 9040
9227
9226

LA RIOJA

9045

9035
✱ BILBAO

PAIS VASCO-EUSKADI

A8

9039
9030
SAN SEBASTIAN

PAMPLONA ✱

NAVARRA
(MAP 5)

A15

A63

A68

9242

9240

9250

9251

MADRID
(MAP 3)

CASTILLA-LA MANCHA
(MAP 3)

ARAGON (MAP 5)

III

Please refer to the numerical index (page 202) for exact campsite page references.

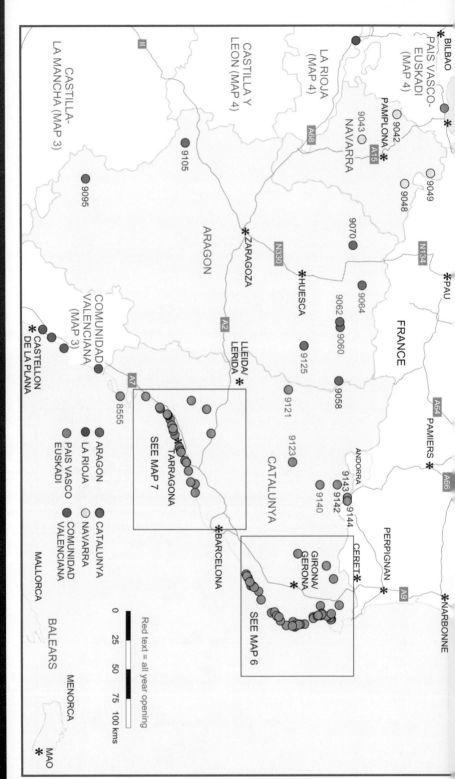

FRANCE

BILBAO ✳
PAIS VASCO-
EUSKADI
(MAP 4)
✳

PAMPLONA
9042

NAVARRA
✳

LA RIOJA
(MAP 4)

9049

9048

CASTILLA Y
LEON (MAP 4)

9105

CASTILLA-
LA MANCHA (MAP 3)

9095

ARAGON

9070

✳ZARAGOZA

✳PAU

N134

✳HUESCA

9064
9062 9060

9125

9058

LLEIDA/
LERIDA
✳

9121

CATALUNYA

9123

ANDORRA

9143
9142
9144

9140

CERET ✳

PAMIERS ✳

PERPIGNAN

✳NARBONNE

GIRONA/
GERONA
✳

SEE MAP 6

COMUNIDAD
VALENCIANA
(MAP 3)

CASTELLON
DE LA PLANA
✳

8555

SEE MAP 7

TARRAGONA

✳BARCELONA

PAIS VASCO
EUSKADI

ARAGON
LA RIOJA
NAVARRA

CATALUNYA
COMUNIDAD
VALENCIANA

Red text = all year opening

0   25   50   75   100 kms

MALLORCA

BALEARS

MENORCA

MAO ✳

Please refer to the numerical index (page 202) for exact campsite page references.

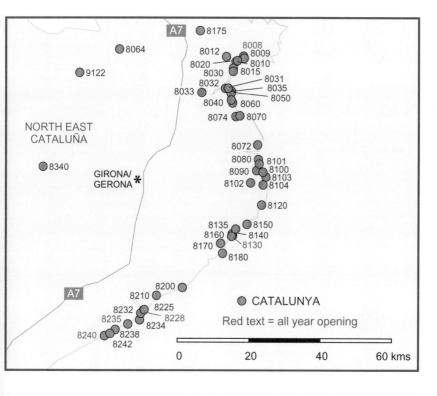

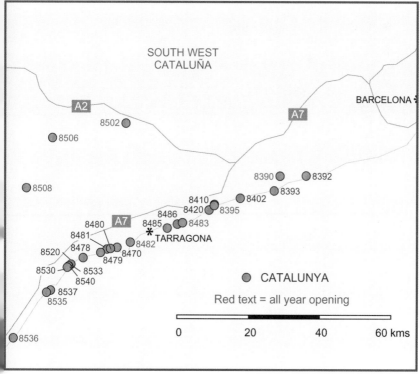

Please refer to the numerical index (page 202) for exact campsite page references.

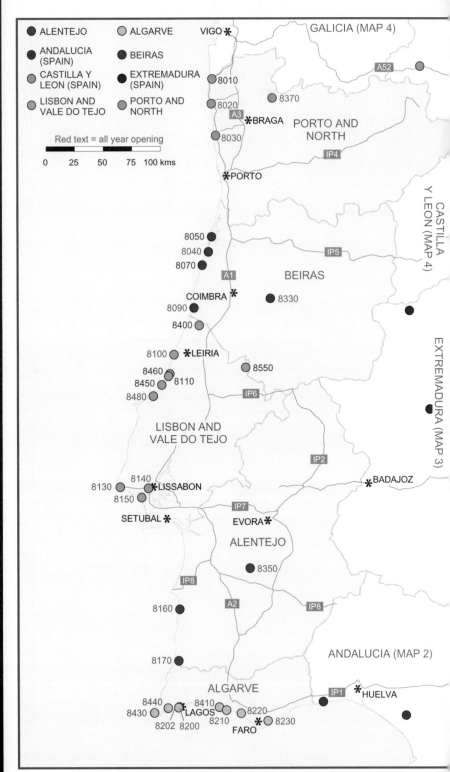

ALENTEJO
ANDALUCIA (SPAIN)
CASTILLA Y LEON (SPAIN)
LISBON AND VALE DO TEJO
ALGARVE
BEIRAS
EXTREMADURA (SPAIN)
PORTO AND NORTH

Red text = all year opening

0   25   50   75   100 kms

VIGO ✳

GALICIA (MAP 4)

A52

8010

8020

A3

✳BRAGA

8030

PORTO AND NORTH

8370

IP4

✳PORTO

CASTILLA Y LEON (MAP 4)

8050

8040

8070

A1

IP5

BEIRAS

COIMBRA ✳

8330

8090

8400

8100   ✳LEIRIA

8460

8450   8110

8480

8550

IP6

LISBON AND VALE DO TEJO

EXTREMADURA (MAP 3)

8130   8140

✳LISSABON

8150

SETUBAL ✳

IP2

IP7

✳BADAJOZ

EVORA ✳

ALENTEJO

8350

IP8

8160

A2

IP8

8170

ANDALUCIA (MAP 2)

ALGARVE

IP1

✳HUELVA

8440   8410

8430   ✳LAGOS   8220

8202 8200   8210   ✳   8230

FARO

Please refer to the numerical index (page 202) for exact campsite page references.

SPAIN

PORTUGAL

INSPECTED CAMPSITES & SELECTED

SPAIN

Widely regarded as the 'Bible' by site owners and readers alike, there is no better guide when it comes to forming an independent view of a campsite's quality. When you need to be confident in your choice of campsite, you need the Alan Rogers Guide.

☑ Sites only included on merit

☑ Sites cannot pay to be included

☑ Independently inspected, rigorously assessed

☑ Impartial reviews

☑ 40 years of expertise

INSPECTED CAMPSITES SELECTED

Tell Us About the Alan Rogers Guides!

We're keen to constantly improve our service to you and the key to this is information. If we don't know what makes our readers 'tick' then it's difficult to offer you more of what you want.

About the Alan Rogers Guides

1 For how many years have you used the Alan Rogers Guides?

Never	1-2 yrs	3-6 yrs	7-10 yrs	Over 10 yrs
❏	❏	❏	❏	❏

2 How frequently do you refer to it?

Never	Each year	Every 2 yrs	Every 3 yrs
❏	❏	❏	❏

3 How frequently do you buy a new copy?

Never	Each year	Every 2 yrs	Every 3 yrs
❏	❏	❏	❏

4 If you lend it to friends, how many others might refer to it?

1 ❏   2 ❏   3 ❏   4 ❏   Over 4 ❏

5 Please rate the Alan Rogers Guides on a scale of 1–10 where 10 is excellent and 1 is extremely poor

1 ❏   2 ❏   3 ❏   4 ❏   5 ❏   6 ❏   7 ❏   8 ❏   9 ❏   10 ❏

6 Do you have any comments about the Alan Rogers Guides?

....

....

7 What do you consider to be the best thing about the guides?

Independent reviews	Honest descriptions	Accurate information	Range of sites	Depth of information
❏	❏	❏	❏	❏

Other ....

8 What do you consider to be the worst thing about the guides?

....

9 How many sites featured in the guides have you visited in the past? *(best estimate)* ....

10 Can you comment on any other campsite guides?

Title ....   Your opinion ....

About Your Holidays

11 a) Do you own any of the following?

Caravan ❏   Motorhome ❏   Trailer Tent ❏   Tent ❏

Other *(please specify)* ....

b) How many times a year do you use it?

1 ❏   2-3 ❏   4-6 ❏   7-10 ❏   More than 10 ❏

12 When on holiday, do you participate in any of the following?

Fishing	Golf	Cycling	Sailing/Boating	Walking	Bird Watching
❏	❏	❏	❏	❏	❏

Other *(please specify)* ....

13 How many years have you been camping / caravanning?

3 yrs or less	4 – 7 yrs	8 – 12 yrs	13 – 15 yrs	16 – 20 yrs	Over 20 yrs
❏	❏	❏	❏	❏	❏

About You

Mr/Mrs/Ms, etc. .... Initial .... Surname ....

Address ....

.... Post code ....

e-mail address .... @ .... Telephone ....
(If you would like to receive monthly e-newsletter with offers and news).

14 **Your age**   30 and under ☐   31-50 ☐   51-65 ☐   Over 65 ☐

15 **Do you have children – if so, how old is the youngest?**
   6 and under ☐   7-12 ☐   Over 12 ☐

16 **Do you work (full or part time)?**   Yes ☐   No ☐

17 **Are you retired?**   Yes ☐   No ☐

About Your Leisure Time

18 **Are you a member of any caravan/motorhome clubs?**
The Caravan Club   The Camping & Caravanning Club   The Motor Caravanners Club
☐   ☐   ☐
Other *(please specify)*

19 **Are you a member of the following?**
National Trust   English Heritage   RSPB   CSMA   Ramblers
☐   ☐   ☐   ☐   ☐

20 **Which (if any) camping/caravanning magazines do you read regularly?**

MMM	Practical Motorhome	Practical Caravan	Caravan Life	Which Motorcaravan	Motor-caravan	Caravan
☐	☐	☐	☐	☐	☐	☐

21 **Which other magazines do you read regularly?** ....

22 **Which newspapers do you read regularly?**

Express	Mail	Telegraph	Times	Guardian	Observer	Sun
☐	☐	☐	☐	☐	☐	☐

Other (please specify)

23 **Do you enjoy any particular hobbies?** *(please specify)* ....

24 **Do you have regular access to the internet?**   Yes ☐   No ☐
If yes, which camping/caravanning websites do you visit regularly? ....

And Finally

25 **Do you have any useful camping/caravanning tips?**
....

26 **If you could change one thing about camping/caravanning holidays what would it be?**
....

We may wish to publish your comments, please tick this box if you would prefer us not to. ☐

Might you be interested in becoming an Alan Rogers site inspector?
If so, please tick the box and we will send you further information ☐

*Camping Cheque and Alan Rogers may use this data to send you information and Special Offers.
Please tick here if you do not wish to receive such information* ☐

**Thank you very much for your time and trouble in completing this questionnaire
Please return to: Alan Rogers Travel Service, FREEPOST NAT17734, Cranbrook, TN17 1BR**